THE AMBER NECTAR

THE AMBER NECTAR

A CELEBRATION OF
BEER AND BREWING
IN AUSTRALIA

KEITH DUNSTAN

VIKING O'NEIL

Carlton and United Breweries wish to thank the State Library of Victoria for permission to reproduce the following photographs from the La Trobe Collection: pages 6, 7, 8, 10, 11, 17, 35, opp. 36 (bottom), 38, 40, 42, 43, 46, 50, opp. 68 (bottom left), 72.

Viking O'Neil
Penguin Books Australia Ltd
487 Maroondah Highway, PO Box 257
Ringwood, Victoria 3134, Australia
Penguin Books Ltd
Harmondsworth, Middlesex, England
Penguin Books
40 West 23rd Street, New York, N.Y. 10010, U.S.A.
Penguin Books Canada Ltd
2801 John Street, Markham, Ontario, Canada L3R 1B4
Penguin Books (N.Z.) Ltd
182-190 Wairau Road, Auckland 10, New Zealand

Published by Penguin Books Australia Ltd 1987
Copyright © Carlton and United Breweries Limited, 1987

Produced by Viking O'Neil
56 Claremont Street, South Yarra, Victoria 3141, Australia
A division of Penguin Books Australia Ltd

Design by Sandra Nobes
Typeset in Garamond by Meredith Typesetting, Australia
Printed and bound by Globe Press, Australia

National Library of Australia
Cataloguing-in-Publication data

Dunstan, Keith.
    The amber nectar.

    Includes index.
    ISBN 0 670 90044 3.
    ISBN 0 670 90046 X (pbk.).

    1. Carlton and United Breweries — History. 2. Beer — Australia — History. 3. Brewing industry — Australia — History. I. Title.

641.2'3'0994

CONTENTS

ACKNOWLEDGEMENTS

Henry Lawson once said the greatest pleasure he ever knew in the world was when his eyes met the eyes of a mate over the top of two foaming glasses of beer. It is by far the most popular drink on earth and I have been a simple devotee for more than forty years. It seemed a very good idea to celebrate the centenary of Foster's Lager and Australia's bicentenary with a history of Carlton & United Breweries. This is not the official history of CUB. It does not record every annual report, every promotion, every director or the starting date of every brew. The attempt here is rather to create a social history of a nation's love for beer, through the story of the remarkable development of CUB.

Nor is this the first history of CUB. There was another, 'Acorn to Oak', written by an employee of the company, Eric Nilan. Although unpublished, it is an excellent work and I drew on it for many good stories.

I deeply regret the many names, thousands of them, that do not appear in these pages. Had they done so the tome would have reached the majestic proportions of Gibbon's *Decline and Fall of the Roman Empire*. The story of CUB was, of course, not a tale of decline, but the story of continuing growth and the combination of at least sixty breweries. There were times when the history seemed never ending and the task of writing it as vast as that tackled by the patient Mr Gibbon.

I have to thank CUB employees one and all, particularly Paul Ormonde whose enthusiasm, wise advice and encouragement finally got me to the publisher. Gary Max put together the illustrations, Erika Petersons dug deep into the resources of the CUB library, Joyce Grimshaw found the long-lost records of the Foster Brewing Company and Ann Williams did the endless copying. Kevin Merrigan and Keith Deutscher provided many historic bottle labels.

There were many others who drew on their memories of events: Sir Edward Cohen, Lou Mangan, Dr Carl Resch, Ted Williams, Bert Williams, Tom Kelly, Brian Corrigan, Eric Thomson, Neville Wigan, Fred Coulstock, Frank Harold, Tim Plant and all the present executive of CUB. I was deeply indebted to Colin Fraser who told of the CUB campaigns with George Patterson Advertising. The co-operation everywhere was splendid.

I toast them all over a glass of foaming Foster's.

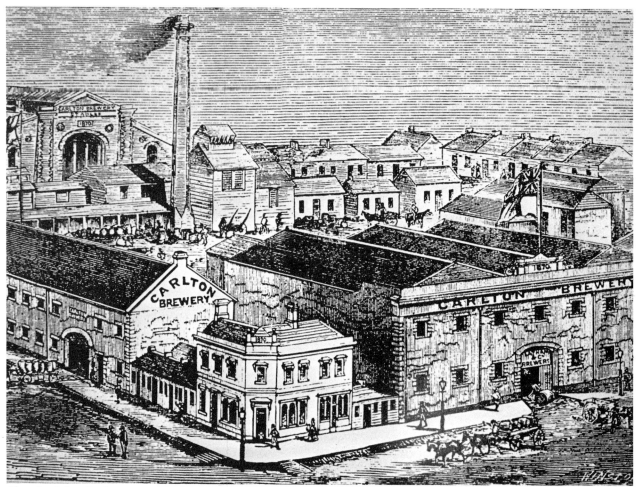

*Sketch of the Carlton
Brewery, before the grand
building project. The old Bush
Inn at the corner of Bouverie
and Victoria Streets was
demolished in 1922.*

INTRODUCTION

The old brewery at Carlton sits up at the top of Swanston Street and dominates. Down the other end of St Kilda Road is the Shrine, a vast Grecian tomb, the memorial to the fallen in two world wars. Over to the left is the Melbourne Cricket Ground, the biggest cricket ground in the world and home for the astonishing Australian Rules Grand Final. There is an old saying that if you understand these three totems you need to understand little else about Melbourne. This triangle holds its heart and soul.

In the early colonial days rum and brandy were the staple drinks. But even as the colonials were building their first racecourses and constructing their pubs, they were brewing beer. It was a hot and dusty climate, always more suited to beer, and beer became our drink. After the Germans, the Belgians and the Dutch we were among the most ardent beer drinkers in the world. Had we been colonised by the French or the Italians wine may have become number one, but English, Scots, Irish and Cornstalks dominated. Although we produced wine, beer always was the drink of the working man.

Melbourne was a noble beer capital. We grew up with a curious sense of inferiority about products, a strange attitude that almost anything manufactured overseas simply had to be better. But not beer. There was not the slightest doubt that beer made in Melbourne, and that meant Foster's, Vic or Melbourne Bitter, had to be the finest beer on earth. We would shudder at the thought of anything that came from Sydney or Adelaide. The ultimate horror was the thin, undrinkable fizz made in the United States.

Those of us who grew up in the inner suburbs were aware of the importance of brewing. A rich variety of smells would flow down the Yarra, particularly on a still autumn morning. The Rosella factory would be in full cry, producing sauce and soup and the heady odour of cooked tomatoes. But best of all, flowing across Richmond and Burnley to South Yarra, Toorak and Prahran, would be the smell of good malt and hops from the Carlton, Abbotsford and Richmond breweries.

In 1871, when Victoria had a population of 800 000, there were 126 commercial breweries. Beer did not transport easily so every little community needed to get it fresh. With the coming of an efficient railway system, brewing became more concentrated so that only the fittest and the best survived. Carlton & United Breweries was ultimately the survivor. Its family tree spreads back through all those 126 breweries and many others across Australia; its roots go back to the 1850s.

As a history of CUB this book is timed for the centenary of Foster's Lager, which has its one hundredth birthday in 1988, the bicentenary year of British settlement. It is also the centenary of the style of beer we drink now, right across the continent. All through the nineteenth century colonial Australia drank the heavy top-fermented English style ales. Foster's Lager was the first successful German-type bottom-fermented lager to be made in Australia. Served clean and cold it set the pattern for the type of beer most of us wanted to drink. It suited the climate.

There have been other good lagers in the Carlton stable but Foster's finally dominated and is now the flagship brew of the company all around the world. When a cartoonist creates a comic strip he fills it with interesting characters. Ultimately one gets out of control and to the surprise even of the creator, it comes alive. It was like that with Foster's.

An air of mystery surrounds the men who gave the beer its name, W. M. and R. R. Foster, brothers, from New York, USA. They came to Melbourne in 1887, started the Foster Brewing Company in Rokeby Street, Collingwood, and began brewing in 1888. They were desperately under-capitalised. They turned it into a public company, sold out their interest within a year and then returned home. By my reckoning they were not in Australia more than eighteen months. They made no waves, held no press conferences; they kept out of sight. Indefatigably I have searched through public records in the United States, but have found no trace of them. They came to Australia, gave us a famous name, and left.

If they are sitting aloft somewhere in a brewers' heaven they will be proud of their Foster's today. Foster's is brewed in Australia, the United Kingdom and Canada. It is shipped to eighty-five countries around the world. There are more than a hundred and fifty outlets in the Middle East in such exotic places as Bahrain, Oman and Abu Dhabi. Look for it in bars in Manchester, Seattle, Hong Kong, Tokyo, Montreal, Vanuatu, Chatanooga or Katherine, it will be there. The one single Australian name that is better known than any other across the globe is Foster's.

CHAPTER ONE

She-oak, the Shearer's Joy

Australians have always been a race of knockers. They have worshipped that mythical place 'overseas'. Anything that came from overseas was always better. Overseas had the style, the sophistication, the know-how. A native sense of inferiority made us feel Australian had to be worse. Sport was one of the rare exceptions, we felt we could run, fight, row, handle a ball and speed a horse better than most people. We also believed we could make beer. No doubt about that, most of us feel that Australian beer is the best on earth. But it wasn't always so. At least until the mid 1890s there was nothing but contempt for colonial beer. If a man could afford it he would buy Bass or Allsopps from England, and particularly the best from Holland, Denmark or Germany. Right from the earliest times the sailing ships came to Australian ports laden with beer.

There was a beautiful range of names for the colonial product: sheep wash, stringybark, shearer's joy, ketchup and catch-up. They called it shypoo, and a shypoo joint was a pub.[1] Another favourite term was swipes. You called beer swipes when it was thin, watery and indigestible. The story of Murphy's swipes was famous.

In 1854 Sir Charles Hotham took over from La Trobe as Governor of Victoria. Hotham was a rear admiral and not over-gifted at the charming niceties of mixing with the colonials. In May 1855 on the Queen's Birthday, after what seemed an unconscionable time, he gave a ball at Government House in Toorak. It was a disaster. The *Age* next day said: 'No champagne, no sherry, no port, no nothing, but Murphy's "swipes" and sour marsala which nobody could drink. People never tasted such execrable beer before'.[2] Murphy, the maker of the beer, was a member of the Legislative Council and the *Age* said never again would he be able to hold up his head. The *Herald* had a very eloquent Geelong correspondent named Marie who wrote:

> It was not a nice pale ale, or any good wholesome malt mixture, but a villainous compound . . . Poor Captain — of the 12th, a very elegant man, took a bold draught, being excessively thirsty, but when he set down his tumbler, he cast a look upwards that was like the beer itself — he seemed thunderstruck.

To make matters worse the Governor didn't ask Marie for a dance, or anyone else, and he served the acid brew out of bedroom jugs. Many of

OPPOSITE PAGE:
Carlton Brewery in the 1870s. The lovely tower is still there, but has long since been hidden by the trappings of the high tech age.

the guests were ill for days. 'Poor Mrs P. and her daughter,' Marie said, 'have been obliged to take a glass of flour and water twice a day and now gruel with brandy in it . . . the doctor says it will be weeks before we are right again.'[3]

Even worse, many believed that colonial beer polluted the blood. In 1871 'New Chum' wrote to the *Argus*:

> Sir, having got my hands and fingers bruised while following my business, and they being bad for three weeks without showing any signs of healing, I spoke to one of my fellow workmen about them, when he aptly said, 'You don't drink colonial beer do you?'
>
> I said 'Yes, two pints per day.'
>
> He said, 'Leave it off, and your hands will soon get better.'
>
> I did so, and in a week they were nearly well . . . In the big city that I come from I never heard of Barclay's porter or Bass's ale polluting the blood.[4]

Colonial beer, it was said, could even do worse than that. In February 1875 a Dr Jenkins died, according to the inquest, from 'indulging in very heavy potions of colonial beer'. Dr Youl claimed colonial beer was brewed from sugar and hops instead of malt and hops; the result was an effusion of fusel oil, a deadly poison. He advised all present at the inquest not to drink colonial beer. The controversy over using sugar instead of pure malt was to rage for the next thirty years.

The *Argus*, which believed that almost every sin perpetrated by mankind was the result of demon drink, thundered that 'Every police court affords daily testimony to the truth of the insinuation . . . the cheap beer of the pub is as vile a compound as it ever entered into the brain of man to concoct'.[5]

The brewers were outraged. Thomas Aitken of the Victoria Brewery in East Melbourne said he had been making beer for twenty-six years and never had he used an ingredient that was in the slightest degree injurious to his fellow creatures.[6] In August there was a government inquiry. William Johnson, the government analyst, reported that they examined 1200 examples of colonial beer. With few exceptions they were muddy and poor in alcohol, but he didn't find that any dangerous ingredients had been added.[7]

The temperance advocates believed wickedness prevailed everywhere in the brewing industry, but it was really the lack of quality ingredients and the ferocity of the climate. Everything had to be transported by bullock waggon so it was cheaper and more practical to make beer on the spot than to import it from the city. Many hotels made their own. There were no railroads, no roads, only tracks. The brewers used anything they could lay their hands on for fermenting: old water tanks, crudely built vats or maybe English hogsheads that had come out filled with beer, whisky or rum. The local water often was saline and the ingredients would have been better suited to making damper or Johnny cakes. But it was a lovely way of making money. There was no one else around to do it.[8]

And how did you cart the beer in the hot sun? An old brewery man explained what it was like back in the 1880s:

> The first brewery with which I was connected was at Sandhurst [Bendigo], and I had to cart the beer from 30 to 40 miles, and sell it at my own risk. Not more

than a third of it bore the ordeal of transportation without deterioration, and it was a frequent subject of inquiry on the part of my customers why the beer I delivered was so bad, and the beer of the same brewing, which they tasted in the brewery, was so good? The reason was that the beer would not bear transportation.[9]

Even in 1890 Dr Carl Rach, a German chemist, wrote with some wonder that no country on earth had to put up with such tough conditions.

Lager brewers will be horrified to learn that a retailer often requires longer than eight days to accomplish the sale of a barrel of colonial beer; that the colonial beer in cask, after being shipped a day's journey by rail must make a journey of 200 or 300 miles to some far off spot in the Australian bush by team, in a waggon drawn by fourteen to twenty oxen or camels under the burning heat of the sun, a journey that may endure six weeks or more.[10]

Not only were the bush brewers in trouble, the climate throughout the Australian continent was an agony for all brewers. Until the late 1880s refrigeration did not exist. Yeast is a sensitive living organism, which prefers temperatures around 25 degrees Fahrenheit. As one writer put it, what do you do in a country where the temperature might be 115 degrees Fahrenheit one day and over 100 degrees for weeks on end? Regularly whole brews would be ruined, thousands of gallons washed down the drain, and brewers would have to suffer the eternal vigil, sitting up all night taking the temperatures of their brews, like nurses watching their dying patients in an intensive care unit. Then, after the beer had been delivered, imperious hotel keepers would return it to the brewery claiming it was unsatisfactory. All this happened at the time of the year when demand was at its peak. The greatest thirsts came during heatwaves, when it was considered impossible to make good beer. So the breweries would work at peak during the winter months hoping to store good brews for the summer. Colder areas like Tasmania were better for making beer.

An English brewer who came to Australia from Burton in 1857 put his entire agony into verse. It was known as 'The Brewer's Lament'.

> The beer that I turned out at Burton
> Gave me cash, credit, fame and renown;
> I've brewed here on the very same system,
> But as 'swipes' it's known over the town.
>
> Capt. Cook, when he found out this island
> Should have asked for some recipes grand
> How to brew beer that will stand the climate,
> Not 'fret' and go sour on your hand.
>
> Wild yeasts are the curse of the country,
> Bacterium sure thrives by itself;
> The weather's hot, murky, and sultry,
> And brewing brings very poor pelf.
>
> Kangaroo 'sheoak's' a very poor article,
> Sugar's the principal ingredient of same;
> Hops and malt make up the smallest particle,
> Chemicals, dirt, yeast, and water make poison the name.

'Tanglefoot', 'swipes', any name you give it,
Won't make it smell sweet or alter its taste;
The 'tang' still remains, the book looks decrepit,
'Tis of energy, time, and material a waste.[11]

An early name for the colonial beer that made your hair stand on end
was 'she-oak'. Several glasses of she-oak allegedly would destroy the system
for a month. Sidney J. Baker[12] says that the fine old word 'shickered' was
probably derived from she-oak, and perhaps it first came from the she-
oak net, a life preserving net, slung under the gangways of every ship
moored to the Melbourne wharves; if you were thoroughly shickered or
she-oaked you toppled off the gangway into the net.

The true story was this. Moss was one of Melbourne's first brewers. In
1838 he had a brewery in Little Flinders Street at the back of the old Ship
Inn. His plant consisted of one 75-gallon copper, a cooler, a mash tub,
and two malting mills. He sold his beer for 2s a gallon or £5 a hogshead
and he called it 'She-oak Tops' in honour of the she-oaks on top of Batman's
Hill. The suspicion was that it even tasted like she-oak juice. T. Capel was
another brewer. In 1837 he had a brewery near Queen's Wharf.[13] Then
there was T. G. W. Robinson, who opened a brewery in 1840. Legend
has it that he made 'a fair imitation of English ale', and this cooled the
demand for She-oak Tops. Tom Robinson was a gregarious hearty
character who covered himself in jewellery. He wore a watch chain composed entirely of gold sovereigns. Poor Tom fell on evil times. He married
the widow of his employer and in a court battle over property he landed
as a bankrupt in the Melbourne Gaol. Late in life he became a 'beer doctor',
moving around the colony, advising, ministering to diseased brews, solving
one desperate ale problem after another.[14]

The early days were difficult. Sydney Town was the headquarters where,
every April, all hotel keepers and brewers had to send their applications
for licence renewal. On 30 June 1839 there was tremendous grief because
all the licences had expired and the new ones had not arrived from Sydney.
So on 1 July, and for several days, all Melbourne's eighteen hotels closed.
A drought of sad proportions set in. According to one journal 'the town
presented a most singular and unlooked for appearance', and the soft drink
shops did remarkable trade. When the licences arrived it was like the relief
when the siege of Paris was lifted. The town of four thousand was strewn
with bottles.[15] Paul Maguire in *Inns of Australia*, described Melbourne
as a hard-drinking town, more American in temper than Sydney which
was more sedate. Hotels were open from six in the morning until midnight.
If these hours seemed miserably short it was possible to get a night licence
and trade twenty-four hours a day.[16]

The first man to have a brewery which could be described as a serious
manufacturing organisation was Henry Condell. He was born in Madeira
in 1799 where his father was a wine merchant. He went to Van Diemen's
Land (Tasmania) in 1822, opened a brewery in Hobart in 1830, then moved
to Melbourne in 1839 to start a brewery in Little Bourke Street, not far
from St Francis' Church. He produced a beer which was called facetiously
'Condell's Entire'. In those days the fancy, expensive beers from London
were 'Entire'. It had been the practice in London pubs to mix the brews
using two different pumps — half bitter and half malty ale — and a brewer

Henry Condell, Melbourne's first successful brewer. In 1842 he celebrated becoming Melbourne's first Mayor with copious quantities of Condell's Entire.

named Harwood had the ingenious idea of putting the two together to avoid all the inconvenience. He called it 'Entire'. His beer was eminently drinkable. Some said if only anyone could ever have a chance to age Condell's Entire a little it could even be superior to English beer. Henry Condell very quickly became one of the richest men in Melbourne and in 1842 he became the first Mayor of Melbourne. Legend has it that the election was celebrated with considerable quantities of Condell's Entire.

Disastrously, on 15 July 1845 the home of Condell's Entire burnt down entirely. A kiln overheated, fire quickly went through the woodwork, the flames licked the fronts of the buildings opposite and the heat was so great the glare lit up the whole city. It was hopeless trying to save the brewery, all they had was the 'miserable little engine' from the Cornwall Insurance Company; the only water came from the Yarra and had to be carted by horse then applied with buckets. In the end the real battle was to save Henry Condell's private house. There was plenty of manpower to do that: the 99th Regiment under Lieutenant Blamire, plus an interesting ecumenical band, the Reverend James Forbes of the Presbyterian Church and Roman Catholic priests, P. B. Geoghegan and R. Walshe, all helped. The Condell home was finally saved at the expense of torn away doors, smashed windows and broken furniture, but Condell made no more beer.[17] The sacrifice of Melbourne's best brewery was enough to shock the citizens into action; meetings took place immediately to find adequate fire protection.

There was a fine amber period when it was difficult to go wrong making beer, everything just kept growing. In 1856 Victoria had thirty-five breweries, and in the city area of Melbourne bounded by Flinders, Spencer, La Trobe and Spring Streets there were 136 inns and taverns. Of course, many of them were just holes in the wall, fearful dens where the she-oaks and swipes could only be imagined. The breweries had evocative names,

Melbourne's first hotel, the Lamb Inn. Watercolour by W. F. E. Liardet. La Trobe Collection, State Library of Victoria.

Sketches, showing the different processes involved in the manufacturing of beer at the Carlton Brewery, which appeared in the Handbook of Victoria, *1886.*

the Dublin, the Cambridge, the Phoenix, the Eagle and the Star. The peak was reached in 1871 when there were 126 breweries in Victoria turning out 13 061 145 gallons, brilliantly impressive for a colony that had a population of less than 800 000. That was 16.3 gallons a head.

Large breweries were, however, already beginning to show their muscle and the power of their balance sheets. In 1873 the Carlton Brewery from Bouverie Street put out a handsomely printed little book, *A Glass of Ale* by John Barleycorn. Such moving prose in praise of beer has rarely appeared in print. 'Beer is the staple beverage of England', it says, 'let an heir be born to a noble estate, the delighted father immediately orders a special brewing . . . A prince of the blood-royal falls ill . . . the first thing he weakly murmurs as consciousness returns is "Give me a glass of ale".' Although 'The ploughman homeward plods his weary way', the truth is 'his mouth is watering in anticipation of his well-earned pint'. Even the London swell 'all whiskers and vanity' must have his 'bitter beah'.

John Barleycorn noted that English beer was still coming to Australia in big quantities.

> We notice in the manifests of newly arrived vessels, hogsheads of draught and barrels of bottled beers, sufficient to accompany the most Gargantuan repasts. Enough, one would think, to wash down all the fresh and preserved meats in Australia.[18]

But Mr Barleycorn lamented it was not suited to the climate. It was

> too heavy, too somniferous in its effects for the heat of our summer days. What is wanted to recoup the waste of tissue, to appease the drouth of sun-baked Australians is a beer that shall be light, yet good, pleasant to the palate, a beer without a headache in a hogshead of it.

And of course, here to solve the problem was the Carlton Brewery, pre-eminently popular in the hands of Mr Edward Latham.

Latham was an imposing gentleman, winged collar, bow tie, neatly clipped beard and moustache. He looked like a cross between Alfred Deakin and King George V. He came to Australia from Liverpool in 1864, bringing with him an invalid younger brother; the sea trip was supposed to restore his brother to health, but he died the day after they stepped ashore.[19] Latham went to Tasmania, married, and returned to Melbourne looking for a business. He spotted an advertisement:

Edward Latham's Prize Ale advertised on a poster by Charles Troedel. Latham's Carlton Ale was supposed to conquer all. La Trobe Collection, State Library of Victoria.

SHERRIFF'S SALE, McGEE V. BELLMAN AT 3 O'CLOCK, 9TH AUGUST 1865, AT
CARLTON BREWERY, BOUVERIE STREET. ALL RIGHT, ETC. IN 90 CASKS OF
ALE, MORE OR LESS, 150 EMPTY CASKS, 4 HORSES AND THE PLANT ON THE
PREMISES. P. F. KAVANAGH, SHERRIFF'S OFFICER, AUCTIONEER.

The first brewery on the site had been conducted by Rosenberg & Co.
in 1858, and they had called it the North Melbourne Brewery. Breweries
failed then even faster than restaurants do now, and this one lasted little
more than a year. John Bellman took over the building, but failed even
faster than Rosenberg, and so Edward Latham found himself a very cheap
delapidated little brewery.[20] Latham went into partnership with G. M.
Milne, but quickly took over as sole proprietor. He hired Alfred Terry,
who undoubtedly was the best brewer in the colony, and output rose from
fifty hogsheads a week to five hundred. According to the advertising copy
Carlton produced a unique beer. There were secrets only known to Mr
Latham and Mr Terry which tended 'to make the Carlton Ale what it
really is, the most wholesome, the pleasantest and hence the most popular
of vintages'.[21]

In 1864 Latham built handsome bluestone offices in Bouverie Street,
Carlton, which stretched all the way to Victoria Street, except for the little
Bush Inn on the corner. The inn came down in 1922 and the present

The oldest known photograph of the Carlton Brewery in Bouverie Street. The photograph was taken in the 1880s.

Alfred Terry, founder of the Carlton Brewery Fire Brigade.

executive offices were built in matching bluestone for a fortune. The main brewery was in Victoria Street and the stables, which were very grand, were over in Ballarat Street. They were

> 80 feet square, 30 feet high and covered with a single span roof. A senior judge walked down Ballarat Street just as the building was approaching completion. He was so impressed he asked the clerk of works, what denomination the church would be, Anglican? Catholic? Methodist? Oh, no, said the workmen, these were just the stables for the Carlton Brewery.[22]

The horses according to the Latham journal were the 'crème de la crème of the equine creation'. Each stall had the name of the occupant above it, 'Kitty', 'Punch', 'Johnny', 'Jennie', 'Jessie', and 'Hector', a huge fellow who won the big prize at the 1871 Agricultural Show. Then there was 'Old Coppin', the most famous of all the horses of the Carlton Brewery. His tail and hooves are still preserved at the old stables plus an 'In Memoriam'. He was named after the illustrious rotund George Coppin, who originally owned him back in 1860.[23]

George Coppin MP, married three times (his third wife was the daughter of his second wife),[24] was a comedian and entrepreneur, the most famous man in colonial theatre. It was absolutely right that a majestic draught horse should be named in his honour. Already in 1873 the horse was more than 30 years old. John Barleycorn recorded that he was

> in as good a state of preservation as though he had lived upon the beer he draws. Thirty years for a horse is more than equal to threescore and ten for a human being, and yet Old Coppin can trot away with his eight hogshead of Carlton as jauntily as the youngest in the stables.[25]

If anyone could be described as the father of Carlton it would be Edward Latham. It was his business and administrative skills that made the Carlton Brewery a success against frightening competition. In 1884 he was a rich man and he lived in a splendid Kew mansion, 'Knowsley'. He sold out to the Melbourne Brewing and Malting Company, but under the terms of the agreement remained for three years as managing director.

The *Age*, maintaining an unending campaign against the liquor industry, reported that in 1883 there were 20 breweries and 1120 public houses in Melbourne, looking after a population of 284 474. The *Age* maintained there were 11 000 total abstainers, estimated the number of children and female non-drinkers, and worked out that less than 100 000 people were spending £2 million a year in 1100 public houses.[26] At this time there were twenty Victoria Hotels, twenty-one Railways Hotels, twelve Albions, nine Bayviews, thirteen Commercials, eight Councils, eight Harps of Erin, and four Foresters. The *Age* said:

Edward Latham, patriarch of the Carlton Brewery.
La Trobe Collection, State Library of Victoria.

> These houses are sometimes so close together it is hard to understand how the occupants get a living . . . one would imagine that the powers that be rule that every street corner should have a pub. At one street corner in Moray Street, Emerald Hill [South Melbourne], there are five corners and each one of them is occupied by a pub.[27]

And the *Age* thundered that many of these pubs were poor indeed: 'low dens in the slums, they are resorted to by besotted drunkards, loafers, vagabonds, thieves and prostitutes'.

Edward Latham retired in 1884. He was a leading figure in the Anglican Church and the *Australian Brewers' Journal* described him as a man of unswerving integrity. 'He is a man whose individuality is stamped on his face; his open brow, clear, honest eyes, are the outward and visible signs of a good and valiant soul within.'[28] Latham travelled the world — USA, Great Britain, Norway, Sweden and all over Europe — and like every other Melburnian in the 1880s he indulged in the most beautiful way ever contrived to make quick riches, land speculation. He bought eighty-seven acres of land at Preston, and with James Munro and B. J. Fink formed the Heart of Preston Land Co. Ltd. They divided the Latham land into blocks, promoted it judiciously and in 1889 made a profit of £33 000.

Edward Latham was deeply associated with the Baillieus. He represented Queenscliff in the diocese of Melbourne, and Queenscliff was the ancestral home of the Baillieus. In 1887 Latham's 22-year-old daughter made what Michael Cannon described in *The Land Boomers* as a brilliant marriage. She married William Lawrence Baillieu, a tall, good-looking, adventurous young banker. That other daring banker, George Meudell, said W. L. Baillieu had an alluring personality and in the palmy days of the land boom was the greatest auctioneer of them all. There was one subdivision called the Town Hall Estate at Malvern. W. L. Baillieu sold it at the rate of an allotment a minute, total purchase price £50 000.[29] W. L. Baillieu was to be very nearly the leading financial power broker of his generation. W. L. and Bertha Latham had four sons and four daughters and they all received Latham as their second name. Their eldest son Clive became a London barrister and was created Lord Baillieu in 1953.[30] The association with the Baillieus did not end there. Edward Latham married twice. His second marriage in 1859 was to W. L. Baillieu's sister; the Baillieus were a large family with sixteen children to James and Emma Baillieu.

As the *Australian Brewers' Journal* put it, Edward Latham was bitten by 'the tarantula of land speculation'.[31] His Heart of Preston Land Company crashed and paid nothing to its creditors. He was also on the board of the Federal Bank which closed its doors in 1893. He made a secret composition with his creditors in 1892 for £32 795 and paid a shilling in the pound. W. L. Baillieu paid sixpence.[32] Edward Latham was now living in Studley Park Road, Kew, next door to 'Raheen', but financially he was poorer than when he first came to Australia in 1864. He tried to make a comeback and bought the Southern 'Ye Olde Tymes' Brewery at Richmond. There was nothing in the brewery but its bare walls. Output was small and he made less from one hogshead than he did from three in the old days. He sold out to the Carlton Brewery in 1902 and died on 4 July 1905, a few days short of his sixty-sixth birthday.

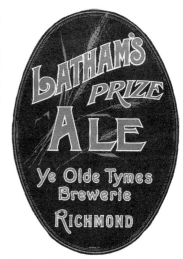

Edward Latham after the bank crash and depression of the 1890s tried unsuccessfully to make a comeback with a new company. The beer produced was the very short-lived Ye Olde Tymes.
La Trobe Collection, State Library of Victoria.

CHAPTER TWO

The Birth of Foster's

During the 1880s Melbourne became like a jet engine on afterburner. Buildings were constructed which decorated the Melbourne scene for the next eighty years — the Federal Coffee Palace, the Grand Hotel, the amazing Rialto office building with speaking tubes going from floor to floor, and, most remarkable of all, Mr Benjamin Fink built a ten-storey office building said to be the tallest in the world. In 1888 the *Daily Telegraph* had a series of articles on 'Marvellous Melbourne' and claimed there had been an expansion of 'social growth, an expansion of wealth and material well being as can scarcely be paralleled in the history of the planet'.[1] Admittedly there were a few flaws. The Rialto, the most modern office building of its time, had urinals which dropped their effluent straight into the gutters. The Yarra, the stream with the lovely Aboriginal name, was just a common sewer.[2] The *Bulletin* in Sydney delighted in referring to 'Marvellous Smelbourne', and the city's typhoid rate was five times worse than London.[3] Yet the Melbourne Telephone Exchange Company listed its first subscribers in June 1880 only four years after Alexander Graham Bell invented the telephone and the first cable tram ran to Richmond in 1880.

Melbourne built the Exhibition Building for the International Exhibition of 1880, a remarkable creation described as hybrid Florentine–French. This affair was spectacular enough but the 'International' was eclipsed by the great Centennial Exhibition of 1888. The building, which remained the biggest hall in the country, was still not large enough. The budget was £25 000 and ultimately it cost £250 000. The organisers had to roof the entire Carlton Gardens, 12 hectares of it. There was some devastation, every tree and shrub in the gardens had to be removed for this vast shed, but the Governor, Sir Henry Loch, described it as the largest area under one roof in the world. Every civilised nation on earth was invited to send exhibits and most of them did. The biggest drawcard was Mr Edison's phonograph. There was a special Centennial Cantata composed for the occasion and the words were remarkable. Part V was titled 'The Present and the Future':

To celebrate winning first prize Carlton Brewery displayed the Exhibition Building on its 1888–96 label (above).

> Where the warrigal whimpered and brayed,
> Where the feet of the dark hunter strayed,

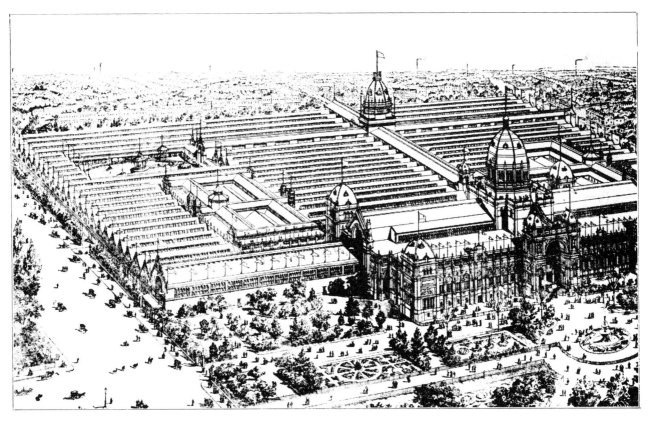

See the wealth of the world is arrayed.
Where the spotted snake crawled by the stream,
See the spires of a great city gleam.
Is it all but the dream of a dream?

The Melbourne Exhibition Building at the time of the great Centennial Exhibition, 1888.

The world's finest in industrial machinery, fashion, invention, came to Melbourne. There was an exhibition of two thousand paintings on loan from Britain, France, Germany, Belgium, Austria–Hungary and there was a vast international parade of beer. There were noble displays of kegs and fermenting vats, and in the Victorian machinery court one brewing firm erected a miniature brewery and actually made beer twice a week. The *Australian Brewers' Journal* pointed out that the public was able to see how their favourite beer was made, not from evil chemicals, but with pure malt, hops and sugar.[4]

The Victoria Brewery and Cascade of Hobart shared a gold medal in the light sparkling ale division. Against all comers world wide Wood & Sons of Collingwood had the best malt bitter ale, but they were about to perish through lack of enthusiasm from the public. Cooper & McLeod of Edinburgh won the pale ale, Cascade shared the strong ale with the Melbourne Brewing & Malting Co. and the Alpine Brewing Co. of NSW, and stout went to Macphlin's of Liverpool. The lager was particularly interesting. The first prize went to a gaggle of breweries from London, New York, Brussels, Bremen, and Hamburg, but included in the list was Foster's Lager from Melbourne, a firm that had only started brewing months before.[5]

McCracken's Australia Bitter label at the end of the century reflected the Federation spirit.

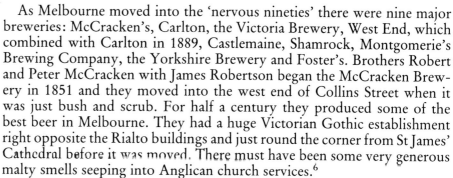

As Melbourne moved into the 'nervous nineties' there were nine major breweries: McCracken's, Carlton, the Victoria Brewery, West End, which combined with Carlton in 1889, Castlemaine, Shamrock, Montgomerie's Brewing Company, the Yorkshire Brewery and Foster's. Brothers Robert and Peter McCracken with James Robertson began the McCracken Brewery in 1851 and they moved into the west end of Collins Street when it was just bush and scrub. For half a century they produced some of the best beer in Melbourne. They had a huge Victorian Gothic establishment right opposite the Rialto buildings and just round the corner from St James' Cathedral before it was moved. There must have been some very generous malty smells seeping into Anglican church services.[6]

The Victoria Brewery was founded by Thomas Aitken. He came from Scotland when he was 19, started a brewery at Geelong in 1851, then established the Victoria Brewery in Victoria Parade, East Melbourne, in 1854. The building was rather charming in the old days, with a tower just like the one at Government House and a garden out the front in Victoria Parade. Right next door he had a stately two-storey mansion with beautiful cast iron balconies. The *Australasian Sketcher*, in its issue of 17 April 1875, described the Victoria Brewery. The writer could hardly have been more moved:

> The principal feature of Mr Aitken's establishment is the brewing tower. Such a tower attached to a church would gladden the hearts of all who worshipped in it, and if beer-drinking were a religion . . . [which] happily it is not, beerists of every persuasion would view it with just pride . . .

McCracken's used the familiar emu on another of its end-of-the-century labels.

There was a theory in typhoid-ridden Melbourne that you could beat the disease by taking Victoria Brewery Malt.

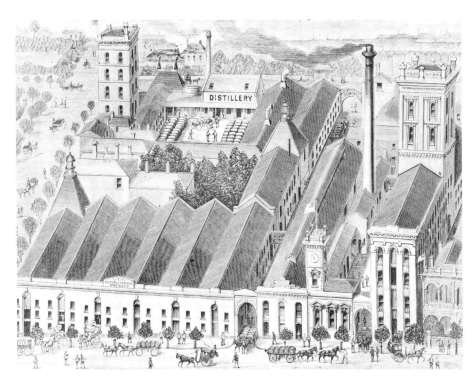

The Victoria Brewery in Victoria Parade, East Melbourne, had a grandeur unequalled by other breweries.

But his passion really got under way when he observed the fermentation in full bubble:

> You lean over the edge of the tub — such a tub as Glumdalalitch might have washed Gulliver in — and with a rapid movement of your hand over the surface of the fermenting mass, bring the gas up to your nose. The shock is innocent and delicious. Teetotallers might experience it without violating their consciences. So beneficial is the effect, that children suffering from whooping cough and other similar ailments are frequently sent to sniff the gas as a remedy.

He told too that Mr Aitken guarded his malt house from rats with a veritable army of cats, 'destroying angels'. Mr Aitken, he claimed,

> doesn't know how many cats he has. He said at one time, mildly, about a thousand; afterwards, that he was personally acquainted with at least fifty, but that there were wild ones in the recesses of his cellars at whose presence he trembled. There must be queer games played on the roofs of a brewery on moonlight nights.

A Victoria label of 1890 commemorated Queen Victoria's long reign.

Mr Aitken died in 1883, and left the business to his sons Archibald and Thomas. Thomas smartly dissipated the money on the horses. In July 1886 he appeared in the Bankruptcy Court. He was described as a commission agent of Hawthorn, formerly a partner in the Victoria Parade Brewery. He had lost £14 000 betting, buying and selling racehorses. In 1888 the business was sold to James and Alfred Nation for £80 000 and they built a grand edifice complete with clock tower, chimney and battlements. Were they fearful that they might have to hold off the invading armies of Temperance?[7]

The Shamrock was one of the smaller breweries, but clearly it was well loved and well managed. They had three acres and a very stately building on the banks of the Yarra at Collingwood. The brewery chimney, 50 metres high, ejected its sweet smells over the district. Their annual picnic was before Christmas and the employees used to go off in four in hand drags drawn by beautifully coiffured horses. There was a load of good Shamrock aboard with 'some soft' for the ladies and they would travel into the bush at Warrandyte.[8] This was their slogan and rallying cry:

> Your doctors may boast of their lotions,
>   And ladies may talk of their tea;
> But I envy them none of their potions —
>   A glass of good 'Shamrock' for me.
> The doctor may sneer if he pleases,
>   But my recipe never will fail —
> For the physic that cures all diseases
>   Is a bumper of good 'Shamrock' Ale.[9]

The Shamrock Brewery acquired its pretty name in 1874 when it was taken over under the name of Boyd & Head. It began at the corner of Simpson's Road and Walmer Street, East Collingwood, in 1865 with Thomas Graham, and it was known alternatively as Graham's or the Simpson's Road Brewery. It suffered internal financial troubles until the skilful Henry Collis Boyd took full command. Mr Boyd was said to be brilliant and witty and most skilful at promoting his product. At annual meetings he would point out that Shamrock was not only nutritious and exhilarating but calculated 'to promote the energy and continuance of muscular exertion'.[10]

The Castlemaine Brewery was in Moray Street, South Melbourne, and it began in 1871. There was some fierce prejudice when it started, as the local citizens thought Castlemaine beer ought to come from Castlemaine. One of the local publicans went into the cellar at Moray Street and asked for a sample of their best brew. They gave him a glass. 'That's rubbish,' he said, 'nothing like the good stuff from Castlemaine'. They didn't tell him the beer had actually come from Castlemaine.[11]

Castlemaine at this time was Australia's most amazing story. Edward Fitzgerald started the brewery in the little Victorian goldmining town of Castlemaine in 1857. He was joined by his brother Nicholas in 1859. They were educated Irish gentry, born in Galway, Ireland. The business expanded like no other brewery in the country. They established breweries in Sydney, Brisbane, Newcastle, Daylesford and Newbridge. They had to go to Melbourne because the orders were so large they couldn't cope with the city demand. Of course, the various Castlemaine companies eventually split and went their own way. Nicholas Fitzgerald became a prominent member of the Victorian Legislative Council and even had a hand in Federation. He was a warm, generous man, brilliantly gifted at flowery speech and he wore a pearl pin in his elegant cravat! He formed the South Melbourne Brewery with J. B. Perrins. They sold out in 1885 to form a public company with Perrins as the first managing director.[12]

There were other breweries: Mongomerie's, West End, and Yorkshire were all destined to fail. The most unusual of all these breweries was the

A Castlemaine Tiger Brand label from the South Melbourne Brewery, 1898.

youngest, the Foster Lager Brewing Company at Rokeby Street in Collingwood. They set out to compete with all the beautifully brewed lagers
that were imported in huge quantities from Germany.

Australian beer was very different then to what it is now. It was sweet,
dark, flat, heavy and warm. In short it was English, top-fermented. In top
fermentation the yeast rises to the surface. In bottom fermentation, exactly
as the name implies, it sinks to the bottom. Lager is bottom-fermented,
requires cooling machinery, and is a much slower process. It takes much
longer to mature; the German word 'lager' actually means storage. The
Australian Brewers' Journal called lager the beer of the future and cam-
paigned for it relentlessly.

> Unquestionably the taste of the Australian beer in the past has been in the
> direction of a sugary beer. We hold that a light gravity, rather than a highly
> hopped beer is the proper beer for this climate . . . So strong is the taste for
> sweet drinks in some districts that a Victorian brewer recently assured us that
> in his district customers at hotel bars frequently ordered a small quantity of
> raspberry cordial to be mixed with their beer.[13]

The normal way of cooling beer was just to pipe it up from the cellar, or
if the keg was on the bar, it might be covered with a wet sack. The
Australian Brewers' Journal estimated that not 2 per cent of hotels, fruit
stalls, or refreshment rooms served ice or even cool drinks on a hot day.
'Why such a state of affairs should exist is difficult to see,' thundered the
journal. 'That the public indignation has not been aroused long ago is only
to be accounted for by the well-known meekness of Australians in sub-
mitting to all sorts of inconvenience and trouble.' Every brewers' cart, it
said, should at least have a canvas cover. It complained that here it was,

*Yorkshire Brewery label,
c. 1889.*

*Castlemaine was so successful
its breweries spread around
Australia. Castlemaine beer
was produced in Melbourne
until 1907. La Trobe
Collection, State Library of
Victoria.*

1890, and there were no ice factories in the suburbs. Fishmongers should use ice, so should butchers, fruiterers, and dairymen. After the milk came down by train at night wouldn't it be improved if it were put in cool storage, wouldn't freshly killed carcases be better in a freezing chamber?[14]

The *Australian Brewers' Journal* kept insisting that lager was the beer of the future.

> . . . the human system craves for cold drinks . . . for warm countries such as this lager beer is undoubtedly one of the most suitable beverages when supplied in the proper way, in bulk, cold and fully charged with carbonic acid, we venture to prophesy that it will be *the* drink of Australia.[15]

The first attempt at the beer of the future looked utterly classic. In May 1885 Messrs Renne, Friedrich and Co. established the Gambinus Brewery in Collingwood. There were so many breweries in Collingwood that it was the brewing capital of the nation. Friedrich and Renne were both Germans, all their staff were Germans and the lager-making equipment came from Germany. Their fermenting cellar was 12 metres underground and the whole operation looked very promising. But competition in the beer business was cruel and tough. Send out your beer to the hotels and you were lucky if you were paid under three months. By April 1887 Gambinus was bankrupt with a debt deficiency of £4637 18s 8d.[16]

Cohn Bros of Sandhurst (Bendigo) also started making lager in 1885 and they called themselves the Excelsior Lager Beer Factory. They were better organised than Gambinus because they made ale as well and catered vigorously for the sticky sweet colonial taste buds. By 1887 they were claiming that they were the only brewery in the nation that was making lager successfully. Mr Cohn imported some massive ice machinery made by J. H. Schwalbe and Sohn of Chemnitz. The steam engine compressed and condensed ammonia gas then turned the ice into oblong blocks a little over a metre long. Soon he was sending his ice all over Victoria. According to the *Argus* his ultimate triumph was a customer in Hay, NSW, Tattersalls Hotel. The ice was packed in wood boxes with a good layer of sawdust inside. By the time it arrived it was all in one solid block. It had to go '100 miles by rail to Echuca to Deniliquin, then 75 miles across the dreary treeless waste called "Old Man Plain" to Hay'. A very expensive operation for a cool drink. Ice that cost 10s at the factory was 30s by the time it got to Hay.[17]

The greatest, the most successful of all the lager makers was the Foster Lager Brewing Company at 15 Rokeby Street, again in the brewing capital of Collingwood. Two brothers, W. M. and R. R. Foster came out from New York in 1886 and went to live at 7 George Street, Fitzroy. They brought with them Mr Sieber, a German American who had studied brewing at a college in Cologne, Frank A. Rider, a New York refrigeration engineer, and everything they needed. They spent £48 000 on a new brewery on an acre of land within 'a stone's throw of Victoria Parade'. The *Australian Brewers' Journal* thought it was very modern indeed . . . 'It far excels any brewery that we have seen in Australasia'.[18] There was a 60-horsepower steam engine of the very latest design to power the ice-making machinery plus the brewing appliances. The freezing apparatus, right next to the engine, had a 25-ton capacity. It could cool all the cellars,

One of the first Foster's Lager labels, c. 1890. From the start the labels sported the now famous Foster's F symbol.

the fermenting room, everything. The cold brine went through 6 miles of pipes. The racking room was marvellous, '68 feet by 54 feet with walls 32 inches thick'. What's more, the lager was stored for sixty days at 35 degrees Fahrenheit before it went out to the customers. Incredible for 1888; most beer suffered barely a week at 60 degrees. Continuing its enthusiasm, the journal said that in the whole of Mr Foster's brewery there was no wood except for doors and stairs. All the kegs and the fermenting tuns were pitched or varnished. So it could be said 'with truth that Mr Foster's Lager never touched wood'.

At the start it was bottled beer only, in the classic heavy bottle of the day with the wired-down cork. Brewing started in November 1888 and the public of Melbourne received their first taste of Foster's from 1 February 1889. Messrs Foster used some high-powered New York hustle. Every hotel that took the new lager received a free supply of ice to go with it. This was a sensation, and Foster's was an immediate hit, particularly as they craftily chose the hottest month of the year. But by the winter things were not going so well. With Foster's Lager on the market, the importers of lager from overseas had dropped the price of German and American lager from 11s and 12s a case to 7s 6d to drive Foster's out of town. A foreign brewery which turned out 480 000 barrels a year with profits of £200 000 didn't mind one bit losing £5000 in Melbourne to score a quick victory.

The Foster brothers led a deputation to the Minister for Customs, Mr J. B. Patterson, and told him they couldn't compete with the lager imports that were coming in from overseas. Mr Patterson was sympathetic enough. He thought Foster's was first class, and no better beer was being imported. Although he doubted it was possible to do anything at the time, he promised to raise the matter in Cabinet.[19] It was the local member for Collingwood, Mr Langridge, who actually did do something. He put the motion that the tax on imported lager be raised from 1s 6d a dozen to 3s. He did not get all his own way. Mr G. Downes Carter, chairman of Carlton, was also a member of parliament. He didn't want this upstart lager taking trade away from his Carlton Ale. This lager beer factory was started by a Mr Foster, said he, who had been trying for a good many months to sell it. Failing in his endeavours to get rid of a bad speculation he came to an innocent member for Collingwood, Mr Langridge, and asked him to try to get an extra duty. If this were conceded he did not see why an additional duty should not be imposed to protect the particular beer in which he was interested — that of the Melbourne Brewing and Malting Company.[20] Mr Carter's eloquence was not sufficient and the Fosters got their extra duty on imported lager. But his message was correct. That extra duty was just what the Foster brothers needed to help them offload their brewery. Two months later, on 13 November, they sold out to a local syndicate. The new directors were Messrs Hart, Thomson and Turner. After that the Foster brothers were never heard of again and they remain a mystery. According to the Municipal Directory they moved out of their house in George Street, Fitzroy. They returned to the United States, having sold far too quickly a lager that was destined to be famous even in their own country.[21]

Two Foster's Pale Ale labels of the 1890s (top and bottom).

The first meeting of the Foster Lager Brewing Company Ltd was at the office of Pavey Wilson & Cohen on 12 November 1889.[22] Alfred D. Hart

An 1890s Foster's label for its stout.

was in the chair. The choice of venue was of particular interest, the office of Montague Cohen. At this stage Montague Cohen was just 35 and a formidable man indeed. Not only did he have a smart financial brain but he had cricket skills almost in the Test class. When he was at Scotch College, a dispute with the sports committee led to L. S. Woolf, who was to become a barrister, and he forming their own team. They collected some smart young cricketers, including John Blackham, one of the greatest wicket keepers of all time and Tommy Horan, the Test player. They were coached by John Conway, manager of the Australian XI in England. Montague Cohen was the team captain and not surprisingly they beat the Scotch XI.[23] Cohen did not persist with his cricket career. He did other things like founding the Swan Brewery and being mastermind of the amalgamation that created the Carlton & United Breweries.

The Foster brothers attended the first few board meetings, just to exchange cheques and technical details. The company did not hear from them again. The first account for payment was £45 440 16s 10d, the purchase price demanded by the Foster brothers.[24]

The new syndicate imported a new head brewer from Denmark, Joseph Preska of Copenhagen. He arrived aboard the steamer *Parramatta* in November 1890. The Foster Brewing Company was hardly dramatic in its output, 1469 dozen for the week ending 16 December 1889, but there was no question about its quality. In 1892 Stephen King and Peter H. Engel, trading under the title of Lange and Thoneman, were charged with faking German beer labels and putting them on bottles of Foster's. The crown prosecutor said they bought fifteen cases of Foster's Lager for 5s a dozen and sold them for 10s all under the label Munchener Brau-Haus Bier. William Kemp, licensee of the Town Hall Hotel in Swanston Street, said he tasted the beer and thought it really was German lager. Mr Mitchell on behalf of Stephen King said there was a prejudice against colonial beer. He believed the local article was superior to the imported and he had attempted — innocently enough — to overcome that prejudice. Stephen King was fined £5 with five guineas costs.[25]

The board minutes of the Foster Lager Brewing Company in the early 1890s show a company in turmoil. Output was small, the debt was huge, and staff were coming, going or being dismissed at an alarming rate. On 20 February 1890 we are told that J. Crossly had embezzled nineteen guineas, which very smartly made him an 'ex-employee'. This left the office petty cash in a parlous state and the unfortunate clerk, Mr Frey, had to pay the travellers out of his own pocket. Frey went to the police and had a warrant made out for Crossly's arrest, but Crossly was not to be found. Frey himself lasted only another month before he was dismissed. The company secretary, Montgomery, resigned. He departed with all 'the advances' meant for the travellers, plus £4 6s in petty cash. The board told acting secretary Farrell to get the money back and put 'the late secretary's indebtedness in the hands of a solicitor'. By April 23, however, Montgomery had called by and paid £30 on account.

Every penny had to be counted. They put on Mr Knott as a traveller, on a salary of £2 a week plus expenses. His horse and trap cost £40. Then there was the question of the ice machine. The Foster Lager Brewing Company, very fortunately, had the services of the brilliant chemist, Auguste de Bavay, a close friend of Montague Cohen. De Bavay told the

OPPOSITE PAGE:
This tribute to the Carlton Brewery Fire Brigade celebrated some of its accomplishments.

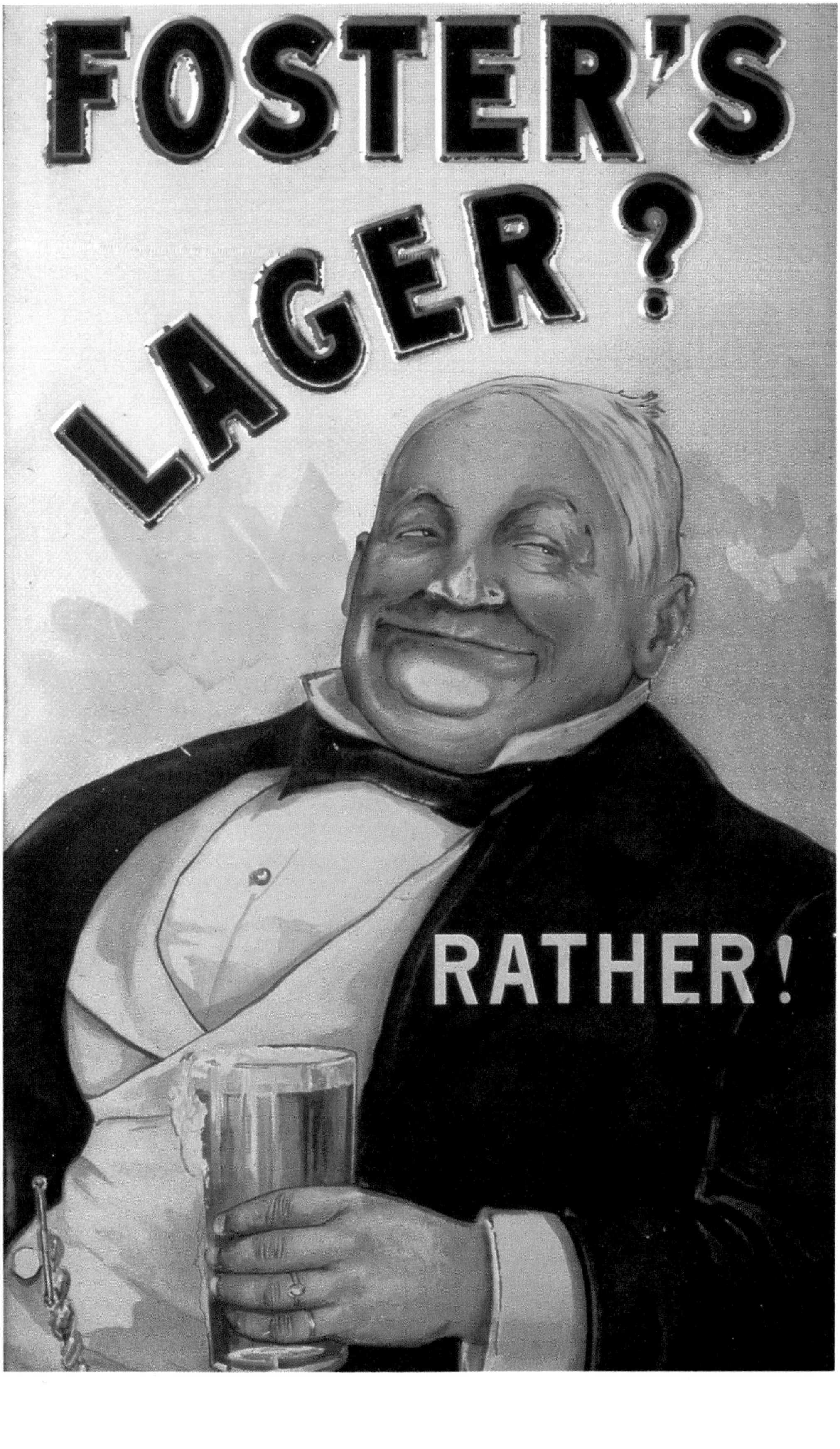
FOSTER'S
LAGER?
RATHER!

board that for two years they had been struggling with the one ice machine. It was likely to break down any minute, then they would be in real trouble. In January 1890 they decided they didn't have the money, but in March they took the plunge and bought a fine machine for £3700. All the time the Bank of Australasia was hovering in the background, demanding that they reduce their overdraft. The debt was £33 000 and the interest rate varied from 6.5 to 7.5 per cent. The board tried everything possible to make Foster's more popular. They bought 360 cases of safety matches with 'Drink Foster's Lager' on the label. They installed beer engines in city hotels. It cost £100 to fit out the bar of Her Majesty's Hotel.

There was a little Foster's advertisement in the *Herald* every day: 'Foster's Lager Beer. Send to your hotel, send to your grocer, sixpence a quart bottle', and occasionally they inserted a little riddle:

> The comparison between Foster's Lager Beer, pure high-class malt and hops, and the ordinary colonial beers is as to sixpence divided into two such parts that when the greater is multiplied by the less the product shall be sixpence. The person first solving the above problem will receive as a prize one case of Foster's Lager Beer.[26]

The lucky winner was Mr R. B. Campbell of South Yarra. The two parts were 4.73205 and 1.26795.[27]

In October 1891 the chairman tried to switch the Foster account to the Bank of Australia, instead of the Bank of Australasia. He met with a polite refusal. The situation did not improve. In December the licensed grocers decided to boycott Foster's, because the price was too high. The company did not have the muscle to resist their demands, so the grocers got exactly what they wanted, but there was worse to come.[28] On 6 June 1892 Mr Sawyer, superintendent of the Bank of Australasia, and Mr Blundell inspected the brewery. They looked at all the accounts, asked for copies of the half-yearly balance sheet and a full statement of profit and loss. On 25 July Mr Blundell told the board that the bank would carry the company's account for another twelve months but the limit would be £17 000 at 8 per cent. At the end of a year, if the bank was not satisfied, the brewery would receive one month's notice and failing compliance with that there would be a bill of sale of all moveable effects to the bank. The bank also demanded that the brewery raise £9600 in uncalled capital. On 4 August there was a meeting of shareholders. They disapproved of the arrangements with the bank and decided on a share issue. Soon Foster's was doing so well the rest of the trade was all against the young brewery. The *Australian Brewers' Journal*, which had been so friendly in 1888, became distinctly chilly. Alfred Lawrence, who produced the journal, also sold beer-making equipment and no doubt wanted to protect the journal's big advertisers.

It was really the taxman who saved the company. In September 1892 the Legislative Assembly introduced a bill which put an excise of 3d a gallon on beer that had been made with sugar. If the beer was produced only from pure malt and hops then the tax was 2d a gallon. All the colonial ales, the dark, English-style, top-fermented brews, which made up most of Victoria's beer, were made with sugar. This was a boon to Foster's, a blessed government gift and immediately sales began to rise. But once the company's fortunes began to improve, it lost some of its old friends, including the *Australian Brewers' Journal*. In 1890 the journal had been

An 1888 label for Foster's patriotic brew, Empire Pale Ale.

OPPOSITE PAGE:
One of the old tinplate poster advertisements for Foster's Lager. These were displayed in hotels around the turn of the century.

saying over and over again that lager was the beer of the future. Suddenly it switched its tack and adopted precisely the opposite view. In 1897 it said lager beer had just been a passing fad. It had had its chance and had failed. It claimed there had been a drop in consumption of 42 818 gallons and said:

> There is not the smallest chance of the concocted-in-Germany swill ever being acclimatised in Australia, and, as usual, shareholders, directors and managers will be left mournfully lamenting their want of judgment as to our public taste. People that drink beer will stick to the decent old Anglo-Saxon stuff, on which Drake, Hawkins, and Frobisher were weaned, which was the drink of their fathers before Norman foot pressed English soil, which was quaffed by British heroes throughout all the glorious centuries of glorious English history.[29]

There was an attempt in 1895 to have the duty reduced on imported lager, because it was such a help to Foster's. Mr Murray Smith told the Legislative Assembly that the duty of 1s 6d a gallon was introduced back in 1889 'in one of those temporary madnesses that seize the Assembly at various times'. He even suggested that because of the monopoly even chemicals, one of them salicylic acid, went into the beer, but the motion was defeated by twenty-six votes. Foster's survived all the assaults.[30]

CHAPTER THREE

The Bankrupt Years

The year 1890 began without any warning or suggestion from party platform, prospectus or pulpit that the nation was on the edge of its greatest financial disaster. Sarah Bernhardt, the divine Sarah, the greatest actress of her day, toured Australia with her customary collection of wild animals, including a tigress. Mr J. C. Williamson paid her £20 000 plus £5000 for a thirteen-week tour of Sydney and Melbourne, a sum almost beyond belief when the official rate of payment for a plasterer, a bricklayer or a carpenter in 1894 was 6s to 8s a day. She opened in Melbourne in June 1891. *Melbourne Punch* recorded that men and women fainted, some had hysterics, some lost portions of their attire, children were in danger of being trampled to death, and there were scenes such as had never been witnessed at a Melbourne theatre. Then, for the 1891–92 cricket season, Lord Sheffield brought a touring England side to Australia with Dr W. G. Grace as captain. The worthy Doctor demanded and received £3000 plus expenses for himself and his wife. Not quite such a large reward as that for Miss Bernhardt, but then the divine Sara did not describe herself as a true blue amateur.[1]

In 1892 share prices dived. The worst year came in 1893. According to George Meudell, twelve banks suspended trading and forty-seven building societies, more than a hundred land banks, properties and investment companies were 'dragged to the dust'. The total loss, he said, was worth £200 million sterling, or nearly half the nation's wealth. The historian P. G. McCarthy estimated that 28.3 per cent of Victorian bread winners were out of work in 1893.[2] There were soup kitchens in the suburbs for the hungry unemployed. Thousands fled the city looking for work, rabbiting, scavenging for gold. This was a popular song of the day:

> Good-bye, Melbourne Town,
> Melbourne Town, good-bye;
> I am leaving you today
> For a country far away;
> Though today I'm stony broke,
> Without a single brown,
> When I make my fortune I'll
>   come back and spend it
> In dear, old Melbourne Town.

McCracken's City Brewery was almost opposite the Rialto in Collins Street.

Nearly every brewing house was in trouble. Through the 1880s the breweries carried on as if the thirst would be eternal. They capitalised without any thought of the size of the market. They built castles in Collingwood, East Melbourne, even Collins Street, reminiscent of Fort Zindeneuf in *Beau Geste*, complete with battlements. The prime example was McCracken's great brewery in Collins Street. Benjamin Josman Fink floated McCracken's as a public company in 1888. He paid the McCracken family £250 000 for the right to float the family company and raised £2 million, one million £2 shares with a guaranteed dividend of 8 per cent for at least three years. Fink kept 130 000 shares for himself then sold them at a splendid profit. Fink was very nearly the greatest land boomer of them all: he was the floater, the starter, the creator of a whole maze of land booming companies, and finally, when the whole edifice collapsed into a pile of worthless paper, he paid a halfpenny in the pound on £1.5 million.

Michael Cannon wrote: 'When he filed his composition, Fink still owed Peter McCracken £113 000 — much of it without security. The honest brewer hadn't been able to keep pace with the swift financier.' Indeed, amongst his debts there was an invoice from McCracken's Brewery for £260 for beer consumed. He paid a halfpenny in the pound on that too.[3]

The board, manager and head brewer of Carlton Brewery, 1898. Standing (left to right): T. L. Parker (manager) and J. R. Ballenger (head brewer). Seated: Dr Lloyd, Hon. S. Williamson MLC, Hon. G. D. Carter MLA (chairman), J. Fulton and W. M. Brookes.

Beer in the 1890s was 6d a bottle, so Mr Fink's consumption from the brewery would have been 10 400 bottles. Rather than an 8 per cent dividend, from 1892 there was no dividend at all, and in 1893 £1 shares were down to 1s 6d.

Carlton share prices also took a dive. Their 15s shares were being quoted at 1s and Wood's Yorkshire Brewery was in the hands of the receiver. The money market had a mood of pending disaster akin to the witches' scene in *Macbeth*. Carlton in 1892 had planned to float some debentures. The rumour spread that the company was in trouble and about to make a call on shares. There was a panic run on deposits and the company paid out £76 000. Yet at the annual meeting on 20 September the chairman, Mr Godfrey Downes Carter, announced they were still able to pay a 5 per cent dividend just like the year before with a 4½d a share bonus.

Carter ran a wholesale liquor business. He was the Mayor of Melbourne in 1884–85, and he had a string of directorships, including a seat on the board of the ill-fated Bank of Victoria. He went into politics and was unlucky enough to be the colonial treasurer at the time of the great bank collapse. The Premier, J. B. Patterson, in consultation with Carter, declared bank holidays on Monday, Tuesday, Wednesday, Thursday and Friday, from 1 May to 5 May 1893. The panic action caused the collapse of the banking system. George Meudell described Carter as 'a whisky merchant, untrained in finance, who had a colossal conceit of himself. . . A man who lost his head at the critical moment. An ignorant man.'[4] His colleagues in the trade were much kinder. The *Australian Brewers' Journal* thought he was 'a gentleman of the best English type — high-minded, sympathetic, upright' with a 'cheery smile and genial manner. . .an ornament to the liquor trade.'[5] He may have been a disaster as a treasurer, and he certainly failed to make his own fortune: when he died in 1902 he left a deficit of £3396.

Carlton Extra Stout label, 1890–1900.

Victoria Brewery label,
c. 1900.

The Victoria Brewery was another in deathly trouble. The public company was floated in 1888 in a beautiful spirit of optimism with Alfred Nation as managing director. The company even guaranteed the trusting and happy shareholders 10 per cent dividends for ten years. By 1892 those happy shareholders found that their 20s shares were being quoted at 3d, and by November the company was in liquidation. But Victoria continued to do an astonishing trapeze act. The brewery was heavily mortgaged to the London Bank, there was a new float in London in 1894 with £100 000 in preference shares and another £150 000 in debentures. Thus the Melbourne Brewing and Distilling Co. Ltd was born. It was a nice example of finances back in the 1890s. Those keen to make money were prepared to believe almost anything.

First there was an acrimonious battle because the acreage of the grand property at East Melbourne was incorrectly stated. Then the prospectus, which went to the willing buyers in 1894, was inaccurate to the point of being dishonest: there was no mention that the company was in liquidation, and it said that average profits from 1889 to 1892 were £26 000. The true figure was £16 000, but there was no explanation of the discrepancy.[6] Finally the Melbourne Brewing and Distilling Co. Ltd was wound up in 1902. The receiver, Mr G. S. Barnes, complained from London how difficult it had been to find out what had happened in Melbourne.

They were remarkable people. Melbourne was in financial ruin, the Victoria Brewery had gone from prosperity to disaster, yet the new London-owned company immediately set about making lager beer. They imported from New York at 'great expense' an entire plant, the Pfaudler Vacuum Fermentation System, plus an expert brewer, A. J. Metzler, to run it. Optimism reigned again. This new lager system, according to the directors, was astonishing. The problem with lager was that it took so long to make. The Pfaudler system reduced the whole process to a fortnight. Mr A. Reid Baird, the assistant manager, an enthusiast for the system, said Foster's was the only other firm making lager. They were getting astonishing results but were only a little brewery. Foster's would never be able to compete because Victoria Lager would not only be produced much more cheaply, it would be an infinitely superior article. 'When the system is in operation at the Victoria Brewery, the sales will simply astonish you,' he said.[7] Sadly, the sales never astonished anyone. The Melbourne Brewing and Distilling Co. Ltd never paid a dividend.

The depression agonies were made infinitely worse by the two terrible Ts — tax and temperance. Temperance began to gain pace in the 1870s and by the 1880s it was a powerful political force. Temperance people believed that if only man would banish alcohol, crime would cease, the jails would be emptied, lunacy would disappear, husbands would remain faithful to their wives, the enormous wealth spent on drink would be spent on culture, and in the new, splendid, dry community Eldorado would be at hand. E. W. Cole, who had the gigantic Bourke Street Cole's Book Arcade with two million books, brought out a book *The Evils of the Drink Traffic*. These were some of its quieter lines:

Intemperance . . . makes wives widows, children orphans, fathers fiends, and all of them paupers, and beggars. It feeds rheumatism, nurses gout, welcomes epidemics, invites cholera, imports pestilence, and embraces consumption. It covers the land with idleness, poverty, disease and crime. It fills your jails, supplies your alm houses and demands your asylums.

A passion for 'local option' swept across the land. In 1885 Sir Graham Berry, a patriarchal gentleman with a white beard, introduced a licensing bill which fixed a statutory number of hotels for each district, one for every two hundred and fifty persons up to a thousand and one for every five hundred thereafter. (Back in the old days of Sandhurst–Bendigo they had a licensed hotel for every twenty people.) One fifth of ratepayers could petition for a ballot and a third of ratepayers had to vote or there was no ballot. Of course, the hotel keepers urged their customers not to go near the polling booth and they always referred to the Berry regime as the Berry Blight. That tactic worked beautifully, but there was a new bill in 1887 which wiped out the one third rule and very soon there was a dramatic reduction in the number of hotels. In North Melbourne thirty-seven out of fifty-seven hotels closed their doors after a poll in 1902.[8]

There was even a 'local option' song to be sung to the rousing tune of 'The Men of Harlech':

> Men of Temp'rance all united,
> Women too, your aid's invited,
> All to noble works incited,
> Listen to the call.
> See the havoc drink is working,
> Everywhere the danger lurking;
> Shout, your victory never shirking,
> Alcohol shall fail!

In January 1890 the government put a ban on all liquor at railway stations and the *Australian Brewers' Journal* said unhappily:

The colony of Victoria seems to be drifting nearer to a policy of prohibition every day, and if some check is not given to the teetotal party, those who make their living by the manufacture of ale or alcoholic beverages will find themselves in a parlous state indeed.[9]

The leader of the Temperance Party and Premier of Victoria from 1890 to 1892 was the Honourable James Munro, committee man of the Presbyterian Church and president of the Total Abstinence Society. Michael Cannon, in *The Land Boomers*, claimed that Munro as much as anyone started the land boom and caused the bank crash of 1893. Munro had the dream that the answer to alcohol was to get rid of the liquor house and replace it with the dry hotel. There was a noble name for such an establishment, the Coffee Palace, and they proliferated all over the country. One of the biggest was the Federal Coffee Palace, another was the Victoria and the most splendid of them all was the Grand. In 1886 James Munro formed a company to buy the Grand which was only two years old, and he formed the Grand Coffee Palace Company with a capital of £250 000. On the opening day there was a fine lunch. The Honourable James Munro was in the chair. He wore a frock coat and in his buttonhole there was a slip of blue ribbon, indicating he was a member of the Total Abstainers' Blue Ribbon League. At the climax of his speech, he paused. Then with great solemnity he drew from his top pocket a long piece of paper. 'Well gentlemen,' he said, 'this is what we think of the liquor license', and he put a match to the licence. It is recorded in the official history of the Windsor Hotel that as the licence burned, 'the anticipation of good fortune for the lot of them went up in smoke'. The next day the newspaper advertisements announced the sale in the refreshment rooms of tea, scones, beef tea, malt extract and fresh milk.[10]

One by one the coffee palaces all went to ruin. By March 1890 both the Federal and the Grand were in deep trouble. The Grand did not regain its licence until 1920 when it re-opened as the Windsor. The last of them to go was the Victoria Coffee Palace in the 1960s when even it succumbed to become the Victoria Hotel. It even has a restaurant, Munro's, named in honour of the Honourable James, no doubt as a reminder of the dangers of returning to beef tea.

The wowser was one problem, but more lethal to the brewer was the taxman. In 1892 the colonial government brought in a bill which the liquor trade found hard to believe, a beer duty of 2d a gallon on beer made with pure malt and 3d a gallon on beer made with sugar. Beer at the time was selling for 1s a gallon wholesale, so it was a 25 per cent tax. In the midst of a depression it caused such a panic that the Castlemaine Brewery brewed three times a day, Sunday included, for nine weeks, a total of 189 brewings. Colonel Ballenger, chief brewer at Carlton, brewed eight times in twenty-four hours and made a total of 700 hogsheads. The extra tax on beer made with sugar infuriated the liquor trade, particularly breweries like Carlton and McCracken's. It wasn't quite so bad for Foster's which used only malt for its lager beer. But there was a belief amongst politicians and the *Age* newspaper in particular, that sugar in beer was impure, evil, and produced all sorts of deadly poisons like fusel oil. The *Age* at various times described sugar beer as slow poison, as addling the brain, wrecking the lives of the community, and even a cleverly manipulated drug. T. L. Parker, a brewer at Carlton, became so upset he brought out a pamphlet in which he pointed out that the House of Lords in England had written a lengthy report which stated that sugar did not alter the character of beer. Parker warned darkly:

> The *Age* is not omnipotent, there is a greater power before whom even they will have to bow, the Australian public which is always outraged when the strong try to overbear the weak.[11]

The truth was that Australian brewers had to use sugar, and they did use it, even up to 50 per cent of the wort. It helped them to brew quicker, to combat the terrible problems of hot climate. They produced less contaminated beer by using sugar, and a lighter ale was more suited to our warm weather drinking.

Sir Graham Berry brought down the beer bill, another ravage of the Berry Blight. Mr G. Downes Carter argued passionately against it naturally, being a Carlton director. He pointed out that Melbourne's two leading newspapers (the *Age* and the *Argus*) were all for it. But those illustrious gentlemen would never take a glass of colonial beer. How cruel it was that when the government wanted more money, immediately it hit those articles used by the working classes. No trade felt depression or good times more quickly than the brewers. Mr Carter explained to par-

Foster's Topaz, named for its pale translucent colour, was one of the first of the light beers. Topaz, advertised here on a tinplate poster, boasted no sugar to avoid the tax on beers containing that substance.

liament that all the talk about sugar was nonsense. When beer was made solely of malt and hops it took two to three weeks. With sugar you could mature your beer in a few days, and when a sudden heat wave could ruin your whole brew this was absolutely essential. His pleas made no difference, the bill quickly went through both Houses and helped ruin breweries all over Victoria.[12]

It was not easy being a brewer in those times. The brewing journals complained time and again of their low social status. The *Australian Brewers' Journal* writing from the agony of the depression said:

> There is without doubt a disposition to look upon the brewers' calling as one that is scarcely legitimate, scarcely respectable; and there are some who go so far as to look upon practical brewers as men who prostitute their talents to the preparing of a beverage wherewith certain of their fellow men make beasts of themselves . . . Our sisters and our cousins and our aunts, who adhere to antiquated notions with a tenacity that transcends belief deplore the fact that we have elected to live by making beer and bitterly regret that we did not adopt the infinitely more refined methods of growing rich by deluding unwary speculators in the share market . . . The confectioner deals in puffs, tarts, lollies and other things which are much more awful in their effects than beer yet we do not imagine that he fiendishly wishes us to allow our offspring to cut short their bright young lives by means of his deadly wares.[13]

Oh, there were other miseries. The brewer loafer for example.

> Scarcely is there a brewery that has not its attendant gang of loafers, who hang round at corners and watch every chance to nip in and 'ave a booze' while the boss is away. These pests are aided and abetted by regular brewery hands. It is a preposterous state of affairs that a man, because he happens to make beer instead of bread or other food is obliged or expected to give a portion of his product away for nothing to any blackguard who is so dead to all sense of independence to ask for it.[14]

Yet right into the 1890s there were complaints, particularly from visitors, about the quality of Australian beer. They had a name for it, 'the colonial twang'. One visiting expert, Dr Carl Rach, blamed Australian barley. He said it was no good for brewing. He didn't like the water. He said it was disagreeable right across the continent and would never be accepted in German beer making. But he was particularly interesting on yeast. 'Without exception, the colonial beers possess a strikingly peculiar aroma, and this aroma, known as the "twang" is in all probability to be ascribed to some product of fermentation developed by the colonial yeast.'[15]

The man who changed all this was Auguste Joseph Francois de Bavay. He was the first man to really apply scientific methods to brewing in Melbourne and more than anyone he lifted the quality of our beer to world class. Born at Vilvoorde in Belgium, de Bavay had a passion for genealogy all his life. He claimed he could trace his family back to 1193. He first graduated as a surveyor then did further study at Gembloux, working as a brewer and chemist and even getting to know the great Louis Pasteur. De Bavay migrated to Melbourne by way of Ceylon and in 1884 he started work at Aitken's Victoria Parade brewery. His salary was £6 a week and he received a shilling commission on every hogshead of good beer. He was a bacteriologist by training, dapper, very dignified, and, according to Geoffrey Blainey, had a hearing problem which seemed to add to his concentration. Immediately he was caught up with the agonies of brewing in Australia, the terrors of wild yeasts, the ruined brews that had to be poured down the gutter. Pasteur had proved the dangers of infection caused by exposure to air and the absolute necessity of sterile vessels, but what could be done about these secondary and tertiary fermentations which rose from the yeast?

In 1883 Emil Christian Hansen created a pure yeast culture at the Carlsberg brewery in Copenhagen. He learned how to clone a cell from a single ancestor cell. On 12 November Carlsberg started to brew with a frightening germ *Saccharomyces carlsbergensis* No. 1. For the first time there was a chance to make beer with a reproducible quality and taste.[16] Hansen published a book in 1884 and immediately two Melbourne brewery chemists, de Bavay and C. W. Muller of Terry's West End Brewery started their experiments. Both men had considerable success, but de Bavay was in close touch with Hansen. In 1888 de Bavay isolated a wild yeast and Hansen was so delighted he named it *S. de bavii* in de Bavay's honour. Hansen, of course, was working in the European style and his yeast was for bottom-fermented beer. Almost certainly de Bavay was the first man in the world to develop a culture for top fermentation. In 1888 he developed 'Australia No. 2' which was the first pure yeast to go into action. Then in 1889 he produced 'Melbourne No. 1' which was to be the great ancestor, you might say the sire, of the Australian beer style. At last the colonial twang had been conquered.

De Bavay remained with Victoria for ten years and in 1894 he went on a tour of England, Belgium and France to study brewing methods. When he returned Montague Cohen, a director of Foster's, persuaded him to join his company as chief brewer. De Bavay was very interested in lager and the shrewd Mr Cohen could not have found a greater expert in the land. De Bavay immediately expanded the operation at Foster's. By 1895 he had moved smartly from selling lager in bottles to selling draught beer right throughout Melbourne's city and suburbs.

He was an extraordinary man, this de Bavay. In 1889 he found out that the city's fire hydrants were allowing sewerage to get into the water supply. This, according to de Bavay, was a direct cause of typhoid and diphtheria. Marvellous Melbourne's sanitation system already was a scandal and de Bavay's revelations forced a Royal Commission. Then, working in the Foster's laboratory, he worked out a process that was to have a profound effect on the history of Australian mining. He developed the de Bavay flotation process for treating zinc ore. He was lucky to have some solid financial backers, Montague Cohen and the financier, W. L. Baillieu. It took five years to perfect the system before it was in action at Broken Hill in 1907, but it helped both Cohen and Baillieu to establish their fortunes. He was into everything. He and Montague Cohen were even partners in a vineyard at Woori Yallock. (There must have been a few beer bottles on the shelf inspired by Melbourne No. 1 there as well.) Even after the First World War he remained a brewing consultant at CUB. He died at his home in Studley Park Road, Kew, in 1944.[17]

CHAPTER FOUR

Amalgamation – Carlton & United Breweries

The brash super-confidence of the 1880s never quite returned. Marvellous Melbourne wasn't marvellous any more and the hangover from the 1890s lasted almost until the 1950s. Much did happen, however, round the turn of the century. For a start there was the South African war. In early March British troops with vast reinforcements took Ladysmith, a strategic town in Natal. Nobody was more deeply moved than the staff of the Shamrock Brewery. According to the *Australian Brewers' Journal* the manager, Mr Boyd, was Irish and always carried a shamrock on his person. What's more, almost all his staff was Irish. Mr Boyd had the steam whistle at the Shamrock factory blowing for a full quarter-hour. He called together his entire staff and gave them a talk of pure Irish eloquence:

> Boys, you know what this demonstration means, Ladysmith has been relieved, and a great blow has been delivered against political greed, oppression and bad government. Remembering that under no government are freedom and liberty so safe and so well guaranteed as under our own, and we are all so sure of this that we are ready to fight to the bitter end to keep our Empire in its integrity . . . There is no distinction in nationalities out yonder on the veldt. Irish blood mingles with English and Scotch to water the dry soil, and Irish genius has solved the problem that at times made us almost despair. This is a glorious day for Ireland as it is for her partners in Empire . . .[1]

Next came the relief of Mafeking. As the journal put it, Major General Baden Powell had 'held the Boer Leader and the myrmidons at bay for seven months'. On Saturday 19 May every brewery had its steam whistle screaming. Many hotels threw open their doors. McCracken's Brewery held open house and rolled hogsheads out into the street. The Carlton brewery was covered in flags. Indeed, Carlton distributed 50 000 photographs of Her Majesty the Queen, proclaimed a holiday for the staff and handed every employee from the manager, Mr R. L. Parker, down to the smallest boy in the bottling department 'a gold portrait of the Queen in the shape of a half sovereign'. McCracken's not only gave the staff holidays on May 23 and 24 on full pay, but all employees plus wives and families received staff tickets to the Princess Theatre to see the show *What Happened to Jones*. Then after the show they all went to one of the McCracken hotels in Bourke Street where beer was dispensed 'on a most liberal scale'. Mr

Carlton Extra Stout label of the Boer War years (above).

Coiler McCracken proposed the toast to Her Majesty and Mr Alex McCracken responded on behalf of the staff.[2]

It was a time of vast change. On 23 January Queen Victoria died and business came to a standstill. The newspapers ran black borders for ten days and some had black borders around every single column. All the stores in the city put up black draperies. The gentlemen wore black hat bands and many of the ladies went into full mourning. The doctors in Collins Street draped their brass plates with black and the clubs respectfully pulled their blinds.

In 1901 the Duke and Duchess of Cornwall and York visited and the new Commonwealth was grandly proclaimed. For a month carpenters and decorators worked day and night to make Melbourne look beautiful. They erected some extraordinary Venetian masts around the city, and built eight enormous arches with names such as the Municipal at Princes Bridge, the King's in Swanston Street and the Queen's in Collins Street. The Queen's at the corner of Collins and Russell Streets was four stories high with Disney-like towers at the corners and a concoction on the top like the Victoria and Albert Memorial. What with all the workmen, troops, officials, a myriad politicians and social dignitaries, the consumption of beer was just splendid. Castlemaine in South Melbourne sent out a thousand hogsheads during the four riotous 'Commonwealth' weeks, an increase of 250 a week on the previous month. All the breweries did similar business. The Carlton Brewery had the contract for the seven thousand troops at Royal Park who went through over a hundred hogsheads while the Duke and Duchess were in town. The troops came from every state and even Fiji. According to the *Australian Brewers' Journal* they all drank with equal valour. For ten days in May duty was paid on 552 422 gallons. The government caterer supplied over twenty thousand bottles of champagne and five thousand bottles of other wines and spirits. 'That is a fair reward for ten thousand people, half of them ladies, for ten days,' said the journal. 'A country that has five thousand men who can vanquish a champagne army of twenty-five thousand strong in less than a fortnight should be able to view the future with confidence.'[3]

Actually the future in the beer business required very careful handling. There were sixty-eight breweries in Victoria in 1892. By 1900 there were only fifty-three and not many of these were making money. McCracken's was doing well, and Carlton had made an extraordinary recovery. At Carlton's annual meeting, the chairman, the Honourable G. Downes Carter was ebullient. He announced that Carlton was now making one fifth of all the beer in the colony and a third of all the beer brewed in the metropolis, a splendid position to occupy, unique in financial history. 'I have never heard,' he said,

> of another company, having lost more than all its capital, and being faced with a deficit of over a quarter of a million, not only pays interest on its liabilities, but yet has the courage to make proposals by which they may be liquidated . . . Well, there is not much to be wondered at. With good management and good beer a brewery does not want a deus ex machina to come to its assistance.[4]

Foster's was also doing well. It was only a small brewery compared with Carlton, and they had only two tied houses in the city, but they had a devoted discerning trade. In 1899 they put out Foster's XXX Light Ale, which the *Australian Brewers' Journal* described as very pale in colour, full of condition and similar to champagne in appearance. They were selling beer in every state, and there was a shipment to South Africa in 1901 and another to Samoa. In Rokeby Street they were immensely proud when they heard that blacks in north Queensland were using Foster's bottles instead of telegraph knobs for ornamentation.[5] The shipment to South Africa was unfortunately a sorry failure. Perhaps as an aftermath of the Boer War, anything from Australia was unpopular. One hundred cases of Foster's pints had to be sold at 1s a dozen and 400 quarts went for 2s.

Foster's Sydney rival in the lager market, the Sydney Lager Bier Company, folded that year. The *Brewers' Journal*, which had a curious distaste for anybody who produced lager, printed a facetious poem of triumph.

> Not a sound was heard save the gurgling groan
>   Of the tap when the last hogshead was filled;
> Not a carter discharged a farewell moan
>   O'er the spot where the last drops were spilled.
>
> The smoke from the stack will never more aris',
>   Nor the mash-tun tumble and bubble;
> We have been caught in the meshes of foreigners' fiz,
>   And must wrap ourselves up in our trouble. [6]

The Foster board received a desperate offer from the Sydney company to sell their brewery, contents, the lot for £40 000. The answer from Melbourne was a firm no. Next they dropped the price to £30 000, but the brewery was into debt for £15 000. The secretary of Foster's replied: 'I am very doubtful whether my Board will entertain any such proposal. The

Brewery workers were passionate about sport. Foster's was triumphant at cricket in 1903–04.

task of managing and resuscitating your Brewery can be described as a herculean one.'

Of course, the classic competitive method for selling beer was to own the hotels and make them exclusive outlets for the product. During the depression many a brewery folded because it had over-extended into a vast chain of unprofitable drinking wells. Some of those contracts were tough indeed. On 13 December 1902 the Carlton Brewery leased the Silver Gate at the corner of Clarendon Street and Sandridge Road to John Drake Pearson. He had to pay £150 down and a yearly rent of £130 in instalments of £10 16s on the first day of every month. He had to keep the place in 'substantially good repair'. In the second and fifth years he had to 'cause to be painted in a proper and workmanlike manner with two coats of the best oil paint of proper and suitable colours all the inside and outside wood and metal work and cement'. But the most serious lincs were:

> And the lessee doth hereby further covenant and agree with the lessor that the lessee will not at any time during the said term buy, sell or dispose of either directly or indirectly or permit to be bought or sold or disposed of any colonial ale, beer, porter or stout other than such as shall have been brewed and bona fide purchased from the lessor. And will also pay on demand for said liquors.

The Carlton 'Hale & Stout' advertisement, appropriately illustrated, appeared in the Australian Brewers' Journal, 1902.

The place had to be open to inspection and should there be any foreign bottles on the premises that was the end of the lease.[7]

Montgomerie's Brewery expired in 1899, and the Victoria Brewery seemed to shudder from bankruptcy to bankruptcy. In April 1898 the general manager of the Victoria Brewery, Mr G. R. Gilfillan resigned and was succeeded by a brewer of great reputation, Emil Resch, who owned the Lion Brewery in Silverton, NSW. Resch was born in Wurtemburg, Germany, had studied at one of the large breweries in Stuttgart, then after doing his compulsory military service had come to Australia. The *Brewers'*

Emil Resch when he came to the new CUB as general manager in 1907.

Journal said he had all brewing matters at his fingers' ends. When the brewery was in deathly financial trouble in 1904 Mr Justice Hodges in the Victorian Practice Court made an appointment of Emil Resch, already general manager, as manager and receiver of the Melbourne Brewing and Distilling Company and so it started again.[8]

It was the age-old problem, there were too many breweries and the competition was savage. Travellers would sell their product anything up to 50 per cent below the going rate. Back in 1890 in the palmy days before the bank crash there used to be a brewers' club. It was more a good place to get together for long lunches, Cognac and cigars than anything else. When the hard times arrived it collapsed through lack of interest. There were attempts to put together a serious marketing pool which almost came to the dotted line in 1896, but Carlton was the difficult one and Mr Downes Carter refused to sign. Carlton, the big seller, did not feel it needed a pool. In 1902 other subtle factors made all the difference. There was the worst drought Australia had seen, costs were high and beer was going out at prices that made profits almost impossible. They were also under attack from an old bogey, the Pure Beer Association, accusing them of poisoning the public by making beer with sugar.

In August 1903 representatives of the big metropolitan breweries got together and formed the Society of Melbourne Brewers. They raised the price of beer 12 per cent to a minimum £2 3s 6d a hogshead. There was a nice arrangement which allowed a rebate of five shillings a barrel if you bought five hundred hogsheads in any one year. Of course it was sufficiently high that hardly anyone could qualify. They made a uniform price of 5s 3d a dozen for bottled beer and set up a sort of sweetheart arrangement: if a brewery sold more than its normal quota it had to kick back into the pool; if they sold less then they could apply for compensation. It must have been like keeping check on Russian missile sites. As Eric Nilan put it: 'They loved and trusted one another, of course'.[9] The *Brewers' Journal* applauded all this, saying that at last the brewers had accepted the advice they had been offering wisely for ten years. As they had the strength, they should make use of it. There was a possibility someone could start a co-operative brewery in opposition, but its success would be problematical and they would have to fight:

> They dont want to fight,
> But by jingo, if they do,
> They've got the pubs, they've got the men,
> They've got the money too.[10]

Two years later that very same journal was accusing the association of having made a colossal blunder, because the hotel keepers did exactly what everyone feared: they started their own brewery.

At first the Tasmanian breweries took advantage of the price rise and in February 1904 they sent over eight hundred hogsheads, neatly underselling McCracken's, Foster's and others. The combined brewers were outraged. They counter-attacked by sending beer to Hobart and they even bought two Hobart hotels where they sold the Melbourne brew at 2d a glass. But this was no more annoying than a summer blowfly. It was the hotel keepers who were really angry. They bought an old distillery at Abbotsford for £3750 and with extraordinary speed created a really modern

OPPOSITE PAGE:
The old Abbotsford Brewery on the banks of the Yarra River (top).
An early CUB advertisement (bottom) showing the raw materials used in brewing: the barley field on the left and the hop harvest on the right. Despite the kookaburra on the left, the influence of the northern hemisphere still dominates the artist's style. La Trobe Collection, State Library of Victoria.

brewery. The men behind it were J. C. Dillon, vice-president of the Victuallers Association, H. F. Young, J. McArthur and Stephen Morell. Morell was to be a very powerful figure in Melbourne and the future brewery chairman. He rowed for Scotch College, and was a member of the Victorian Champion Four in 1896 and the Champion Eight in 1896 and 1897. He had a string of hotels including the Orient at the corner of Swanston and Collins Streets. The Morell hotels were famous for their counter lunch: roast beef, ham, cheese, fish, rissoles, sheep's trotters, ox tongue, corner beef, sausages, vienna rolls or bread slices, pickles and condiments, your choice of these viands with a full pint of beer, all for 3d.[11]

Brewing at the Abbotsford Co-operative began in July. The Society of Melbourne Brewers said they wouldn't be able to compete, never would they produce a good beer. How wrong they were. The new brewery was a success from the first day, largely due to the brewing skills of James Patrick Breheny. Breheny was one of five brewing brothers, who began an extraordinary dynasty in the beer trade. There was J. J. Breheny who studied brewing under de Bavay at Victoria, then went to the Volum Brewery at Geelong. There was Peter who trained with his brother at Volum then went to the Barley Sheaf Brewery in Ballarat. There was Tom, also at Volum, who became brewer at the Royal Standard in Ballarat. There was Edward who launched Breheny Bros' own brewery at Sale and James who came to the Abbotsford Co-operative after training at the Barley Sheaf.

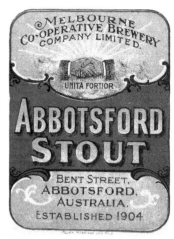

An Abbotsford Stout label of 1904.

The Co-operative Brewery sold its beer at the same price as Carlton and the rest, but they promised that there would be a rebate per hogshead out of profits to all shareholders and customers. Hotel keepers, naturally, were keen to look after their own brewery. The brewery put out its first balance sheet in March with a net profit of £5952.[12] So a beer war started exactly when the brewers did not want it. The Society went back to where it had started. It reduced bottled beer to 5s a dozen and dropped the price of a hogshead to £2 17s 6d.

Melbourne never again recaptured the boisterous super-confidence, the ebullience of the 1880s, when it had felt it had the drive to equal and surpass anything in the old world. Recovering from the bank crash depression was a slow, painful process. Even in 1907 Alfred Buchanan wrote:

The original Abbots Lager label, 1904.

> Commercially Melbourne is not what it used to be. It has lost the sparkle, the animation of other days. Yet, whatever else it has lost, it has retained its consciousness of former prosperity . . . Diminished prosperity has caused it to hold its head higher.[13]

The breweries were accused of rash over-capitalisation. The *Lone Hand*, for example, said they overloaded themselves with hotel properties at ridiculous boom prices.[14] What's more, they borrowed to do it. Only one brewery was really making money and that was Carlton. Eventually the inevitable happened, the breweries which had formed the Society of Melbourne Brewers got together and amalgamated. It was a long, agonised battle which took two years, a battle sorting out shareholders and debenture holders both in Australia and England, tortuous debt problems covering leases of property, mortgages on hotels and deciding which of the six flourishing breweries were to be closed down for ever.

OPPOSITE PAGE:
An early CUB advertising poster which already boasted of overseas success.

On 23 January there was a definitive meeting. The chairman was Alex McCracken in his role as chairman of the Society of Melbourne Brewers. Montague Cohen represented Foster's, Nicholas Fitzgerald and E. Fanning were there on behalf of Castlemaine, Carl Pinschof for Carlton, and David Elder for Shamrock. In the light of events that were to take place seventy-eight years later it was ironic that an Elder should be present. David Elder, born in Dundee in 1850, was an accountant and former general manager for the New Zealand Loan and Mercantile Agency Co. Ltd.[15] There was a fascinating discussion on what should be the title for the new combine:

A. McCracken: Could we not get a better name than Consolidated?
D. Elder: I suggest the Union and Carlton Breweries Pty Ltd. We know that there is in the air the idea of a Union Company being formed, and this is practically the union of all the breweries.
A. McCracken: Would it not be better to start with the Carlton?
M. Cohen: There is a good deal in the name after all.
D. Elder: I like the name Union . . . My idea is that if we are going to bring this concern into being the sooner it is done the better.
A. McCracken: How would 'The Carlton and United Breweries Pty Ltd' do?
N. Fitzgerald: If the word 'Union' were in, the beer would be known as the union beer, and the question is whether that would do.
M. Cohen: Yes, you don't know how the Trades Hall unions would take the name.
C. Pinschof: If I had to choose between 'Carlton and United' and 'Carlton United' the latter would seem to me to express the same with one word less. The shorter the title the better.
D. Elder: I think you must have the word 'and' in.

Unanimously the meeting agreed that the name would be 'Carlton and United Breweries Proprietary Limited'.[16]

In April 1906 it was formally announced that the Carlton Brewery Ltd, McCracken's City Brewery Ltd, Castlemaine Brewery Co. (Melbourne) Ltd, Shamrock Brewing and Malting Co. Ltd, The Foster Brewing Co. Pty Ltd and the Victoria Brewery Pty Ltd were interested in combining into one company. The new company, Carlton & United Breweries Proprietary Limited, was registered on 8 May 1907 and all parties signed the agreement on 30 June 1907. The capital of the new company was £1 million in £1 shares and, of course, Carlton was the big deal. Carlton had two directors including the chairman, while the other companies had one; Carlton also had the majority of shares. This was the distribution:

Carlton	80 000
McCracken's	37 000
Castlemaine	20 500
Shamrock	14 500
Victoria	33 500
Foster's	14 500

The full board was C. L. Pinschof (Carlton) as chairman, W. L. Baillieu (Carlton), Nicholas Fitzgerald (Castlemaine), William Brookes (Victoria), Montague Cohen (Foster's), James Thomson (Shamrock) and Alex McCracken (McCracken's). Carlton & United was to make the beer, while

A 1904–05 label for Abbotsford Sparkling Ale.

This label was used by the Abbotsford Brewery in the second decade of the twentieth century.

OPPOSITE PAGE:
The annual Eight Hours Day celebration was a great event for the workers. Carlton always played a major part in the grand parade down Swanston Street, as these photographs of 1903 (top) and 1904 show.

Top men in the brewing trade just before amalgamation: Emil Resch, Victoria Brewery, Alex McCracken, McCracken's Brewery, Montague Cohen, chairman of Foster's, and G. G. Crespin, Shamrock.

The *Melbourne Brewing Trade*

EMIL RESCH ESQ.

A. Mc CRACKEN ESQ.

Men at the Helm

MONTAGUE COHEN ESQ.

G.G. CRESPIN ESQ

the others were to be brewers in name only, a fascinating situation where companies like Shamrock and McCracken's, no longer making beer, continued on as companies with their own directors, annual reports and meetings for many decades.

For some companies it was a very sad tale. The *Australian Cordial Maker* commented on 27 July that McCracken's, floated by B. J. Fink in 1888 with a capital of £2 million now, nineteen years later, would not fetch half a million and the ordinary shareholders would receive 1s 10d for each £1 share. The journal added:

Taken all round Australia has proved a very graveyard for capital and we venture to say that proportionately more businesses have come to grief here in the past fifty years than in any other country in the world. All Australian businesses are uncertain but brewing seems to be the worst of the lot.

Carlton and Victoria had the biggest plants for the large-scale production of beer, so it was their job to do the brewing for CUB. The Foster Brewery was small but very modern. That was to remain available for emergency brewing. All the others eventually were to close down. McCracken's, a wonderful property taking up a large slice of Collins Street, was to be sold at once.

Of course, there was some melancholy grief about the imminent departure of some of the grand old names. The *Australian Brewers' Journal* wrote:

No old Victorian beer drinker will think, without a pang of regret, that the days of McCracken's are numbered. And never in the history of the City Brewery did it turn out better beer than it is brewing today. There is no beer in Melbourne which has a better finish than McCracken's.[17]

There was even a lyrical ode composed to some of the combining breweries:

> Here's a long life to Carlton,
> Which I'll ever hold me dear;
> If I get outside six glasses,
> Not the devil will I fear.
>
> As for Shamrock, dear old Shamrock,
> O, the fun I've had with you —
> Never finer glass of nectar
> Did a goddess ever brew.

An export shipment of Foster's leaving the Victoria Brewery, c. 1907.

Montague Cohen, chairman of the Foster Brewing Company and the great architect of amalgamation in 1907.

There's another one I'm fond of —
'Tis McCracken's City Ale:
For a drop of good City,
Bet your boots I'll never fail.

Castlemaine, you ask me next, sir,
'Tis a drink that's fit for kings.
I could drink it, sir, for ever
But alas! for other things.

Want to know which I like best, sir,
Why I like the blooming lot,
When I give up taking all, sir,
Have me, like a soldier, shot.[18]

The man who master-minded CUB and brought together all the disparate ailing breweries was Montague Cohen. But for his tact and patience never would they have come together. Montague Cohen was educated at Scotch College, studied law at Melbourne University and in his young days he ran a law and debating society which included such stars as Alfred Deakin and Theodore Fink. He became a partner in the firm Pavey, Wilson & Cohen, better known as Pavey's. He was more than just a lawyer, however. He was a founder of the Swan Brewery in 1887 and he was there at the birth of the Foster Brewing Company. He was a good footballer, a good cricketer and passionate about cross-country running. He was a founder of the Amateur Sports Club of Victoria and he presented a shield for an annual 10-mile cross-country run to get young men interested in long distance running. He was ahead of his time.[19]

As for the first CUB appointments, Emil Resch, general manager at the Victoria Brewery, became general manager at CUB. T. L. Parker, who had been manager at Carlton, came in as manager, R. H. Lemon, secretary

Carlton Brewery staff in 1907. Top row (left to right): C. Thomson, A. H. Baker, W. Robinson (foreman yard), G. Davidson (head bottler), A. Cathie, G. Thomas. Second row: T. Walsh, G. Deeble, G. Phillips, F. Reid, H. Kingston (traveller), R. B. Brinkley (assistant brewer), J. Levi, T. Parker (traveller), H. Fletcher. Third row: P. Joske (traveller), E. McLean (traveller), P. Webb, C. W. Fletcher (manager's secretary), J. G. S. Baker (accountant), J. R. Ballenger (head brewer), H. T. Wardle (head cashier), F. W. Oakley (assistant accountant), W. Christison (traveller), T. J. Davis (country traveller), J. B. Gromann (traveller). Front row: W. H. Parker (Williamstown Depot), F. Hamilton, W. Parker, W. H. Richardson (assistant cashier), D. Shine, H. Bell (delivery clerk).

of the Liquor Trades Defence Union, the man who held the ramparts against the assaults of temperance, became the secretary. H. J. Dalley, formerly secretary at Foster's was the new accountant. There was real trouble in the brewing department. The chief brewer was Colonel John R. Ballenger, assisted by J. C. E. Farmer and R. B. Brinkley both formerly at McCracken's. Colonel Ballenger had been chief brewer at Carlton, an efficient, some said kindly, autocrat. He was a soldier, a horseman, a skilled fox hunter and he looked the part. He had an immense moustache with a splendid gold chain and pendant, which decorated his stomach. He was gazetted as lieutenant in the Victorian Volunteer Artillery in 1876 and rose to become the colonel in command of the Field Artillery Brigade. So he was used to commanding men. He was at Carlton for forty years, head brewer for twenty and he did not take kindly to becoming a second ranker

MR. R. H. LEMON.
Secretary.

Mr. Lemon was formerly for some years Secretary of the Liquor Trades' Defence Union and the Hotel Property Owners' Association of Victoria.

Some
Members of the Staff
of the
CARLTON
and
UNITED
BREWERIES
PROPRIETARY
LIMITED,
MELBOURNE.

LIEUT.-COL.
J. R. BALLENGER.
Head Brewer.

Who for a great number of years has brewed with conspicuous success and ability at the Carlton Brewery, Melbourne.

MR. EMIL RESCH.
General Manager and
Superintendent.

In addition to the gentlemen included in this group, mention must be made of Messrs. Thomas L. Parker, the Manager, and Messrs. John C. E. Farmer and A. H. Woods, who have also been appointed to the Brewing staff.

MR. H. J. DALLY, Accountant.

MR. R. B. BRINKLEY, Assistant Brewer.

The new team that launched Carlton & United Breweries in 1907, as depicted in the Australian Brewers' Journal.

The enthusiastic Colonel John R. Ballenger in his role as brewery fire chief.

under Emil Resch in the combine. He felt he was little more than an advisor, rather than being head brewer, so with great drama he departed. The workers at Carlton presented him with a set of silver dishes and a soup tureen.

The Colonel proved he really was a fighting man. He decided to meet the new combine head-on by buying Wood's Yorkshire Brewery in Collingwood and launching the Ballenger Brewing Company. The *Brewers' Journal* reported that its beer was an excellent drop, well produced. The Colonel timed his launch for the visit of Admiral Sperry's Great White Fleet when it was expected that a million people would be in Melbourne. He brought out a special poster: Bacchus seated astride a cask of Ballenger's XXXX holding aloft the Australian and American flags. Then on the curtain at King's Theatre in Russell Street he had the message:

> To Australia, the Empire and our American cousins
> We drink Ballengers Famous Beer
> The Stimulant for All.[20]

It was very appropriate. This was one of the biggest things that ever happened in Melbourne. There were sixteen American battleships on tour and the greatest of them all was USS *Connecticut*, 16 000 tons, 74 guns, 18.8 knots, 41 officers and 815 men. Our public buildings were illuminated with sixty thousand incandescent bulbs, there were six curtain arches across Elizabeth Street and across Flinders Street Station there was a superb arch with an illuminated picture depicting the battleships.

Over twenty thousand people went before dawn to Queenscliff and Point Nepean to see the ships go through. The crush in Melbourne was so great that two hundred doctors from the medical corps had to treat all the fainting cases in the city. One of the strangest events was the Commonwealth Government Banquet hosted by the Prime Minister, Alfred Deakin, at the Exhibition Building. A staff of 130 worked all night getting it ready and 2500 American sailors were invited. At 7 p.m. the tables were set and two hundred dozen bottles of beer, presumably good Carlton and Ballenger's, were already opened. Alas, only a lone American sailor, plump and young, turned up and he was too terrified to go inside. Somehow they had confused the nights. Mr Deakin quietly went home at 8.45 p.m. Police, army and fire brigade were called in to drink the beer and eat the 2500 dinners.[21]

The might of the Great White Fleet was insufficient to assist the redoubtable Colonel Ballenger in downing the infant Carlton & United Breweries. Prices were too competitive and the Colonel's output was too small. He never had a chance. He went into liquidation on 23 November 1909. There was a meeting of creditors and he paid 15s in the pound. CUB bought all the casks, all the important assets, plus the unexpired portion of the lease. The bitterly disappointed Colonel went into the hotel business and eventually finished as licensee of the Conference Hotel at the corner of Flinders and Queen Streets.[22]

Of course, a great many brewery workers were no longer necessary. The board decided that the Shamrock Brewery would cease operations on 12 July. Those described as 'first class' at Shamrock, and there were two, received £50 each, not in cash but as credit at the savings bank. The eight

Colonel Ballenger's short-lived brew, 1909.

second class received three months' full wages, payable weekly. Third class, boys and travellers earning less than 25s a week, parted with a lump sum of £5. The last Shamrock brew showed that Carlton unquestionably was the superpower at the time of the amalgamation. Carlton produced 1167 hogsheads, Victoria 640, McCracken's 462, Castlemaine 78, Foster's 263 and Shamrock 73.[23]

CHAPTER FIVE

Crown Seals and Automobiles

The Edwardian era had its charming aspects. Beer was still delivered by horse, and magnificently. Bottles had tie-down corks, beer pulls were splendid with ivory handles and there was no such thing as a Pluto hand gun. The glory of the age, adored by the beer drinking public, deeply regretted by the hotel keepers, was the free counter lunch. One journal described its beauty in these terms:

> A leading Swanston Street hotel makes a great feature of the counter lunch. It is but 11 o'clock, yet biscuits and cheese, Fritz sausage, cold corned beef, salads, pickles, black and white puddings, and bread are spread out for the benefit of the morning 'supper'.
>
> At midday the regular lunchers begin to arrive. If they patronise the front or side bars they are welcomed by the appetising odour of hot pigs' cheek. In the back bars hot roasts or hot boiled joints are on the table. If corned beef happens to be 'on', carrots are served with it. From midday until after 2 p.m. a barman stands behind the counter lunch table, and serves food out to customers. But this is not all. At 1 o'clock hot fried sausages and saveloys make their appearance, and, later, in the afternoon this is repeated. At certain times Welsh rarebit is served, and this kind of thing goes on until closing time at night.

Not every customer who bought a drink distended his interior with a couple of pounds of free food, said the journal, but it was a fact that between 11 a.m. and 2 p.m. almost every customer to be found in a Melbourne hotel appeared to be in a voracious condition and gorged himself as though this were his last meal. It was a mystery how the hotels managed to make a profit. Said the reporter:

> We are informed on reliable authority that the cost of providing counter lunches in one city house amounts to £1000 yearly, £500 of which is paid by the brewery as a subsidy to draw one brand only.
>
> 'How in the name of heaven do you manage?' we asked a seedy-looking wreck who accosted us for the loan of three half-pence. 'Well, Sir' replied the tattered remnant of what had once been a man, 'I always manages to get one real good feed every day. So long as I can get hold of a trey bit I can have a pint of beer and a square meal.'

Invoking the Empire continued to appeal, as this Carlton label used between 1907 and 1913 shows (above). La Trobe Collection, State Library of Victoria.

This was entirely a sexist activity; there was no chance for a lady or a female tattered remnant to distend her interior. Both bars and counter lunches were for males only.[1]

The temperance organisations fought a constant battle, claiming that barmaids were a monstrous evil. In 1912 they staged a deputation to the government, and told a patient minister that young men were lured into bars by the promise of food. First they had a ginger ale or lemonade. Next they were on to a shandy. Then inevitably they would drink beer and you would see them later walking the streets with 'illuminated countenance and unsteady walk'.[2] But it wasn't the temperance people who killed the free lunches, it was the licensed victuallers and the brewers. In Brisbane they ended in July 1912 and in Sydney a month later. In Melbourne they held out until 1918 when Montague Cohen, of Carlton & United and chairman of the Brewers' Association, announced their Victorian demise. He said people were actually living on the food provided. They would have a substantial meal at 11.30 a.m. then another at 5 p.m., all for the price of a pint. It was costing some hotels £3000 a year. He didn't know any part of the world where that sort of thing went on.[3] The *Bulletin* wrote a special counter lunch dirge:

A Carlton Bitter label, 1910.

> The corned beef torn as if by dogs
> The slashed and riddled cheese,
> The gnawed and nibbled feet of hogs,
> Farewell! Farewell to these.
>
> The merry days are past and gone
> When Bung kept open house
> And spread good food to lure us on
> To banquet and carouse.
>
> We thought he liked to see us eat —
> To watch us gaily stuff
> With crumbs and bones about our feet,
> Until we'd had enough.
>
> But now we know that ev'ry plate
> We piled with bread and ham
> Was sauced with bitter rage and hate
> And poisoned with a damn.[4]

Bottles to brewers, like a pain in the small of the back, have always been an eternal problem. Before the turn of the century many brewers would not even contemplate the idea and sold everything in bulk. Bottles weren't all that necessary. If you wanted a beer at home it was the normal thing to send one of the children down to the corner pub with a jug to be filled with the best draught, a shocking thing to the temperance folk. Large breweries like Carlton bottled less than 10 per cent of their product. Bottles were always in short supply. The best came from Europe or America. They arrived full and were re-used, or the brewery would import them specially bearing its own imprint at great expense. The local breweries despised 'colonial' bottles because they used to crack when pasteurised. Bottles were expensive because they had to be hand blown, and each bottle had to be blown individually. Michael J. Owens of the USA developed the first automatic bottle-making machine in 1903. The original cost of a hand-made bottle was 3d and when you consider that beer sold at 6d a bottle, the bottle was a majestic item. The old fashioned 'bottle-o' who toured the suburbs with a waggon or handcart, was a power in the land. The *Brewers' Journal* said in 1897:

> The bottle-o is now one of the most profitable trades going in the city and suburbs. It is doubtful if such a large and quick return is to be got out of any colonial investment. If he gets into your yard he won't get out unless you are a bigger man and have heavily soled boots, and then he has the impudence to offer you fivepence or sixpence a dozen for the bottles you have carefully stored away, while there is not a man in the trade who will hesitate to give him at least one shilling and sixpence for his spoil.

Some breweries started to put their names on the bottles with the hope of getting them back. Then the bottle-os refused to buy them. Once that happened, the customers turned to buying beer only in unbranded glass, so much money was to be made on returns. It was a vicous, thirsty circle.[5] The marine dealers (old empty bottles were called dead marines) virtually had the breweries in a state of ransom. When summer approached and the situation was desperate they could charge what they liked. In 1904 the breweries formed the Manufacturers Bottle Company of Victoria, which was to be taken over by CUB. It had the job of collecting and rehiring all the bottles.[6]

The elaborate method for keeping bottled beer in good condition was an additional cost. The popular system was the tied-down cork, but corks too were costly; they had to be well washed or they coloured the beer. By 1904 there was the screw-down stopper. The brewery journals were advertising Harrison's Lignumvitae Woodscrew Stopper for 5s a gross. 'As hard as ivory, recognised as the cleanest most durable stoppers. Have you accepted it yet or are you still in the middle ages, using corks or internal stoppers?' On 23 April 1903 brewery people received an invitation from the Crown Corporation Ltd to a demonstration at the Rowland's cordial factory in Sydney. This was the first arrival in Australia of the crown seal, invented by William Painter in Baltimore in 1892. The Sydney report said:

Victoria Lager Bier.

> The system of corking bottles is both cheap and simple. The cork consists of a small metal cap, lined with cork, which is fastened automatically over the mouth of the bottle by machine pressure. Among the advantages claimed for it are that it is cheaper than the old system, and in no way injurious. By means of a small metal hook, which can be carried on a key ring or fastened on the wall, the cork can easily be removed.[7]

At first the crown seals contained expensive cork discs, but in 1912 the composition disc arrived and by 1913 Carlton & United was using nothing but crown seals.

Meanwhile the brewing scene went through its astonishing metamorphosis. In 1907 there were thirty-seven breweries in Victoria. Back in 1871 there had been 126. Carlton and Victoria were now the two big producing plants for CUB. McCracken's and Foster's still kept on brewing in 1908, but by 1910 McCracken's in Collins Street was being remodelled to accommodate Alex Cowan & Sons, wholesale stationers, and the rear was being subdivided into offices and factories for printing and hardware firms. Shamrock was being used for the manufacture of compressed yeast, Ballenger's Yorkshire Brewery was for the company cooperage, and on 13 December the Foster Brewery in Collingwood was to go under the hammer. According to the reports: 'The buildings are very spacious and are erected throughout of brick. They are so arranged as to afford every facility for easy conversion into well-lighted stores or factories.'[8]

Brewing at Foster's in Rokeby Street actually ceased on 8 May 1908. For some months all Foster operations were in peril. The famous name could easily have disappeared altogether, as it was more convenient to handle only the big sellers like Carlton or Victoria Bitter Ale. According

The Yorkshire Brewery in Collingwood became the place of work for the CUB coopers. The 1920 photograph shows a cooper completing a barrel.

to the board minutes, however, some members argued that they could not stop brewing Foster's because they had orders to fulfil in Western Australia and Queensland.[9] So Foster's Lager, Empire and Foster's Bitter Ale were produced in the extended brewery at Victoria.

The labour problems caused by the amalgamation were not as serious as might have been expected. There were six hundred employees in the six breweries; some retired, but many were employed to cope with increased production at Carlton and Victoria. Just as the hotel keepers had formed their successful brewery, the trade unions thought they could do the same, so they issued a prospectus for the Trades Union Brewery Company Limited, nominal capital £25 000 pounds in 100 000 shares at 5s each. They even appointed provisional directors, J. A. Gaynor of the Liquor Trades Union, Henry Johnson, secretary of the Engine Drivers and Firemen's Association, Andrew Serong of the Coachbuilders Union, John Hampden and Isaac McClure of the Federated Factory Employees Union. But the brewery failed before it ever started. The real customers, the hotels, were already tied either to CUB or to the Co-operative Brewery at Abbotsford.[10]

The speed with which Emil Resch consolidated all operations at Carlton and Victoria in less than eighteen months was a masterpiece of organisation. Mr Resch was a precise operator. When the *Brewers' Journal* sent a reporter to interview him in 1908, Emil Resch allotted the time that was available and as soon as it expired he announced 'Time's up', whereupon, said the journal, 'Our reporter grasped his hat, ejaculated a word of thanks, wished Mr Resch "Good Morning" and left forthwith'. Resch explained that at the time of amalgamation they had not been equipped to take on suddenly

The Victoria Brewery in 1911 with additions just completed by CUB. The young trees have long since grown into a fine avenue.

this huge new brewing capacity. They had to provide more accommodation for staff and directors, put in extra cellarage, build a fresh tower 'entirely new, and when completed the equal to anything of its kind in England, America or on the Continent'. The capacity of the new plant, he explained, would be three hundred hogsheads a brew, so the plant would be able to turn out 3600 every forty-eight working hours. He also created history at Carlton when he installed a laboratory containing all the latest equipment with Auguste de Bavay as 'company laboratorist'. The laboratory was an absolute necessity, according to Resch. The brewer's work could not be by rule of thumb any more, he had to know the effect, the active value of the material he used. There was no other trade where exact knowledge was so entirely essential.[11]

The net profit for the financial year ended 30 June 1908 was £62 433. The dividend was being paid at 3 pcr cent for six months or 6 per cent on the full year. There were some grumblings that this was hardly enough, but considering the costs of amalgamation it was a good performance. At the annual meeting in 1910, Mr Theodore Fink commented on the absence of shareholders. 'It was a good sign we did not see shareholders at annual meetings. It showed they were satisfied.'[12]

No longer were there complaints about the quality of Victorian beer. The *Australian Brewers' Journal* was somewhat suspect, never saying an unkind word about a good advertiser, but even so the editor could be most eloquent:

> The ordinary Carlton is a most pleasant, fragrant beer, gratifying to the taste, exhilarating without 'muddling', and is a pronounced favourite with beer drinkers over the wide metropolitan area, in every corner of which Carlton Ale proclaims the presence of the beloved of the people. As for our own private taste, we confess to a sneaking affection for the Four X which is a full bodied ale of nutty flavour, a grateful bitterness and aroma redolent of the hop.[13]

Much of the beer's success was due to the head brewer, R. B. Brinkley. John Farmer had been the head brewer at amalgamation but within a year he had retired and Brinkley took over with H. L. Torpey as his assistant. Brinkley had been at Woodbridge in Suffolk and had worked for fifteen years at the famous Bow Brewery in London, makers of the India Pale Ale, created for the troops in India. He had emigrated to Australia, had become head brewer at McCracken's, and then assistant brewer to Colonel Ballenger at Carlton. The Brinkleys were very musical. He was a founder and president of the Melbourne Banjo Club. His two sons, Len and Cyril, were also brewers.[14]

Beer deliveries to Williamstown and Footscray went out from the old Artillery Brewery at Williamstown, which had been absorbed by Terry's West End Brewery in 1883. The beer went there on a steam barge, the SS *Oscar*. Will Parker was the commander at the Artillery depot and he did all his rounds in a gleaming horse and buggy outfit. City and suburban deliveries were by horse-drawn lorries right up until 1948, but in 1911 CUB sent Mr Wimble out by motor vehicle to see whether there was any future in this type of transport. The board received the report:

> The car left the brewery at 10.30 a.m. on Thursday, arriving back at 4.30 p.m. on Friday. As the night, from 8 p.m. until 10 a.m. the next day was spent at

Kyneton, the actual running time was sixteen hours, during which eighteen places were visited and forty-five hotels called on. This trip was part of the round of Mr Thomson, and by train travelling and hiring it took him a week to do, and then not so thoroughly as was done by Mr Wimble.

Eric Nilan commented that after this report the affection which Mr Thomson had for Mr Wimble might not have been very deep, however Mr Thomson had left the firm's employ several weeks earlier. The company decided to buy an automobile, but a few months later there was a change of mind. The secretary, Mr Lemon, found that the traveller had to be chaffeur driven and the cost was too great. The company bought its first motor lorry in 1912, a fascinating lesson in semantics — a car wasn't to be bought, but a lorry was permitted.[15]

There were three types of brewery lorry available. There was the British Karrier with an enormous chain drive, the Thorneycroft, or the massive Daimler. They all had solid rubber tyres, brake and gear lever were outside where the driver could grab them with his right hand, and there were great brass oxy-acetylene lights. But most travellers were still getting round by horse and buggy. A serious discussion by the board on 21 July 1911 shows that the chairman was fed up with Garton's Livery stable which was anything but satisfactory. Some travellers were offering to sell their turn-outs to the company. O'Connell wanted £30 for his, Champion £20 for his, and Kingston £20 for his. Mr Joske actually offered Kingston his £20 but the hind wheel of his buggy came to pieces while passing along St Kilda Road, so he withdrew his offer. They decided to offer the travellers £2 2s 6d a week and accept their offers for horses and buggies.

Every year, usually the last Saturday in March, there was the brewery picnic. Carlton & United hired the lovely old pleasure steamer *Hygeia* for all staff, wives and children. They went by train to Port Melbourne and

One of the first chain-driven brewery trucks used by the Melbourne Co-operative Brewery in Abbotsford. There were no such things as cartons in the 1920s. Bottles travelled in wicker baskets.

A sparkling Abbotsford delivery vehicle loaded with barrels, c. 1920.

A Carlton sales representative before the First World War almost always did his rounds by horse and trap.

then, at 9.30 a.m., they set sail for Sorrento. The Richmond City Band with twelve performers was aboard, and they were so good, according to one picnicker, even those with gout took to the dance floor. Progressively more lyrical, he said:

> They can say what they like about the beauties of Sydney Harbour ... but give us the noble expanse of Melbourne's bay for preference. It has bold scenery along its shores hard to beat, and with the blue sky we had glimpses of the distant Dandenongs, the You-Yangs, the bold outlines of Mt Martha, entirely satisfying to the modest lover of the picturesque.

On arrival at Sorrento some went by horse and trap to the back beach, but most went to the sports ground, 'one of the prettiest spots on the shores of Hobson's Bay where over the twinkling waters one could see the dim mass of Macedon', and here there were all kind of races for both foot and cycle. Mr Pinschof, Mr Resch, Mr Parker, Mr Torpey and the genial Mr Gus Cole, head brewer at Victoria, all were there. Mrs Peterson and Mrs O'Brien beat all the other married ladies in the 50 yards.

> Not during all the proceedings of the day was there a single instance of excess. It would have been well if some detractors of the trade had been present; they would have found as much decorum as in a Methodist Conference — more honest fun.[16]

The favourite brewery sport was tug-o-war and at this the Carlton team was utterly triumphant. The Carlton team went to Sydney in 1912 and won an international challenge defeating Swedes, Danes, Russians, and New Zealanders, winning over £500 in prizes. 'Brewery men are quite as respectable and certainly more muscular and well nourished than the employees of most other trades', said the *Brewers' Journal.*[17] The famous anchor man of the Carlton team was Big John Noonan. He used to train by pulling single-handed against a draught horse. Noonan, '20 stone', came to Australia in 1899 with the Irish team and had the reputation of being the strongest man in the world. The World Championship Pull was at the Exhibition Building before a crowd of ten thousand. Ireland beat Australia in the final, and of course the local Irish went mad and stormed the stage. Naturally after this there had to be a world's strongest man contest. Big John Noonan had a man-to-man contest against 'Mighty' Tom Herlihy, a Melbourne sugar carter. Hundreds of pounds were laid in side wagers. The two men, Big John and Mighty Tom, took up their positions on wooden cleats, which were like a heavy ladder laid flat on the ground. Noonan had so much power in his legs he often broke the rungs. It was said to be one of the longest and most agonising pulls in the history of the sport, but eventually Noonan outlasted Herlihy and retained his title. Noonan settled in Melbourne and joined the Carlton brewery. The story goes that 'the strongest man in the world' had the easiest job in the brewery. This was to go round with a small can and top up the casks. A strong man has to look after himself.[18]

The new combine of the six breweries continued to be an outstanding success. Under the terms of the original agreement dividends had to be held to 3 per cent for the half year until all debentures were finally paid off, a rule that did not please some shareholders. On 31 March 1912 the

The invincible Carlton Brewery tug-o-war team, 1912. Top row (left to right): T. Leonard, H. Shine, T. Kelly, J. Noonan, J. Webb, F. O. Francis, W. Williams. Middle row: C. Williams, J. Smith (captain), W. Robinson, E. Sullivan, T. Gorman. Front row: D. Jordan, J. Robinson, Y. Cagney.

McCracken's Brewery tug-o-war team, c. 1912.

McCracken's AK Light Ale label, 1908.

CUB's Imperial Pilsener Lager label, 1907.

company reduced debentures by £48 888 and mortgages by £3531 leaving debentures to 'outsiders' at only £3703. 'Since the union of the breweries the tale told has been one of continued progress' said the *Brewers' Journal*, and 'the beer of Melbourne has never been better than at this moment'.[19]

It was just as well they did not decide to abandon Foster's. When sales in 1910–11 were compared with those in 1909–10, McCracken's AK had gone up by 5 per cent, Victoria Bitter by 2.2 per cent, Pilsener, Imperial Lager and Carlton Export had gone down, and Foster's Lager showed an enormous increase of 41 277 dozen, equal to 83.8 per cent.[20]

In January 1913 CUB made an issue of 100 thousand 7 per cent preference shares and became a public company. There was an uneasy feeling in the air. Even as early as 1911 there was talk of a coming war. Emil Resch sailed to Europe in the *Grosser Kurfurst* on a six-month European tour. He went mountain climbing in Switzerland and climbed both Pilatus and Righi. He went home to his native Wurtemberg, toured all the top breweries and commented:

Brewing is in the great current of evolution. The brewer is no longer a mystic. He is a working scientist. The beer drunk now is immeasurably superior to the beer of a few years ago, and there is now more beer consumed all over the world, because it is recognised amongst all civilised people as man's natural beverage.

He was asked about the possibility of war and he said:

There was far more talk of war and rumours of war in Australia than in Europe itself. People are getting too wise in these days to think of the arbitrament of war, which is the stupidest of stupidities ... A war between England and Germany would be unprecedented and almost inconceivable. There is more community between the peoples of the two countries than ever, and the common bond of race is recognised everywhere.[21]

CHAPTER SIX

War and Six O'clock Closing

The First World War broke out in 1914. On 4 August the *Age* reported:

> Scenes of wild enthusiasm were witnessed outside the newspaper offices last night. All day long and throughout the early part of the evening there was always a crowd extending out on to the roadway reading the cables as they were posted up, but as the hour grew late, so the crowd grew denser and spread right across Collins Street. It needed only a single voice to give the opening bars of a patriotic song and thousands of throats took it up, hats and coats were waved and those who were lucky enough to possess even the smallest of Union Jacks were the heroes of the moment, and were raised shoulder high.

The *Australian Brewers' Journal* was quite overjoyed. 'Nothing short of the marvellous' had been achieved as a result of the war. The Irish problem suddenly was solved, Liberal and Laborite had ceased to fight each other, the French Canadian was showing his fierce loyalty to Britain, and Indians formerly seething with discontent were volunteering now by the thousand. In Australia, Messrs Cook and Fisher cried to the motherland, 'Here's our Navy — it's yours. We have men — take twenty thousand of them'. 'America remains as the sole unlovely example of trade selfishness overshadowing the more sacred obligations,' said the journal. The old belief that German lagers and German ingredients were always better was nonsense. We didn't need them any more, and the brewers and the hotel keepers had their part to play:

> When the whole immortal story comes to be written, when 'the tumult and shouting die,' when a poor wearied humanity shall seek rest and quiet from the unthinkable strife, then and only then shall we learn the part that the trader — be he brewer or hotel employer or employee — has played in the most superhuman struggle of all the ages.

By October CUB had launched an advertising campaign throughout Australia for Foster's Lager. 'The Teutonic brands which have been exported here by the enemy are taboo. Our lagers are equal if not better than their fancy brands,' reported the journal.[1] The tragedy, of course, was that England had given Australia its taste for ale, but the lager skills had come almost entirely from Germany, and the many fine people in the

industry had to suffer the anti-German, anti-Austrian mood. The *Brewers'* *Journal* was prepared to make a few concessions. It conceded there were some Germans who were good, honest, loyal British subjects, there were Germans in Australia who wanted to see Germany come out on top but were sensible enough not to parade their feelings, but there was a third class 'against whom Australians may very well set their faces. These are people who are blatantly pro-German and it is astonishing how comparatively numerous such people are.'[2]

Emil Resch, general manager of CUB, went overseas again in 1913. Mr and Mrs Resch had five daughters and two sons. One son died aged 12 months, and Carl, born in 1907, was later to become general manager of CUB like his father. Carl used to go to the brewery with his father on Saturday mornings and he can just remember the first introduction of crown seals. They were thumped on to the bottles by hand in the same way that home brewers do it now. The Reschs were in Stuttgart, not far from the old family home, when war broke out. Emil Resch was buying equipment for the brewery, which was shipped home. He also bought two grand Mercedes automobiles, one for himself and one for the brewery, but they never left Germany. Before they were shipped the army had commandeered them for the war effort. Carl Resch recalls it took a long time to get home. They had to wait for transport out to Holland and then for a ship to take them to Australia, via Canada. They arrived home at Christmas to find the scene very different. Emil Resch's services were no longer required at Carlton & United. The rival Co-operative brewery was spreading the message: 'You wouldn't drink beer brewed by a German would you?' Carl Resch recalls that his father received a retirement payment of £3000, 'quite generous for those days and told he wasn't wanted any more'.

The Reschs lived at 'Belmont' in Studley Avenue, just over the road from 'Raheen', home of Archbishop Mannix, unquestionably the place to live in Melbourne. The mansion was set in 12 acres and even though Emil Resch was a naturalised Australian, the government considered it not right for a German to own so much land in wartime so he had to sell off 8 acres. The man who had masterminded the astonishingly complex problem of welding six ailing breweries into a brilliantly successful combine was out of a job, aged 56. He had a chauffeur, an old German retainer, and two Irish helping hands. There in the rich land of Kew he kept fowls and grew vegetables, managing to keep most of his friends in produce for the rest of the war. He was fascinated by clocks, grand old German clocks which he used to service and keep in good repair. There was something ticking and chiming in every room of vast old Belmont. He died in 1929, aged 71.

Carl Pinschof, CUB chairman, fared only marginally better. He had come to Melbourne as the Austrian Commissioner for the Great Exhibition of 1880. He had thought the country had so much future that he had returned home, and after settling his affairs he became the consul in Victoria for Austria-Hungary. He was a striking, good-looking man with an impeccable upper-crust English accent. He had a curious resemblance to the Emperor of Austria and many were convinced he was an illegitimate son. He was godfather to Carl Resch, and lived just two doors away in Studley Avenue in another great mansion, 'Studley Hall'. Young Resch used to watch the noble gentleman walking along, rather like Chaplin, with his

OPPOSITE PAGE:

The Foster Brewing Company liked to associate itself with all of man's greatest loves.

The Foster's Export Lager Beer label, 1913–30.

A Victoria Brewery label, 1910–15.

feet angled at a quarter to three. Pinschof married Madame Wiedemann, a great singer and a teacher at the Conservatorium of Music, and for forty years they shared a passionate love for music and the arts. His financial skills brought him to the brewery. He was the originator in Australia of the Credit Foncier system. He expounded the subject in lectures and pamphlets and saw it adopted successfully by the State Savings Bank. Maybe it was just a little better for him being an Austrian rather than a German, but eventually his position as chairman became untenable and he resigned in 1916. He died in Cape Town in 1926, aged 71, while making a trip to England.[3]

The new general manager was Mr W. H. Clarke and Mr S. B. Joske became the new chairman. Mr W. L. Baillieu, because of the pressure of work, resigned from the board. His brother, Mr R. P. C. Baillieu, took his place. Resch and Pinschof were not the only wartime casualties; the board decided unanimously to dispense with the services of all employees of German extraction. Board minutes in January 1916 stated: 'Each will receive today a week's pay in lieu of notice, a fortnight hence another full weeks pay and on each of the two succeeding weeks a full weeks pay. Thereafter weekly payments as the board deems desirable.' On 2 March E. Braemar asked the board to 'commute your generous allowance into a lump sum to enable me to make a fresh start in this country on a small farm as it is almost impossible at the present time to obtain employment'. Braemar earned £2 5s a week with the brewery and he had eight children.

On 8 February the Federated Liquor Trades Union had sent a deputation to the board. The union secretary, Mr Gill, pointed out that twenty-two Germans had been put off, fourteen of them naturalised and eight of them born here. The men were all members of the union. The union took no heed of a man's nationality. They had been discharged without any explanation. They had always done their duty and so they felt a grievous wrong had been done to them. The acting chairman, Mr Thomson, told the union the directors had not discharged the men because their work had been unsatisfactory. There had been no complaints to the board on that score. But the association of Germans with the manufacture of food — and beer had been so classified — was held to be most undesirable and a menace to the public. The pressure of public opinion, of which the deputation must be cognisant, had forced itself on the directors' notice, and compelled them to take action, which they did. To have ignored the popular prejudice would have been tantamount to committing business suicide. Their actions may appear to be harsh and unjust but there had been accusations by Carlton's competitors that the lager was made by Germans. Mr Gill told of men suffering hardship — Schell, Riedel, Beck, Kohlmann, Otto, Neubecker, Dormann and Tillack.[4] Hardship cases continued to receive payments from the brewery until 20 October.

The tough treatment of Germans did not end with employees. On 18 March 1916 a circular went out to all shareholders from Pavey, Wilson & Cohen pointing out that they could not transfer shares to aliens under the War Precautions Act. Shareholders with German names had to make declarations as to whether they were natural-born Australians or otherwise. Furthermore dividends to shareholders of enemy origin, under Regulation 49DD, had to be paid to a public trustee.

As the war progressed conditions were hard for the brewers. In 1915 the government doubled the excise duty on beer from 3d to 6d a gallon, and coal was so short that Carlton was producing only three hundred hogshead of beer a day, Victoria one hundred.[5] Times were not easy for Colonel Ballenger either. He was running the Austral Hotel at the corner of Queen and Flinders Streets and was in danger that his lease would not be renewed. He was battling to pay off a debt of £75 a quarter. A licensing inspector called on 18 May 1917 and laid fifteen charges against him. One of these was for having a drunken person on the premises, three were for selling liquor after hours, two were for having an extra bar without the consent of the licensing court, and one was for having the bar open after hours. He was fined £23 with four guineas costs. The Colonel was in debt to the brewery for £2093. He owed £61 in interest and his beer account was £128. The chairman, Mr Joske, went to see him and agreed to settle his debt for 13s 9d in the pound, saying that had they made him insolvent they would have been lucky to get even that much. Ballenger asked the brewery for another loan of a £1000, which the board refused. But in the next mail came a letter to the board:

> I have to tender my warm and heartfelt gratitude to me [sic] in the liberal treatment over the settlement of my indebtness to the company. This is no mere letter writing, but from the bottom of my heart I fully appreciate what you gentlemen have done for me and my family.[6]

He died two years later on 29 November 1919.

The forces of temperance now were in full cry. The war was the finest emotional weapon yet discovered in the battle against the demon drink which must particularly be kept away from the fighting man. In October 1914 Broadmeadows Army Camp near Melbourne was utterly dry and it evoked this agonised message:

We're a weary lot of wowsers — dry and dismal,
And we musn't have opinions of our own;
We are plunged and lost in blackest depths absymal,
And our officers are adamant as stone,
We have answered to the frantic call for battle,
And we're spoiling for a bit of German fight,
But they've armed each soldier with a baby's rattle,
And with milk and buns they feed our appetite.

Lemonade and frosted cake,
Where the guns their music make;
And it's oh for just a tot of whisky neat!
For there's nothing like the liquor
Just to give the heart a flicker,
And to work your soldier up to fighting heat.[7]

There was a wave of patriotic anti-drink fervour, and the example came from the highest places in London. In April 1915 King George V banned wines, spirits and beer from the royal household for the duration of the war. Now all the members of Mr Asquith's cabinet followed suit. Lord Kitchener banned drink from his house and Mr Lloyd George, Chancellor of the Exchequer, went further than anybody: 'To settle German militarism we must first settle the drink question. We are fighting Germany, Austria and DRINK, and the greatest of these deadly foes is DRINK.' The *Bulletin* commented: 'Soldiers with their tongues hanging out will be singing, "It's a long-long way to Tipple-ary".'[8]

Hotels in Victoria were open daily from 6 a.m. to 11.30 p.m. and the feeling was that if only they would bring in shorter hours, the Kaiser would be more easily defeated. The Victorian Chief Secretary made this very clear when he introduced his Temporary Restriction Bill in 1915. It was a lovely name for the bill: it was a temporary restriction that was to hang on in Victoria for precisely half a century. 'The demand,' said he,

> everywhere is for sobriety; and when you try to enforce that on the troops should not the people who do not go to the front be cheerfully willing to display equal abstinence . . . Is the blood which our people have shed on three Continents going to appeal to us in vain?[9]

South Australia was the first to go for six o'clock closing. New South Wales was vastly helped by dire war news, for on 7 June, just before a referendum, came the news that Lord Kitchener and his personal staff had been lost aboard HMS *Hampshire* on their way to Russia. LONDON STAGGERED BY THE BALD ANNOUNCEMENT, said the headlines. So New South Wales voted overwhelmingly in favour of six o'clock, and Tasmania went the same way. The *Bulletin* thought the whole thing illogical and absurd: 'Why should milk shake and ice cream and vaudeville and Shakespearean tragedy and picture show and tea meeting not come under the same rule?'[10]

Victoria started by introducing 9.30 p.m. closing on 6 July 1915. This sent consumption up by 22.9 per cent, but nobody took any notice of mere statistics. The plan was to hold a referendum like NSW. Now that the Battle of the Somme was at its height, however, the Premier, Sir Alexander Peacock, decided the situation was too grave and could not wait another day, so he put it to the House in a straight ballot and the bill which was to leave Victoria with six o'clock closing for forty-nine years went through by forty-two votes to eight on 25 October 1916. The immediate effect of six o'clock closing was a boom in the sale of bottled beer and a desperate shortage of bottles. Sales just kept going up and up — sixty-one million gallons in 1915–16, sixty-three million in 1918–19 and seventy million in 1919–20.[11]

The temperance battle was unrelenting. There was a serious attempt in 1916 to introduce 'anti-shouting' legislation. The Australian custom of every man having to stand his turn and buy a beer at the bar was a monstrous evil, according to the wowsers. Many an innocent soldier was being driven to drunkenness because of it. Mr Blackburn introduced a bill in the Victorian Parliament on 28 November 1916 which would

> make it an offence for any person in any licensed premises or club to sell liquor to be drunk on the premises, unless the liquor were paid for by the person supplied; and also an offence for any person, other than the person who paid for the drinks to consume them.

The legislation was defeated thirty-seven votes to ten.[12]

The move to outlaw barmaids was more effective. Archdeacon Boyce of NSW, in his book *The Drink Problem in Australia*, summed it all up:

Wanted a beautiful barmaid
To shine in a drinking den
To entrap the youth of a nation
And ruin the City men;
To brighten destruction's pathway,
False gleams with dark fate to blend;
To stand near Despair's dark gateway,
To hide Sin's sad bitter end.

South Australia brought down anti-barmaid legislation in 1908, Victoria in 1916. Only women who had been barmaids for three months prior to the passing of the act could be registered. Otherwise only the hotel keeper's wife, sister or daughters could be employed. Moving the bill, Mr D. Smith told of the fearful corrupting influence the drink trade had on women. Apparently it was all right for the licensee's family to be corrupted.

The theory was that the present barmaids would remain in employment, but their numbers would steadily decline. It actually took the last barmaid a very long time to disappear. Twenty years later there was still a large number on the registration list — they seemed to have the secret of eternal youth. The truth was that the registration certificates were doing the rounds, being bought and sold like taxi registrations or seats on the stock exchange. In 1943, because of the labour shortage, the Women's Employment gave permission for barmaids over 35 to be used for the duration of the war. So in the First World War Victoria banned barmaids to help defeat the Kaiser, and in the Second World War it brought them back to help defeat Hitler.[13]

The temperance forces were powerful: any failure by the troops, every sign of unfitness or lapse of duty was blamed on the demon drink. In 1916 Carlton put out a non-alcoholic beer, which was undoubtedly ahead of its time. It had the patriotic name Camp Ale. The Co-operative Brewery, Carlton's aggressive rival, fought back, fighting non-alcoholic glass with non-alcoholic glass. They called their brew Neer Beer. Production of Camp Ale continued right through until 1940.

The brewers did try to keep before the public the undoubted quality of their beverage. For example this item appeared in 1916:

A remarkable recovery from dumbness is stated to have been made by an Australian soldier returning on a transport. The use of his speech was restored to him after he had drunk several glasses of beer, much to the astonishment of his shipmates, particulary those of teetotal principles.[14]

Another poignant story was reported:

During the warm weather on Sunday evening a clergyman's horse collapsed after an over long drink at a water trough. Bystanders suggested giving the horse a drink of beer and after he had consumed several bottles he survived and continued his journey.

While commending this action the *Brewers' Journal* was puzzled how the horse managed to get a drink on Sunday night.[15]

Of course, Carlton & United was intensely proud of its war effort. It contributed to the war loans. If brewery workers enlisted and were

Nothing is new. Non-intoxicating CUB beer was available in the 1920s.

receiving less money than they had earned at CUB then the company made up their pay. If a man was on active service, irrespective of whether his pay was more or less than his brewery wage, the company paid an extra amount equal to a quarter of his weekly wage. On 25 September 1915 the company gave a farewell 'smoke social' at Sargent's Cafe in Elizabeth Street, Melbourne, to sixty employees who had 'answered the call'. The company secretary, Mr R. H. Lemon, said, 'During the year we have sent many brave men to the front. Almost twelve months ago I bade farewell to my own son, who I am proud to say has departed on the same glorious mission for which our guests tonight are departing.' Already, he explained, two Carlton & United men had 'fallen'. One was Captain W. D. S. Manger, the first wounded Australian to die in England. Mr R. B. Brinkley, Carlton's head brewer, said the company was 'prepared to stand to the last by the honour and integrity of its employees in the fighting line. Only 5 per cent of the total population of the country had enlisted, but 12 per cent of the firm's employees had "answered the call".'[16] Actually seventy-five employees joined the forces and fourteen were killed. One of the volunteers was Harold E. Cohen, who became a colonel while serving overseas and later became company chairman.

On 8 November 1918 Australia was agog with the news that the war was over. The crush was so thick in the city that all traffic was stopped except for the trams. Brigadier General Williams, commandant of the Third District, put out an order under the War Precautions Act, closing all hotels and bars. The feeling was that drink would have a bad effect on the roistering public. The Baptist Union which was meeting at the time passed a resolution that immediately upon Armistice all hotels should be closed for a week.[17] At 3 p.m. official news came through denying an Armistice had been signed and hotels had to be open again.

Peace came on 11 November 1918. The *Australasian* said: 'From henceforth November 11, 1918, will be regarded as the greatest day in history'. The *Argus* said: 'The end at last, what words can tell adequately of the wave of relief that will sweep the civilised world. Heads that for years have been bowed with suffering will be raised with thanksgiving.' Crowds rushed into the city. One mob derailed a tram in Carlton. Another lot pushed a tram through the front window of the Australian Electric Company's office. The thing to do was to keep on making a noise, beating kerosene tins, blowing whistles, jumping up and down on tin roofs in Swanston Street. Any soldier in sight was a hero. He was kissed by the office girls and lifted on the shoulders of the crowd in triumph. The government declared 12 November a holiday, and the hotels were indeed closed until 6 a.m. the following day. The *Argus* reported that never was a holiday conducted like this one. There were enormous crowds in the city. The *Argus* quoted one man: 'We'll never beat Germany again, we hope. Let us celebrate this licking for all that we are worth.'[18] Celebrations continued with crowds singing anthems and patriotic songs. There was hardly anyone in the city who did not wear a flag. The *Age* published an appeal by the Defence Department asking people to stop exploding big bungers; a great many soldiers were still suffering from shell shock.

The terrible agony was over, or was it? As 1919 began Australia was hit by the world-wide flu epidemic. As if the war had not been bad enough, influenza caused 11 552 deaths. The disease spread with such rapidity that

A Foster's label, 1918.

hospitals soon overflowed and the Exhibition Building became an emergency centre for victims. People in trams, trains and buses wore white masks in the hope of warding off infection. On 6 February with 12 dead and 740 in hospital, State Cabinet banned all race meetings. Then, on 12 February, all hotels within 15 miles of the GPO were closed. Eight hundred hotels had to close. The secretary of the Licensed Victualler's Association, Mr A. D. Grant, said:

> During the past few years the liquor industry has suffered more than any industry I know of. Just as we were looking forward to the near future, when it was hoped our trade life would become normal again, we find the ravages of this unknown disease making its presence felt.

A Carlton Ale label, 1918–25.

The *Argus* thought it was a strange anomaly that the hotels closed while restaurants and cafes remained open. There was more risk of infection in a cafe than in a hotel bar. Schools which should have opened again remained closed and first term in 1919 was a month late in getting under way. The newspapers were filled with tragic stories. A widow living in Kew lost three children, twin boys aged 3 and a daughter aged 5, all in one week. There was an intense summer heat wave which seemed to speed the disease. On 5 March, after being closed for three weeks, hotels opened once more. The worst of the epidemic was over. It had been one of Melbourne's most dreadful periods; people had been frightened to go to town, the whole city had seemed like a morgue and CUB had had little need to conduct beer deliveries.[19]

CHAPTER SEVEN

CUB Takes Abbotsford

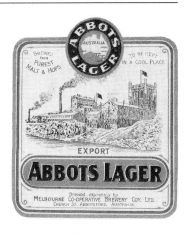

The 1914–18 war was one thing, the battle over 'the demon drink' was another. At Carlton & United they had no doubts about the health-giving qualities of their product, and besides, now they had Cubex and that wonder product of nature, yeast. The brewery launched Cubex in 1918. It was a triumph of the laboratories, enthusiastically pushed by H. L. Torpey who was to take over from R. B. Brinkley as head brewer in 1923. Cubex was a byproduct of yeast. Always it had been a problem what to do with used yeast, the Yarra-brown waste left over after it had done its job of fermentation, so CUB created Cubex, the health spread. Paste it thinly on toast, use it in sandwiches, add it to gravy. Those mysterious ingredients, riboflavin and thiamine, had not been isolated in 1918, but everyone was unanimous about its health-giving qualities; there was nothing it could not cure. But Cubex was never a vast success; never did it become a household word known to all like Foster's or Vegemite.

Vegemite, produced in South Melbourne by Frank Walker, was first created in 1923. Walker believed he could do better than the English Marmite. For a time he even played with the idea of calling it 'Parwill' as an antidote to Ma-mite, but not many caught the joke. Early advertisements called it 'the World Wonder Food' and they depicted a scholarly academic young man in cap and gown, peering into a jar of Vegemite with a magnifying glass, clearly trying to analyse its extraordinary powers. Frank Walker died in 1933 and Vegemite sold out to Kraft Foods. Cubex went out of existence and CUB found it easier and more profitable to sell its yeast waste to Kraft. Carl Resch recalls that for many years afterwards a strange, usually unidentified piece of machinery remained on the floor at Bouverie Street. It was the centrifuge for making Cubex. Vegemite now has become world famous and part of the Australian ethos. Australians when far from home inevitably pine for their Vegemite or take jars with them. American customs officials frequently have been deeply disturbed by the sight of this exotic black paste. It is a fascinating thought that much of the brew, very likely, began its life at Carlton.

There was another outlet for yeast, well remembered by old brewery workers. Yeast was acknowledged everywhere as having magic powers. Anyone suffering from boils or skin eruptions of any kind was advised

A Melbourne Co-operative Brewery label before 1924 (above).

OPPOSITE PAGE:
The Melbourne Co-operative Brewery at Abbotsford was a tough competitor until CUB took it over in 1924.

to take yeast. In 1886 Melbourne had a typhoid plague and Auguste de Bavay made a statement that if anyone brought patients to him, he would cure them with yeast. The offer wasn't accepted. Thomas Breheny, one of the famous Breheny family, reported on yeast when he was head brewer at Tooth & Co, in Sydney in 1924. He said they had three thousand yeast patients at the Kent Brewery in four years. They came with eczema, indigestion, boils, tuberculosis, anaemia, ulcers, jaundice, heartburn, constipation, catarrh of the stomach, kidney and bladder trouble and diabetes. Thomas Breheny reported remarkable success: boils, two thousand cases cured, eczema, eighty-nine cases in all stages, nearly all complete cures.[1] CUB always sold yeast at the door. The queue would form right at the truck entrance gate in Bouverie Street with billy cans, jugs or jam jars to be filled for 3d on production of a doctor's prescription. Some people used the yeast for baking bread, and some took it home to brew their own beer, which is what killed it. The sale of yeast at the door came to an end in 1950. By then it no longer had the romance of old, we were moving into the new era of antibiotics.

In 1918 the United States brought in Prohibition and once again the temperance battle raged all over the world. There was a real belief that what was good for the USA was good for Australia. The year 1920 was significant. On 17 August the *Argus* reported that the Licences Reduction Board was celebrating its thirteenth birthday by closing down seven hotels in South Melbourne. Mr Barr, the chairman, pointed out that altogether his board had closed 1358 hotels in thirteen years, two a week, or over a hundred a year. But the real battle came with Victoria's own prohibition vote on 21 October 1920. The electors had to choose whether hotels in

The chain-driven bottling line at the Melbourne Co-operative Brewery in the 1920s.

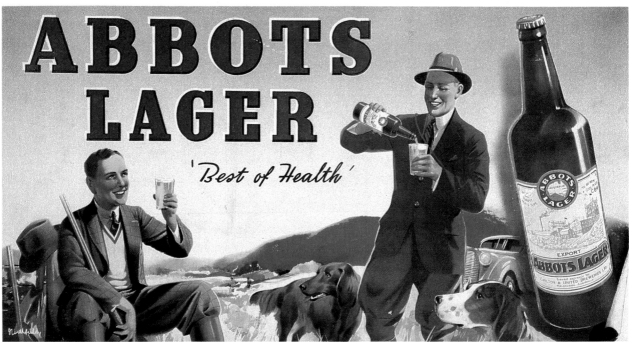

their district should continue, be reduced or closed. The newspapers were filled with stirring advertisements. Mr J. J. Liston on behalf of the liquor trade had the dramatic story about the Prince of Wales being derailed while aboard the royal train near Bridgetown, Western Australia. When asked whether he was hurt, he said: 'Hurt? Bless your heart, NO! And I'm glad to say the WHISKY FLASK is not broken either.' The Viticultural Council made the passionate plea:

CUB advertising emphasised patriotism. Australian Farm and Home, *20 September 1923.*

IT LIES IN YOUR HAND
IT IS FOR YOU TO SAY TOMORROW
WHETHER YOU WILL RUIN THE VIGNERONS OF VICTORIA

They are the men on the land — as settlers everything that can be desired, sober, industrious, prosperous.

Meanwhile at the Collins Street Baptist Church, Miss Grace L. Holder was horrified by a poster put out by liquor interests which had the message: A DROP OF BRANDY WOULD HAVE SAVED HIM.[2]

The result of the vote was:

Continuance of licences	278 702
For no licence	212 234
For reduction	36 025

Booroondara, which contained the large well-heeled suburb of Camberwell, had an unusually high proportion of Presbyterians, Baptists and Methodists and its representative in the Legislative Council was Mr E. W. Greenwood, president of the Anti Liquor League. Booroondara scored 63 per cent of votes for prohibition and Nunawading 65 per cent.[3] The City of Camberwell had seven hotels, two wine saloons and one licensed grocer. They all had to close, but there was a nice irony in this — Camberwell had been named after a pub. George Eastaway had established a hotel in 1853 at what is now Camberwell junction. The crossroads reminded him of Camberwell Green back home in London, so he had called his pub the Camberwell Inn and gave the district the name. In 1920 that same hotel closed its doors for ever and was demolished. Geoffrey Blainey records that the wreckers found an old wine-corked bottle of English ale in a dry well under the hotel, but the anti-liquor forces were triumphant even then, for the bottle broke, untasted.[4]

OPPOSITE PAGE:
Advertising in the period between the wars was innovative and often amusing.

The redoubtable Montague Cohen led the liquor defence battle and the ultimate triumph came when the Premier, Mr Lawson, introduced a bill on 28 November 1922, which killed the old agony of the three-yearly option poll. In future the poll would be held every seven years, and there would be no poll until 1929. The Associated Brewers showed their gratitude by presenting Montague Cohen with a cheque for £5000; £3300 came from CUB.[5]

The mid 1920s was a time of extraordinary expansion. Everything seemed possible. In 1924 the first air mail service began between the capital cities, Andrew 'Boy' Charlton won the Olympic Gold Medal in Paris for the 1500 metres, export trade in sugar began, and, to our shame, two million koala pelts were exported from the eastern states, resulting in their near extinction in New South Wales and Victoria. The following year the first

Melbourne Bitter: top seller from the Co-op Brewery.

coal briquettes were made at Yallourn. In the space of two years CUB doubled its financial power and strength. The general manager was W. H. 'Nobby' Clarke, a tall man with a husky voice who was capable of inspiring terror when he gazed down over rimless glasses. He adored his Clydesdales and there were notices all round the brewery threatening destruction to anyone who harmed the beasts. Wirth's Circus came to the brewery with a request for some hogsheads to use as pedestals for elephants in a head-balancing act. The answer was an abrupt, hoarse no. He felt for elephants almost as much as he did for Clydesdales.[6]

H. L. Torpey, who at one time had been head brewer at Castlemaine, was head brewer at Carlton & United. His hair was cut short, he wore tight little stiff collars, and journalists complained that it would be easier to extract information from a Tibetan monk. But he was amiable and he had a sense of humour. Most of the beer for interstate went out in the great 238-litre hogsheads. The custom was to put them on the interstate loading bank which was just a nice height above road level. One afternoon a character rushed into the office and reported that a mob out in Ballarat Street had a hogshead of beer. They had smashed into it with an axe and now everyone in sight was there filling up, using jugs, jam jars, billy cans, even chamber pots. The clerks in the order office thought it was a joke and took no notice. When the man kept coming back with further bulletins they thought it must be true, so they went to investigate. It was true all right. Two men had disguised themselves as brewery workers. They had

The CUB Clydesdales hard at work delivering beer in the 1930s.

OPPOSITE PAGE:
A Co-op idea of 1923 that was to return fifty years later: beer as a reward for hard work.

S. G. Elliott, Echuca, was one of the breweries taken over by Carlton.

put on the utterly correct leather aprons, rolled a hogshead off the interstate ramp, out the door into Bouverie Street then round the corner to where the picnic party was waiting. The news was relayed to Mr Torpey who said: 'Well, if they had the brains and the nerve to do that, they deserve to get away with it. Send someone round to bring the cask back.'[7]

It was take-over time again. In 1924 CUB paid £130 000 for Hodges Brewery at Geelong. Twenty-one hotels went with it.[8] Then in January 1925 CUB acquired Fitzgerald's Brewing & Malting Company at Castlemaine. This meant another twenty-three hotels at Castlemaine, Bendigo, Echuca and in the Riverina. The Castlemaine brewery was the famous establishment started by the two Irishmen Edward and Nicholas Fitzgerald from county Galway in 1857. Not only did they become the greatest power on the goldfields but the Castlemaine breweries spread to Melbourne, Sydney and Brisbane. By 1925 the brewery in Castlemaine could no longer compete with Melbourne and was going into debt. CUB took over the hotels and the brewery closed down.[9] There were vigorous rumours that the company was about to acquire another brewery in Bendigo. Naturally they were denied both in Bendigo and Melbourne. In early March of 1925, Carlton & United absorbed Cohn Bros Victoria Brewery Ltd in Bendigo for £120 000. This included forty hotels in northern Victoria, but not the Cohn Bros cordial and soft drink plant. Cohn Bros was the biggest brewery in the north, and had been established by Danish brothers Jacob, Moritz and Julius Cohn in 1857. According to Frank Cusack, they made the first lager in the Australian colonies and catered for the Germanic thirst on the goldfields.[10] Magnus Cohn, the managing director of Cohn Bros, joined the board of CUB.

CUB shares soared on the stock exchange with the announcement. The *Brewers' Journal* signalled it as virtually the end of country brewing in Victoria. Only half a dozen remained. It said:

The 1922 Abbotsford cricket team. Back row (left to right): G. Bryant, W. Raabe, K. Lloyd, F. Woodman, J. Hughes. Second row: J. Edwards, P. Breheny, R. Coburn, W. Erickson, T. Hele, H. Beyers. Seated: L. Weate, J. Keenan, E. Dynes, W. Cockburn, W. Bowtell, T. Ansell, A. Kerr. Front: A. Gration.

In some ways it is a pity, and there are many persons in the State who have pleasant memories of the old time brews, now, alas, no longer obtainable, but it must be realised we live in the age of standardisation and it must be admitted that as far as quality of beer is concerned there was no time when a better and more uniform beverage was brewed.

It was comforting, added the journal, that there was one national product which was simply above reproach.[11] But there were rumours abroad even more astonishing. Melbourne's two big remaining breweries, CUB and the Co-operative at Abbotsford were about to merge. Both companies denied these rumours with splendid conviction. On 2 April 1925, however, Messrs Pavey, Wilson & Cohen, solicitors, announced all had been arranged. No changes were contemplated. The capital was £2 million of which two-thirds would be held by CUB and one-third by the Co-operative. Once again Montague Cohen had been using his masterly negotiating skills. Six days after the announcement of the merger the CUB board voted him a special grant of £10 000 for 'the continued success of his schemes, both in politics and trade'.[12]

All the other mergers and take-overs which involved CUB did not raise an eyebrow. They were inevitable. But the Co-operative at Abbotsford was large, healthy and well run. Its annual profit since 1921–22 had risen from £77 000 to £120 352 in 1923–24. Rivalry between the two companies was intense, even bitter. Carlton & United and Co-operative travellers fought each other for custom. The Co-operative was ahead of Carlton in installing fountains in many hotels and many believed Abbots beer drew better than Carlton. Finance writers were puzzled that the Co-operative should be willing to lose its identity. The Co-operative had begun, however, as a protest by hotel keepers against the rise in price of beer. The non-tied houses had got together and started their own brewery. In

A Melbourne Bitter label before the take-over.

The Abbotsford Brewery about the time of the CUB take-over.

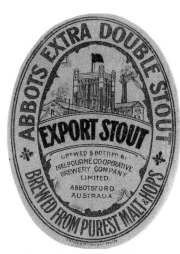

Abbots Stout label before 1924.

The extraordinary James Richardson, hotel owner.

twenty-one years times had changed. More and more of the crusading hotel keepers sold out their shares for a good profit until the Co-operative was owned just by a few very wealthy hotel men, some of them quite elderly. These principally were Stephen Morell, Henry F. Young and James Richardson, all originals in 1904. The Morells were of Spanish origin and Esteban Morell, like his son, was a successful hotel man and restaurateur. Stephen was successful at everything he touched; he was popular, affable and shrewd. He owned property in Queensland, and from 1911 he was a director of Windsor Pictures. He took over the Princes Bridge Hotel (Young & Jackson's) in 1914 and he represented Gipps Ward in the Melbourne City Council from 1901. Yet somehow he had never become part of the Melbourne Establishment. The trade-off of the Co-operative Brewery helped him to achieve this. In 1926, the year after the merger, he became Lord Mayor, and was there in office to entertain the Duke (later King George VI) and Duchess of York in 1927. That year he was knighted.[13]

It was Henry Young who sold Young & Jackson's to Stephen Morell. Speaking at the Early Colonists and Natives' Guild he said that he had come to Victoria in 1849, and when the ship arrived in Port Phillip Bay there was a crier in uniform who walked the streets and proclaimed through a trumpet: 'The Good Ship *John Mitchell* has arrived'.[14] Mr Young died six months after he joined the CUB board.

James Richardson was an extraordinary character. He had the largest chain of first class hotels in the southern hemisphere, which he sold in 1944, all except his first and last purchases, for half a million pounds. He was born in Ayrshire, Scotland, in 1865 and he came to Australia when he was 21. He started work as a 'useful' at the Hotel Wentworth in Sydney. His next job was barman at the Hotel Windsor in Melbourne, but he was no ordinary barman. In six years he saved enough money to buy the lease of a hotel. And so it went on. He bought another, and another, and another . . .[15] His first purchase was Morell's Hotel, originally the Australia Felix, at the corner of Russell and Bourke Streets, owned by Esteban Morell Sir Stephen's father. Old Esteban liked him so much he helped him with the finance. The name Richardson was there on the door until the hotel came down sixty years later to make way for a bank.

Even though he was extraordinarily rich, there was never any display of wealth with James Richardson. He was a bachelor and he lived at Morell's Hotel until he died in 1951 at the age of 87. He was a little man with a white goatee beard, quiet both in dress and manner. He used to get about town in a battered utility truck with a driver. There are legendary stories at the brewery about his overcoat, a pale moss-green antique, faded across the shoulders. One day as Melburnian weather turned bitter during a board meeting, Mr Richardson sent a boy to fetch his coat from the hotel. When the hotel manager produced the famous Richardson coat the boy would not believe it.

'But I want MR RICHARDSON'S coat.'

Said the manager: 'You've got it son. It's the only one he has.'

James Richardson was not a social man about town. He could see only one point in an overcoat, as an article to protect him from rain and cold. Yet he was not mean. When the driver of his old utility truck was ill, Richardson used to visit his home every Thursday to deliver the full week's wages.[16]

The annual reports listed board members in an interesting fashion. For example there was Clive Baillieu, gentleman; Montague Cohen, solicitor; Harold Edward Cohen, solicitor; Alexander T. Creswick, solicitor; William M. Hyndman, gentleman; Sidney Brewster Joske, gentleman; George A. Kay, gentleman. Then, when new members came on the board, Stephen J. Morell was a gentleman, Norman J. Carson was a gentleman, but James Richardson was a Russell Street, Melbourne, merchant. Could a person be a solicitor or a merchant and also be a gentleman? Whatever the terminology, under the new set up Sidney Joske resigned as chairman in 1926, stayed on as vice-chairman, and the new chairman was Colonel Harold Cohen. James P. Breheny, head brewer at Abbotsford, carried on his old job. T. V. Millea, former manager at the Co-operative, became joint general manager with W. H. Clarke. CUB had a share issue of 800 000 shares at £1 each to absorb the Melbourne Co-operative Brewery. Things were going very nicely for CUB. Its preference dividend in 1920 was 7 per cent, now it was 15 per cent and the ordinary dividend also had been increased from 10 to 15 per cent.[17]

Pearl Lager Pilsener Special label, 1926.

Canberra officially opened to become the national capital on 9 May 1927. There were many knockers. The Governor-General, Lord Stonehaven, did not want to live there. As far as he was concerned, it had one virtue. It was only 300 miles from Melbourne.[18] *Truth* newspaper said it was a gigantic frost. It was better to forget the £10 million that had been spent, the task was hopeless. The area wasn't any good for agriculture, let alone anything else.[19] Worst of all, at the behest of King O'Malley, the minister in charge of Canberra's construction, the Australian Commonwealth Territory was a dry area. King O'Malley was passionately against liquor. Once he made a famous speech in the South Australian Parliament claiming that as long as the barmaid system remained 'they might as well try to tame and manage a huge rattlesnake, an Indian cobra, or an Australian tigersnake, without extracting the fangs and the poison pouches'. All this was 'bespattering with mud the golden mantle of the loving moon-eyed goddess of democracy'.[20] A man with a good turn of phrase, was King O'Malley.

The *Brewers' Journal* lamented the sorry situation that a dry capital had to pander to the fads of this federal minister, this 'gentleman', who had a genius for self-advertisement. 'Today', continued the journal,

A Foster's label of the mid 1920s.

> Canberra is theoretically dry and no liquor may be manufactured or sold within the commission's territory. Actually it is quite the reverse and judging from the harvest of empty bottles, which at present represent the only crop gathered in the territory, the inhabitants have not much difficulty in getting all they want . . . Of course in a city where everything, from the colours of one's letter box to the width of a footpath is regulated, it would be a grateful change to be able to obtain a glass of beer which in composition, colour, cubic contents, manner of serving, was free from departmental regulation.[21]

On 1 September 1928 there was a reprieve. Canberra had a liquor poll — 1991 voters wanted a system of private licences, 1086 wanted all drinking under government licence, 801 wanted no licences at all and 211 wanted total prohibition.[22]

Carlton & United was always known as 'the combine' and the combine now was so powerful most people believed nobody would ever be brave or foolish enough to tackle it in combat. They were wrong. In November 1929 Peter Grant Hay, who had the old established firm of Coulson, Hay & Company, hop merchants, launched the Richmond Nathan System Brewing Co. Pty Ltd. The hop company was in Church Street, Richmond. Grant Hay bought land immediately behind it adjacent to the river and built a large modern brewery in twelve months. It was Richmond 'Tiger' beer with a splendid Tiger on the label. There was a deep chauvinistic desire to ally it to the district and above all, to the powerful Richmond football team. There was no price cutting. You could get your Tiger beer delivered home for 12s a dozen. It cost 1s 1d a bottle in a hotel, 5d for a long glass or 9d for a pot. The experts reckoned that Mr Grant Hay would be taken over or be out of business in three months.

The finest beer battle since 1904 got under way. CUB introduced Foster's Lager on draught for the first time since the old Foster Brewing Company introduced it back in 1895. Richmond did not join the Brewers' Association, so CUB played it hard. Hotels which were not tied had to make a choice. If they bought Richmond then it would be considered a breach of their agreement with the Brewers' Association and they would receive no beer. Yet some hotels and several big ones in the city did reject the combine. Richmond took its battle to Sydney and sold there in competition with Tooth's and Toohey's. What's more, as soon as the drought broke in Canberra, Richmond went to the ACT. Not only did Richmond survive the first three months, but on its third birthday there was a formal announcement that they had quadrupled their plant and there was a great birthday party at the brewery for twelve hundred of their friends. There was just one problem, the managing director, Mr Grant Hay, was not there. He had run into the great Australian ailment — a shipping strike — and could not get back from Queensland.[23]

The decade ended in yet another classic Victorian happening, a referendum on liquor. This one was fought even harder than the battle of 1920. The prohibitionists had a picture of a happy child playing with a spade on the beach.

> MOTHERS! FATHERS!
> which means most to YOU —
> The Publicans 'monetary ruin'
> or
> A Drink Ruined
> Life for Your Child?

The Reverend C. Irving Benson of the Wesley Church asked

> How would Jesus Vote if he were here today. It wasn't germaine to the question whether he drank fermented or unfermented wine. If drunkenness had been a social evil raging in Palestine as it was in Melbourne, if it had turned homes into hells, broken into the love of a father for his children and a husband for his wife, it is unthinkable that he would have countenanced it.[24]

J. J. Liston of the Liquor Trades Defence Union used brilliantly a cartoon which Percy Leason did for *Table Talk*. It was a play on the famous Carlton poster 'I allus has wan at eleven'. It showed the old digger leaning

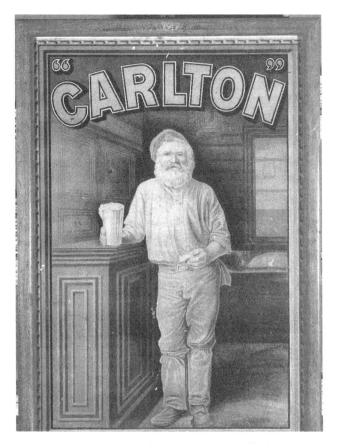

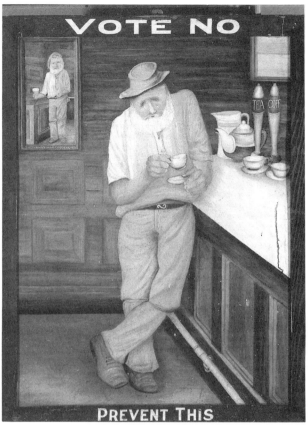

against the bar. One beer pull is labelled tea, the other is labelled coffee. Clearly he is weeping into his beard, as miserable as a man can be. As he lifts his cup from his saucer he says: 'And to think that I allus uster have one at eleven'.[25] The original poster dates from the turn of the century. In about 1897 a Carlton traveller was doing his rounds and he called in at McVeigh's Hotel, Walsh's Creek at the head waters of the Yarra. There he found Sam Griffin, an old gold fossicker from Wood's Point. Sam was the perfect bushman, complete with whiskers, red shirt and bowyangs. Paddy McVeigh introduced Sam to the traveller. Sam waved his pot and said: 'I allus has wan at eleven'. The Carlton man thought he looked so perfect he asked if he could take his photograph. Very soon hoardings throughout Victoria were depicting life-size pictures of Sam advertising Carlton Ale. According to the *Australian Brewers' Journal* of 1909, Sam Griffin was eager to see his own picture but he died a few days before the start of the advertising campaign.[26]

The CUB publication *What's Brewing* has another story. It reports that Sam Griffin was actually paid a small royalty for every poster published with his picture. He died in McVeigh's kitchen, choked by a piece of ox tail. The Wood's Point mailman agreed to bury Sam for £4, but he failed to arrive because of heavy snow. So Paddy McVeigh made a coffin out of packing cases. The boards carried various messages, 'This Side Up', 'Stow Away From Boilers', 'Beer Boxes' and 'Keep in Cool Place'. They put the coffin on a spring cart and in pouring rain they set out for West Warburton, 25 miles off. On the way they picked up Tiger McGinn, Sam's cousin from

Carlton's most famous poster, 'I allus has wan at eleven' (left), became part of the liquor defence in 1930 with a miserable Sam Griffin weeping into his tea, 'I allus uster have wan at eleven'.

East Warburton. It was a rough trip. While crossing the timber-line at Warburton the horse fell and the coffin dropped from the cart. They met Dick Geddis at the cemetery, but there was another problem — no parson. Because of the rain he had been unable to make it through the mud. They found the grave full of water. Two men had to hold the coffin down with sticks to keep Sam from floating away while another shovelled in the clay, and a fourth man read the burial service. As they were leaving the cemetery, the parson arrived. They told him it was all over, but the reverend gentleman was very unhappy. This would not do at all. Sam Griffin must have a Christian burial and besides he was entitled to his 10s fee. So back they went and did the burial service in its proper, correct, Christian fashion.[27]

It was a bitter referendum campaign. Two Archbishops, Archbishop Head of the Anglican Church and Archbishop Mannix of the Roman Catholic were in rare agreement and spoke in favour of 'no licence', but maybe Sam Griffin so long in his wet grave, helped to play a part. The prohibitionists were soundly defeated 507 024 votes to 388 833.[28]

CHAPTER EIGHT

CUB Heads North

People dream that they only have to be associated with the liquor industry for riches to follow automatically, but few riches were available in the early 1930s. The Federal Government increased its excise duty to 2s a gallon in July 1930 and company profits for that year were the lowest in five years. By late 1928 unemployment was on the rise and by 1930 Australia was deep into the depression. 'Susso' for the sustenance worker was a new word in the language and the unemployed reached a peak of 30 per cent of the work force. It was like the 1890s all over again; thousands left the city and took to the track. Others begged from door-to-door around the wealthier suburbs.

On Christmas Day 1930, Mr Sidney Myer, the city's leading retailer, gave the greatest Christmas dinner Melbourne had seen. He fed eleven thousand of the poor and unemployed at the Exhibition Building. At first he planned to limit the dinner to ten thousand and he issued tickets, but when it was almost over he walked outside and found a thousand people waiting there, silently, so he invited them inside. Over three hundred of the Myer staff helped: shop girls, departmental managers and Mr Myer himself. Constantly he walked from table to table, making sure everybody was fed. They did feed too. They ate, among other things, three-quarters of a ton of ham, half a ton of corned beef, half a ton of butter and they drank a thousand gallons of beer.

Carlton & United was proud that not one member of the staff lost their job because of the depression, but they went close. CUB warned the unions that with reduced output it was not possible to run the brewery at a profit, 10 per cent of the staff would have to go. There was a mass meeting of the employees of the Liquor Trades Union. They agreed to accept an 8 per cent reduction in salary and so the crisis was averted. Employees who earned £5 10s or under took a salary drop of 8 per cent. Those earning more dropped 10 per cent.[1] In 1929 CUB produced the equivalent of 3 439 912 dozens of beer. In 1932 that was down to 2 649 166. Beer, even at 6d a bottle, was a commodity too expensive to drink.[2]

It was a very different world in the 1930s. CUB had three main breweries, the Victoria, the large and modern Abbotsford, formerly the Co-operative, and the Carlton in Bouverie Street. All these were active in producing beer. There was also the stately old Yorkshire Brewery in Wellington

Jack Robinson (left) and Paddy Dernin in the hop store at Carlton, c. 1925.

Street, Collingwood, established in 1858 by John Wood, and held onto by CUB for two reasons. First, it was a useful back-up brewery in case of fire or disaster at the other breweries, and second, as long as CUB owned it, then no other competitor could. So the Yorkshire was used for storage, maintenance, and above all the repair and manufacture of wooden barrels.

There was no fixed retiring age at CUB. As long as a man was fit he could stay on for ever. In 1932 there were 140 employees who had been there for a quarter of a century. William Jackson had been there since 1877 and Joe Justice, aged 76, had been a Carlton worker since 1876. He told reporters he proposed to stay on another twenty years. Maybe it was the beer, maybe it was the hard work; certainly, to be a brewery worker one needed muscle.[3] The work was extremely labour intensive. All the malt and sugar came in bags which weighed about 31 kilograms. Men pulled them off the horse-drawn lorries and carried them in on their backs. The hops came in bales which weighed over 60 kilograms. Ted Williams, former chief brewer at Carlton recalls that he was the first to introduce forklift trucks. His successor Neville Wigan remembers:

> We needed masses of space and masses of men. When the brew was made up we had to count out the number of bags of malt that we wanted and tip them into a hopper which went down to the mills to be crushed. All these bags had to be trolleyed across to the hopper, cut open and tipped. The same with the sugar.

The delivery line-ups at the Abbotsford Brewery (top) and the Victoria Brewery, c. 1930: a combination of petrol power and horse power.

There were sixty Clydesdales at the Carlton stables. There were no such things as cardboard cartons, no packs of stubbies stuck together in plastic. The bottles went out in specially designed baskets, two dozen to a basket. It took genuine muscle to lift them. Those going interstate or overseas were packed in wooden boxes, each bottle in its own straw sheath. Barrels came in firkins, nine gallons; kilderkins, eighteen gallons; halves, twenty-

A 1920s label from Geelong's Volum Brewery Co.

seven gallons; barrels, thirty-six gallons and hogsheads, fifty-four. They would use hogsheads to send beer to Queensland or big customers like Young & Jackson's, the Princes Bridge Hotel. Goldie Melbourne at the old Volum Brewery in Geelong, says it was a great work of art to get those immense barrels off the lorry and down into the hotel cellar. It could all be done by one man. He would take the barrel off the end of the lorry on to a dump bag, wheel it across to the door of the cellar, then use skids, metal cleats, and a great lowering rope. He would brake it on a rope as it went down and you could see the smoke rising from the strain.

The biggest problem was keeping an eye on the publicans. Carl Resch said:

> In the early days there were lead pipes from the casks and they were bloody dangerous. There was lead from the vats to the drawing equipment with a pulling gadget on the bench. They were hardly ever clean. The brewery had to appoint its own team of plumbers to do the cleaning. They were given a special name to differentiate them. They were called hotel plumbers. Their job was to make sure connections were good and the equipment was clean. Even if they were clean you could pick up lead into the beer. The original casks were all big, hogshead size, which meant that the beer would be standing in the pipes for a long time. Then the hotel keepers would send back barrels saying the beer had gone off. Sometimes they had left barrels standing out in the sun, or in extreme cases they even poured slops back into the barrel.

Labelling of bottles was all done by hand.

> We used to have a conveyor, six bottles wide. Four men sat along the conveyor and put them on one by one. It was bloody marvellous how fast they got. They moaned when we started putting in the machine labelling. That came to the Victoria Brewery about 1935.

A McCracken's Invalid Stout label of the period.

Perhaps most fascinating of all was the curious business of the tax stamps. The Victorian Government first introduced the beer duty, rate 3d a gallon, in 1892. The tax was collected 'by obliging the brewer' to buy beer stamps which he had to fix to every barrel before delivery or to delivery dockets in the case of bottled beer. When the states federated in 1901, naturally the new Federal Government was delighted with this idea and adopted it as its own. So it continued for the next fifty-seven years. The denominations of the stamps ranged from two gallons to four hundred gallons.[4] A prime job at the brewery was that of paste boy. He would take up his position with a paste brush and a pile of stamps. Later when the cool rooms were installed they had to use a piece of wire gauze and staple the stamp to the barrel.

Output and value of stamps had to balance every day, and the cost of stamps ran to hundreds of thousands of pounds. Therefore the brewery was loath to buy too many in advance. There was a visit to the old Customs House in Flinders Street every few days. In the mid 1930s Brian Corrigan, as a very young man, had this job. He retired as assistant general manager properties.

> One of my jobs was to go down to the Customs House and buy the stamps twice a week. I would carry a leather case, very heavy, with all the stamps in

it. If it was £10 000 I had to go to the ANZ Bank first and get the cheque cleared before I went over to the Customs House. There was always a constant procession of horse-drawn brewery waggons heading down to the wharf and the railhead. So I would always get a ride, a lovely trip on a sunny morning. We would even call in at the Phoenix Hotel and have a pot. Then there was another ritual—we would call in at the bottling room and collect half a dozen bottles to take to the Customs House.

Carlton label, c. 1934.

Mr Corrigan explained that the operation always went through more smoothly if you had a few bottles in hand, and sometimes he was able to save a few bottles for a party of his own. The whole excise operation was under inspection and the government had and still have their excise officers at the brewery. All the stamps had to be cancelled and publicans were under threat of heavy fine if the stamps were not cancelled before the beer was used. Brian Corrigan said: 'A lot of the boys used to try to wash the stamps off and use them again. They used to wash a stamp at times, put it on another barrel and whip one barrel out'.

The excise tax has always been strict. It has to be paid even on beer drunk in the brewery premises, and paid on all beer given away as gifts. The Cricket Club had its own beer barrel. The company was only too happy to donate the beer, but the club had to pay the excise. Neither the management nor the excise people knew that the coopers kindly shaved out the inside of that barrel so that it held a few extra gallons. The staves were so thin it required very gentle and loving treatment when it went in for cleaning. The excise people kept a close watch on the amount of beer produced and the amount of tax paid. If there was a discrepancy there would be a demand to 'Please explain'. Ted Williams said:

> Loss of beer in bottling always caused me concern. Men being what they are pilfering was always going on. It was very hard to track it down. I noticed that many of them were bringing their lunches in Gladstone bags, large enough to carry their food needs for a week. Well, it's a pretty sensitive area, going around accusing people of theft.
>
> Well I put in a cloak room, a bag room, and all bags had to go in there. I got hold of the Liquor Trade Union President, Bert Roberts. I told him what was happening and I was responsible for the excise on this stuff. We stood by waiting for them to pick up their bags.
>
> There were fourteen bags unclaimed that night. We opened the bags and I sent them all to some charity, minus the beer.

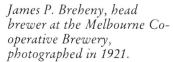

James P. Breheny, head brewer at the Melbourne Co-operative Brewery, photographed in 1921.

It was not easy getting rid of the archaic stamp tax system. The company made its first approaches to the Department of Customs in 1956, kept up the pressure for two years, and finally the government agreed that in future duty could be paid on the total gallonage estimated to be delivered on the following day. The new system began on 1 August 1958. On the evening of 31 July a photographer took an historic photograph for *What's Brewing* magazine of the last stamp being pasted on the last kilderkin. Few people noticed the mistake, a 9-gallon stamp was fixed on to an 18-gallon cask.[5]

The brewing industry was larded with remarkable characters. Two of them, James P. Breheny and Montague Cohen, died in 1931. James Breheny was the best known of the extraordinary Brehenys. In 1915 the *Australian Brewers' Journal* listed twelve Brehenys all working as brewers around

Australia.[6] Jim Breheny was the man who made the Co-operative Brewery such formidable opposition for CUB. He was so good that Abbots Lager at times even outsold the redoubtable Foster's. He remained as head brewer at Abbotsford after the amalgamation almost until his death at his home in Lisson Grove, Hawthorn, on 24 February. His two brothers Peter and Tom also worked with him at Abbotsford. He had a whimsical, Irish sense of humour and there is a legendary story that once he asked the brewery carpenter, Bob Vaughan to make a kennel for his dog. Mr Vaughan looked upon his head brewer with a vast sense of awe and made a magnificent dog kennel. Indeed it was a miniature mansion, gabled roof, dormer windows, balconies, porticoes. Jim Breheny looked at the kennel in wonder: 'Bob, that's wonderful. I didn't expect anything as fine as that. But tell me, where does the bloody dog get in?' Vaughan had forgotten to include a door.[7]

Breheny had three sons and five daughters. His son Brian, also a brewer, became general manager of CUB. Breheny was succeeded at Abbotsford by Hans Trunschnig. Trunschnig was first employed at the Victoria Brewery, but like all the Germans, come the First World War he lost his job and was interned as a potential danger to security. After his release he went home, did a course in brewing and migrated to Australia for the second time in 1925.

Montague Cohen died on 17 October 1931 at his home in Melbourne Mansions, aged 76. He was replaced on the board by Maurice H. Baillieu. Although Montague Cohen was always the dominating power in the company, he was never the chairman. His son Colonel Harold Edward Cohen joined the board in 1926 and Sidney Joske stepped down so that he could immediately take over as chairman. Colonel Cohen was rich, powerful, and a success at everything he touched. There was no question about his authority at the brewery. Eric Nilan recalled in the ledger room there was a special box of elongated, gold-plated J nibs kept for the use of the chairman, Colonel Cohen. Mr Millea, who was joint general manager with W. H. Clarke, had a box of scribbler nibs, made merely of common steel.

Harold Cohen was born in November 1881, went to school at Xavier College, Melbourne and had a brilliant career at Melbourne University. In his freshman year he took the Bowen Prize, then final honours in law and the Supreme Court Prize. In the First World War he commanded the 6th Army Brigade, left Australia in 1915 and did not return until 1919. He was twice wounded, and won the DSO and the CMG. In 1921 *Melbourne Punch* wrote a profile on him:

> Enormously rich he nevertheless lived as simply—not to say as uncomfortably— as his humblest subaltern. He liked to see the men smartly turned out and was a stickler for clean harness and burnished chains. Yet his own costume in and out of the line consisted of a complete issue outfit, including a ruined overcoat on which no badges were worn. Having occasion to visit an English artillery potentate at an adjoining headquarters he was refused admission by an impeccably attired young staff officer. Not until unforgettable words had been spoken by the unfortunate lad about the notorious disorderliness and lack of discipline of Australian soldiers did it occur to Cohen to prove his identity by removing his overcoat. The subaltern nearly swooned at the spectacle of a crown and two stars and the CMG, DSO plus other ribbons ... With his

Harold Edward Cohen who
was chairman of CUB in
1926.

fighting record and social and political influence, he could certainly have had a division for the asking after 1917. He preferred to stick to his Brigade.[8]

Cohen returned to Australia to become Chief Commissioner of the Scouts. He was chairman of CUB and the Swan Brewery in Perth at the same time. He was a state member of parliament for fifteen years, first in the upper house, then as member for Caulfield in the Assembly. He became Solicitor General and Minister for Education. In the 1920s and early 1930s he lived in a large house in Wattletree Road, Malvern, opposite where the Cabrini Hospital is now. Daily he would go to the city in a chauffeur-driven car. The chauffeur would drop him off while he walked through the Botanic Gardens. His son Edward remembers him as a workoholic. In those days directors had to sign the pay cheques. The Colonel would bring home a pile of cheques, feet high, from the brewery and he would sign them through the night. He remained in the Army Reserve and in May 1944 he was appointed brigadier.

Another great figure in the 1930s was F. W. J. Clendinnen. He joined CUB in June 1922 as a university student. The board decreed that he was to receive £300 a year and he was to have time off for his lectures in biochemistry. This was a time when brewers were self-taught. They did not go to university, and this young boffin was treated with suspicion. He was always quiet and reserved, but few men had a more profound effect on production at Bouverie Street. Particularly with his work on yeast, and isolation of yeast cells, Clendinnen defined the quality and style of CUB beers for the next forty years. In 1923, at a cost of £102 000, CUB established a low yeast section. The yeast cultures came directly from the Carlsberg Brewery in Denmark. Professor A. Jorgensen in Denmark, one of the great revered scientists at Carlsberg, wrote:

> I am very glad to hear that your new Low Section is working so satisfactorily and that my yeast cultures may put a little deal of progress to their credit. We shall, of course, try to do our best to suit your demands at every time in the future.[9]

Ted Williams remembers the arrival of the first yeast, culture 1226. It came out in a little Hansen flask and the whole consignment was smaller than a cigar box. The first consignments from Denmark in 1923 have been cultivated ever since. They have gone on growing and growing through countless generations, providing the yeast for the billions of litres of beer and stout that came from Carlton breweries in the following six decades. Brewers Ted Williams and Brian Breheny went to Copenhagen in 1957 and visited Jorgensen's laboratories. They spoke to Dr Eric Helms, the scientist in charge. They asked him about the Jorgensen yeast, whether he had the original culture. 'Oh no,' said Helms, 'the Germans came through here during the war and smashed everything.' So the oldest Jorgensen strain is not in Copenhagen, but in Melbourne. Clendinnen installed the first proper laboratory inside the building at Bouverie Street. In the 1930s it was just a small room, fitted with Bunsen burners, very different to the multi-millon group technical centre that exists today.

Melbourne beer was shipped to north Queensland almost from the turn of the century. Maybe it was dissatisfaction with Brisbane beer, maybe it was almost as cheap to ship beer to Townsville and Cairns as it was to sell it in Melbourne, but Carlton Ale, Foster's Lager, Empire Ale, all went

Ted Williams at the Carlton Brewery laboratory bench, 1925. He became head brewer in 1949.

to north Queensland. CUB used to distribute through four firms, Cummins & Campbell, Samuel Allen, Joseph Pease, and Burns Philp. Eventually it became simpler to acquire these firms, so CUB bought control of them, all except Burns Philp which was too large. Carlton was the only brewery in Australia that sent draught beer to north Queensland. It all came by ship in wooden kegs, hogsheads and half hogsheads. It was difficult maintaining quality over such distances and frequently the beer arrived cloudy and in poor condition, but any beer was better than no beer. Theft was an even greater problem. Wharf labourers took their share, railwaymen took theirs. Often they would drill holes to prime a leak and barrels would come back to Melbourne with more holes than a porcupine.

In 1931 CUB bought a controlling interest in Northern Australian Breweries Ltd, originally the Cairns Brewing Company. The first meeting of the Cairns Brewery had been held on 24 June 1924 and the first directors were J. L. Breheny, chairman, P. T. Cahill, E. S. Williams, W. J. White and A. L. Nevitt, secretary. Ned Williams was the father of Sidney Williams, the north Queensland businessman. The original brewery was built by A. L. Hargreaves of Portland Cement using railway lines for the foundations. Local hotel keepers desperate for more convenient supplies were the main shareholders. J. L. Breheny, of Toowoomba, one of the famous Breheny family of brewers, was the brewer.

The company was under-capitalised. They found brewing desperately difficult in tropical conditions. Breheny had to mortgage his house to send out the first beer. He did not even have the money to buy excise stamps. Brewing began in July 1925 but in early 1927 the funds ran out. It was too hard to get paid. F. C. Odel was appointed liquidator, but late in 1927 they had another try. The Cairns Brewing Company became the Northern Australian Breweries Ltd and the original shareholders received one share for every share they had had in the old CBC. New money came from investors in Sydney and Melbourne. Auguste John Charles de Bavay came from Melbourne to be brewer manager. He was the son of the scientist de Bavay, pioneer of Foster's. De Bavay jnr had been at the front in the First World War and insisted on being called Captain de Bavay. The new board was D. Headrick, chairman, A. J. C. de Bavey, A. Devine, P. T. Cahill, W. P. Listner, H. L. McKenny, secretary, F. C. P. Curlewis and R. T. McManus. The Cairns Brewery supplied beer as far south as Cardwell, just beyond Innisfail, a very small market, and the new company suffered all the agonies of the old. In 1930 de Bavay resigned as brewer manager. Carl Stefanson, the under-brewer, took his place. Stefanson was a Dane. He had started as a labourer with no qualifications and in just a few years he was the brewer. Tony Devine, one of the original directors took over as acting manager.

Tom Kelly started with the brewery as a delivery clerk in 1929, became general manager in 1957, then Queensland state manager for Carlton in 1961. He says legend has it that R. F. G. Fogarty (later chairman of CUB) started his famous brewing career in the following way. A group of directors was drinking in a Cairns bar, bemoaning the fate of the failing brewery, when Fogarty, an old friend of Tony Devine, said: 'I'll fix it for you'. Fogarty did not lack confidence; he thought he could fix anything. Fogarty and Devine had been in the artillery together, they were old wartime pals, so the deal was on.

Executive staff of the Cairns Brewery. Top row (left to right): W. H. Houston, Ted Williams, C. Stefansen. Bottom row: H. McKenny, R. F. G. Fogarty, V. Ennis.

Reginald Francis Graham Fogarty was born in the tiny town of Normanton on the Gulf of Carpentaria on 24 November 1892. He had little education, but his remarkable organising skills were revealed early. He went away with the 1st AIF, became adjutant of the 11th Field Artillery Brigade, and rose to lieutenant. After the war he became a commercial traveller, dealing in soft leather goods and such things as ladies' hand bags. He dealt in ladies' shoes, boiled sweets, and one time was an agent for King Tea. He always considered himself an expert on tea.

Geoffrey Blainey in his book *Mines in the Spinifex* tells a story of Fogarty. After the floating of Mt Isa Mines in January 1924 three men who held the Rio Grande lease sold out for £5000 and insisted on cash, not shares. They called for their cheques at a Cloncurry bank and began a spree. They boarded the train for the coast with an ice chest crammed with beer and spirits. They invited a commercial traveller, Fogarty, and a railway guard to join the party. The guard obliged and hung a placard marked RESERVED on the carriage door whenever they came to a station. At Richmond the floods had washed away the line, and they spent four days fighting and drinking and being ejected from hotels. 'Fogarty', wrote Geofrey Blainey, 'delighted his cronies by mounting a balcony and haranguing the crowd as an evangelist'. Even then he had a reputation as a good drinker. When Fogarty came to the brewery he was the representative for Express Parcels in Townsville. Tom Kelly remembers him in those days as an extraordinarily good-looking man, handsome, with an excellent singing voice. One time he even formed a choir among the girls on the staff.

CUB had a large cool store in Townsville, which became a distribution centre, and so battle was joined with Northern Australian Breweries. Much later when he was Sir Reginald, Fogarty used to tell stories of those days before 1930. The Cairns Brewery was selling its beer at 6d a glass. CUB dropped its price to 3d. Fogarty did not give in. There was loyalty to the local product, so they managed to keep on selling at 6d. He went all over the north, drumming up trade. He would appeal to hotel keepers to pay cash, and he recalled the days when he would go on the train just to get the cash from the hotel keepers, so that he could meet the weekly pay cheque at the brewery. Eventually it was an uneven battle. CUB owned almost all the hotels through its four distribution companies, leaving Fogarty with no outlets. The end came in 1931. CUB now had a real beachhead in Queensland, and like the Normandy invasion it was to become very much larger. Tom Kelly remembers the sale vividly.

> Arthur Fadden, later Sir Arthur and prime minister, was a great friend of Fogarty's. Fadden was an accountant in Townsville and Fogarty engaged him to arrange all the transfer of scrip. I was seconded from the brewery to help him and it was all done in the back room of the Commercial Bank in Cairns. Fadden was a great humourist. Half way through he would stop and tell yarns. He said he had been a referee in a football match between the Palm Island Aboriginals and the Mainland. It was a curtain raiser to a visit of the English team, Rugby League. They brought them on a launch to town. They had to go back straight after the English game. One Aboriginal from Palm Island went through and got on the grog. He woke just as the launch was leaving for Palm Island.
>   He called out, 'Who won the bloody game?'
>   His mate yelled back, 'We beat the bastards thirty-three to nil and they wouldn'ta got to nil only Artie Fadden was referee.'

Tom Kelly said Arthur Fadden offered him a job to go and work in his office for 30s a week.

> My father advised me to talk it over with Fogarty. I said to Mr Fogarty, 'Your friend Mr Fadden has offered me a job.' Well, he blew his top. He got on the telephone and told Fadden to come right over. He abused him and they both got on the grog. The upshot was that he matched the bid of 30s a week. I started on 17s and was getting 22s at the time. The secretary received £8 and Carl Stefanson got £10.

Tom Kelly said Fogarty would have his drinking bouts. Amongst his employees was Billy Grimes, who had been a boxer almost in world class. After drinking bouts Grimes would act as masseur and give Fogarty a rub down on the board room table. Always Fogarty demanded absolute loyalty. Tom Kelly said he had a favourite saying, 'You can buy geniuses from the university but you can't buy a loyal man'.

The general manager at CUB, W. H. Clarke, sent Ted Williams to be a brewer in Cairns and he stayed for five years. Fogarty's organising skills were as good then as they were to be in Melbourne when he became general manager. Ted Williams says they made no packaged beer, only draught, and in the first few years their profits were so large they were able to turn a quarter of a million pounds back into the brewery in improvements. Yet these were still depression years. When times were tough and you had no work, it was better to be penniless in a warm climate. Ted Williams vividly remembers young men with their blueys jumping the rattler in Cairns, often with police in full pursuit. But it could be hilarious, usually the young men were far too athletic for the steaming, overweight police who tried to catch them.

R. F. G. Fogarty was an enthusiast for public works. In Cairns he not only resurrected from chaos the Returned Servicemen's League, he became a life member. He founded Cairns Legacy, became the first president, and was district governor of Rotary. He also staged an agricultural show, not an easy job. Ted Williams remembers that the unemployed had occupied the fair grounds and were living in sheds where there should have been prize poultry or cattle. Furthermore they refused to move.

> The police plus helpers moved in to take the grounds by force. There was a real battle and all morning ambulances were taking the injured back to hospital. Of course, some of the evicted weren't too happy and they blamed the brewery. There were even threats that they would burn it down. So we had to mount guards round the clock and at night we used big 500-watt bulbs to floodlight the place.
>
> We had one fellow on guard who had been in the 1914–18 war and he was a bit shellshocked. It was raining this night and suddenly there were explosions like gun fire. This fellow came running in : 'They're coming! They're coming!' It was just the 500-watt bulbs exploding in the rain. However the agricultural show, like most things Fogarty did, was a big success. It became an annual event.

Wal Fisher, later executive brewer for CUB, was brought up in Brisbane, went to Queensland University and started work at Cairns in 1945. He said that Fogarty always wore a homberg. He was everything you expected an old time beer baron to be. He was a hard task master, tough and he expected everyone else to work hard.

> He used to work with a series of buzzers to all his staff. When he buzzed he expected you to arrive on his doorstep, quick and lively. Yesterday almost. He used to press the buzzer for Victor Ennis, the engineer, who was in the office underneath him. He knew very well what Victor was up to. As soon as Ennis heard the buzzer he would rush out of the office, pretending he wasn't there. Fogarty woke up to this. He would look out the window and see Ennis disappearing at a great rate of knots. He would yell, 'Where are you going, I want to see yer'. Every now and then he would pull himself up to the table. He was pretty rotund and his stomach would go against all the buzzers at once. Then everybody would arrive in his office. 'WHAT DO ALL YOU FELLERS WANT?'

The brewery survived the very difficult depression years, then in 1940 all shipment of beer from Carlton & United to the north came to an end. There was no shipping space. Tom Kelly said Carlton & United had beer barrels all over north Queensland. Now Cairns was on its own and it had to take them over. Of course, it did not have the capacity to cope; it had to supply not only the north but the troops as well. The beer was going out only two or three days old, practically green. In those years the brewery came of age. Tom Kelly remembers the Cairns pubs before and immediately after the war. They did not have any refrigeration. The kegs would go straight on to the bar, reasonably cold from the cool room at the brewery. The pubs would expect instant service. Sometimes they had to send across kegs three or four times a day, say, at seven, nine, eleven and four o'clock.

R. F. G. Fogarty was not the only one to have his troubles during the

Wally Fisher, executive director of brewing, before his retirement in 1986.

Stoking the boilers at the Abbotsford Brewery in the 1930s.

depression. The effect of the 1930s depression on beer consumption in Australia was startling. In 1927–28 Australia produced 74 035 000 gallons. In 1930–31 it was down to 55 654 484 gallons, a drop of 24.66 per cent.[10] Business began to improve in 1934, sales picked up, and CUB actually made a bonus issue to shareholders on a one for two basis and nearly a million shares were distributed. There were changes afoot. Carlton was mainly equipped to produce top-fermentation bulk beer, the old fashioned English ale. But the public taste had changed. On 27 April the brewers reported to the board that the public taste now was largely for bottom-fermented beer or lager. As far as they could see, the change was permanent. Those with long memories could possibly recall how the *Brewers' Journal* used to say that the Australian working man wouldn't drink this stuff even if you gave it to him. 'There is not the smallest chance of the concocted-in-Germany swill ever being acclimatised in Australia.'[11] New equipment had to be installed immediately at Carlton and Victoria at a cost of £28 000. There was an interesting class distinction in tastes: old hands have reported that top-fermentation men and bottom-fermentation men didn't quite get on together, they even drank at different bars.

There were further signs of prosperity. In 1937 CUB bought the Royal Arcade Hotel in Little Collins Street, Melbourne, for £85 000. In 1938 the company bought the Queensland Hotel at the eastern end of Bourke Street and promptly changed the name to The Carlton. But the most interesting purchase was the ancient Port Phillip Hotel just over the road from Flinders Street Railway Station. It was a strange labyrinth of little bars. It used to have power-operated punkas, which always operated on roasting north-wind days, sending little eddies across the surface of the beer. It had an oyster bar where it was possible to get a dozen delicious oysters for 2s 6d, plus a glass of beer.

CHAPTER NINE

The Second World War

On the night of 3 September 1939, the Prime Minister, Mr R. G. Menzies, made an announcement in a radio hook-up throughout the nation. He said:

> Fellow Australians, it is my melancholy duty to inform you officially that in consequence of the persistence of Germany in her invasion of Poland Great Britain has declared war on her . . . We are therefore as a great family of nations involved in a struggle which we must at all times win, and which we believe in our hearts we will win. Where Britain stands there stands the people of the entire British world.

The newspapers printed photographs of the British Prime Minister, Mr Chamberlain, along with his historic words: 'This is a sad day for all of us. Everything that I have worked for and believed in has crashed in ruins. I trust that I may be permitted to see the day when Hitlerism has been destroyed.' It was very different from 1914. There were no 'demonstrations of enthusiasm', no displays of patriotic fervour in Collins Street. In fact there was a sublime twilight period which lasted for almost two years. While Australians died in Syria, Greece and Crete, the cosy comfort of Melbourne, Sydney, Brisbane and other capitals was beautifully unchanged. Indeed with the production of munitions and more jobs for women, Australia for the first time in more than a decade had full employment.[1]

On 8 December 1941 came the news of the Japanese attack on Pearl Harbour, followed on 19 February by the devastating raid on Darwin. Now Australia was really at war. It was a strange Christmas. At the height of the Christmas shopping rush the government brought in the black-out. It was not easy to get used to the darkness, the awful gloom of Bourke Street, the complete absence of neon lights. Black paper was pasted over the windows. There was a 'Dig for Victory' campaign. Hideous trenches, so-called air-raid shelters began to appear in the all public gardens and vacant allotments.[2] Melbourne Grammar, Wesley, Macpherson Robertson Girls' High School all became offices for the armed forces.[3] The Americans took over the Melbourne Cricket Ground. Even the Melbourne Cricket Club secretary, Vernon Ransford, couldn't get in there unless he had a

A poster, made by Buckle Bros, placed by deeply thirsty Diggers outside Tobruk during the Second World War.

properly accredited pass from the US forces. The new name for the MCG was Camp Murphy.[4]

The making of beer went on in the comfortable, normal manner it had always done until this extraordinary telegram arrived from the Collector of Customs:

> CANBERRA 26/3/42
> Rec'd Customs House
> Melbourne 9.30 a.m.
> 27/3/42

> COLCUSTOMS MELBOURNE
> REFERENCE LIQUOR CONTROL AS FROM FIRST APRIL BREWERS ANNUAL PRODUCTION QUOTA TO BE BASED ON TOTAL PRODUCTION FOR JANUARY AND FEBRUARY 1942 LESS ONE THIRD DIVIDED BY TWO AND MULTIPLIED BY TWELVE STOP BREWERS MAY PRODUCE AS CONVENIENT TO THEM BUT MUST NOT EXCEED ANNUAL QUOTA ESTABLISHED ABOVE STOP DELIVERIES TO BE BASED ON MONTHLY QUOTAS ESTABLISHED ON FOLLOWING BASIS NAMELY TOTAL ESTABLISHED PRODUCTION FIGURES TO BE DIVIDED BY TWELVE AND FIGURE THUS OBTAINED TO BE MONTHLY QUOTA FOR JANUARY FEBRUARY MARCH APRIL OCTOBER AND NOVEMBER STOP FOR MONTHS MAY JUNE JULY AUGUST SEPTEMBER MONTHLY AVERAGE ESTABLISHED FOR JANUARY ETCETERA TO BE REDUCED BY TEN PER CENT STOP FOR DECEMBER THE MONTHLY AVERAGE WILL BE INCREASED BY 40 PER CENT STOP THIS BASIS WILL NOT ENTIRELY ABSORB TOTAL PRODUCTION QUOTA BUT WILL LEAVE A SMALL SURPLUS WHICH MAY BE USED TO CORRECT ANOMALIES AT THE DISCRETION OF THE COLLECTOR STOP CANTEENS OFFICERS AND SERGEANTS MESSES BOTH AUSTRALIAN AND ALLIED ALSO EXPORT TRADE NOT TO BE DEBITED AGAINST EITHER PRODUCTION OR DELIVERY QUOTAS STOP COLLECTOR IS EMPOWERED TO SETTLE ANOMALIES ARISING FROM CHANGES IN POPULATION OR OTHER CAUSES BUT WHERE CONSIDERED NECESSARY HE MAY CALL IN NOMINEES FOR BREWERS ASSOCIATION AND LICENSED VICTUALLERS ASSOCIATION STOP UNDER NEW ARRANGEMENT HOTELS WILL BE RATIONED ON THEIR AVERAGE TRADE FOR JANUARY AND FEBRUARY LESS ONE THIRD WITH VARIATION FOR DIFFERENT MONTHS AS IN CASE OF BREWERS STOP APRIL DELIVERIES TO BE PERMITTED COMMENCE IMMEDIATELY STOP PLEASE CONVEY FOREGOING INFORMATION TO BREWERS PROMPTLY .... (Sgd) ABBOT

> COMPTROLLER GENERAL[5]

Unquestionably the telegram was a public service masterpiece and it needed a public servant to understand it. Churches, temperance groups and welfare organisations received the news with enthusiasm. They had an ally in Sir Keith Murdoch, chairman and managing director of the Herald & Weekly Times Ltd, who wrote a series of articles under his own byline. He said the restrictions did not go far enough.

> A great deal of damage is being done throughout the country by the misuse of liquor, and it is not at all certain that the weakening of the war effort and morale may not be fatal. At the lowest estimate, it is lowering the good fibre of the nation, causing a sickening rate of casualties on the social front and breaking down the basis for a great nation in the future.[6]

This was not necessarily the answer. Soon it was difficult to buy a bottle of beer at the regular price, 1s 7d. Sly grog operators or hotel keepers who were prepared to sell out the back door were doing splendid business. The sly grog price was 3s or 4s a bottle.[7] The *Herald* published a story by an American news correspondent who staged a hunt for a bottle of Scotch. At the first two hotels he met with no success. One told him: 'Sorry Yank. You Americans have drunk it all up. We haven't got our next month's rations yet'. But with the aid of a taxi driver he went to the appropriate pubs and found he could buy Scotch at £2 a bottle and Australian for 30s. The correct price was 19s 3d and 10s 3d.[8] These were not record prices. The pubs believed that the thirsty American would pay anything. Prices like £9 for a bottle of Scotch and 10s for a bottle of Foster's were even mentioned. This cynical piece of verse titled 'U.S. General to His Love' did the rounds:

> Come live with me and be my bride
> And you'll have orchids five feet wide,
> Unrationed robes from Saks to swathe in
> And Chanel No. 5 to bathe in.
> With sheer stockings by the mile on
> You'll be my serpent of the Hylon.
> We'll take a flat in Darlinghurst
> Big enough for Randolph Hurst;
> At breakfast, as we sip our Bourbon,
> I'll tell you how I met Miss Durbin
>
> And when I'm back in USA
> I'll send a cable on Mother's Day.[9]

If the general public was rationed, brewers were expected to keep up full production to supply army messes and to send beer to troops in the field. While Sir Keith Murdoch was writing 'the plain fact is that we will pass under the bondage of the Japanese' because of the demon drink[10] the humble opinion in many points north was that just a simple bottle of Foster's would do more for morale than anything except a War Office message that you were to be shipped home on the next boat. At some camps the ration was two bottles a week; further north closer to the battle line, or maybe Borneo, one was lucky to receive two bottles a month, or even every six months. The most dearly loved creature was the teetotaller who was prepared to trade his bottles. Fred Archer, author of *The Treasure House*, history of Menzies Hotel, told on radio his experiences as an army cook in New Guinea. The troops desperate for something to drink asked him to make some of the fearsome jungle juice:

I said to them, I can't make jungle juice, all I can do is make beer. Well they said, WHAT, make beer! I said, yes, I could make beer. So I allowed them to talk me into making beer. Unbeknowns to them, a girl friend of mine had sent me two bottles of Foster's through the post in the ordinary manner in a box. It arrived, no worries . . .

Well, I hadn't drunk it because I couldn't cool it. And it was beautiful beer, Foster's Export, lovely beer — best beer in the world, perhaps. So I just hid it quietly.

When they asked me to make the beer, I pretended to all right. They rushed around, they all helped me in the kitchen, everything. So they got me a little barrel. I put in some blue boiler peas — it was a hard dried pea — put some

A Foster's label from the 1940s.

A label for McCracken's Extra Stout familiar during the 1940s and into the 1950s. The Khaki label reflected the nation's preoccupation with the experiences of the Second World War.

water on, and it makes froth and it smells like hops. And every time they'd be watching me. On the sly I'd put a few more things in to pretend. I told them on Christmas Day we're going to drink the beer.

I got six of the accredited drinkers and lined them up, and said, well I'll taste it first. Of course, I'd thrown out the rubbish I had pretended to make and put in the real beer. I tasted it, spat it out. No good, it'll poison you.

Of course, they'd smelt it, anything that smelt that good couldn't be poison. They all tasted it; and you should have seen their faces. They said, my God, it's marvellous — it's nearly as good as Foster's. Aw Gawd, they said, we could make a fortune out of this, a fortune, fifty quid a barrel from the Yanks.

They kept on asking me to make it again, but of course, I couldn't. It had all gone.[11]

Actually beer was not allowed into New Guinea until 1 August 1944. Each man was permitted to buy two bottles a week from army canteens. New Guinea had been a dry area and under the new arrangement they received the same ration as the men in Darwin.[12]

But was beer good for morale? The Melbourne North Methodist Synod did not think so. They held an indignation meeting in fury over remarks by Senator Keane. The unfortunate Senator, the Minister for Customs, had pointed out that beer was not a luxury to men after fighting in the steaming jungles of New Guinea, or working in the blazing heat of northern Australia. Nor was it harmful for men to have a few drinks after long hours of arduous labour in war industries. Consumption of liquor had been a part of British national life for centuries. It had even been said that Britain grew to powerful nationhood on roast beef and old ale. Lord Louis Mountbatten, Commander in Chief, East Asia, had authorised the construction of mobile breweries to keep beer supplies up to the troops, even at battle stations.[13] The Senator did add however that he believed beer was the most popular Australian commodity. He had received forty-five thousand complaints of alleged injustices in delivery and protests that supplies were inadequate. 'I have brushed aside all complaints, because I have not received one that indicated that a person had died because of the beer shortage'.[14]

The Baptist Union agreed with the Methodists that the abolition of liquor was the obvious way to beat Hitler. The government did not think so. Brewing was a reserved occupation. Neville Wigan, later head brewer at Carlton, volunteered for active service. He volunteered to go to a munitions factory as well. The board would not release him. His vital war work was in the brewery.

Wigan said all supplies were short. No longer could they get fine white sugar. 'We had to use brown sugar and we got some pretty treacly looking stuff. It didn't really hurt the beer, but it became sticky and it was a business getting it out of the bags.' At times barley was in desperately short supply with the result they went short of malt. At times they even had to make their malt out of wheat. They needed bottles to send beer to the troops, but bottles were as scarce as they were in the days when they were made by hand. They had to hound the marine dealers to bring in as many as possible. Coal was rationed. Brewing was an essential industry and they received their ration, but it was never enough. They used brown coal and when they couldn't get that they used wood. Neville Wigan said:

I'd be brewing and the tower pressure would go down. So I'd ring down to the boiler house, and make a great fuss. 'I can't boil the brew because the pressure's too awful.' They'd reply, 'Can't do any better, the wood won't burn'.

So one day I went down below and they had big logs sticking out of the furnace, logs with big leaves attached to them. Wood was hard to get too.

Regardless of the agonies and the labour shortage the output of beer in Victoria during the war years was still wonderfully impressive. The following figures are in millions of gallons:

1938–39	29
1940–41	34
1942–43	29
1943–44	29
1944–45	30

Carlton Viking Head Stout label, 1944.

Much to the chagrin of the keep-them-dry movement the government decided on December 1940 as the base period for the 30 per cent cutback for civilians. But 1940 was the year of the greatest beer production on record. There were huge orders for the canteens in the Middle East. Beer was on just a slightly lower priority than ammunition. So if you take 1938–39 as normal, they did not really drop at all. The greatest hardship was the bottle shortage. Most orders for the troops were in bottles and they took three-quarters of the entire output. So the longer the war lasted the more the civilian had to show devoted kindness to his hotelier or licensed grocer.[15]

Beer was something akin to diamonds. On 11 October 1943 this report appeared in Melbourne's *Sun News Pictorial*:

Precious Melbourne brews boosting the morale of the 13th platoon, D Company, 21st Machine Gun Battalion, Ikingi, Maryut, Egypt, 1941.

Police are searching for 1656 bottles of beer which disappeared on Friday on the way from the Carlton and United Brewery to a firm of carriers at Richmond.

A driver employed by a city firm of cartage contractors picked up the beer, which was packed in sixty-nine crates at the brewery, with horses and lorry. The beer failed to reach its destination at Richmond, and at 10.30 p.m. on Friday the lorry and horses were found abandoned in Powlett Street, East Melbourne.

No trace has been found of the driver, who did not return to his residence.

Many people just took to making beer themselves. In April 1944 Maurice Thomas Weeson of Barnard Grove, Kew, was on a charge of having contravened the Beer Excise Act. The police raided his garage. They found a great quantity of crown seals, four large barrels of fermenting beer ready to go, stacks of malt, hops, raisins and barley and twenty-eight dozen full bottles. It was potent stuff, according to a chemist, 10.5 per cent proof, compared with commercial beer which was ranged for 3 to 7 per cent proof. Weeson told the court he was just making beer for his friends. They had asked him to do it and they had even given him the ingredients. The deal was six dozen each. Mr Nicholas P.M. thought twenty-eight dozen on the premises was rather too much of a friendly order and fined him £70 with two guineas costs.[16]

In 1944 there was a Gallup Poll on the liquor shortage. Three out of five people thought it ought to be rationed like meat, sugar and chocolate. The government never got round to that one; it thought it had more important problems on its mind.[17] Petrol was rationed in 1940. Private cars were allowed enough petrol for 16 miles a week. Many citizens installed gas producers, which consisted of a large tank on the rear bumper. They were hideous devices which burned charcoal, blackened the face and hands, reduced power by 50 per cent, and if lucky gave a range of 100 miles. Then came the rationing of clothes, tea, sugar and meat. But if you wanted beer or cigarettes you stood in a queue and waited and waited. The Chief of the Traffic Branch, Inspector Tom Morris complained bitterly in 1944. He said the beer and tobacco queues were a bigger menace than the theatre queues.[18] Journalist Lois Lathlean wrote that the only hope of getting cigarettes was to go to that kiosk where she was well known, and buy a whole raft of things she did not want, a box of matches, a nail file, a tube of toothpaste, licorice all sorts, a bottle of cleaning fluid. Then the lady in the kiosk would say: 'Come back on Tuesday week and I may — mind I don't say I will — have a small packet'. Not everybody was patient, she reported. One man who was refused tobacco picked up a 'No Smokes' notice, tore it in pieces and hurled it across the pavement.[19]

Colonel Cohen, now brigadier, went to the Middle East and served as honourary Red Cross Commissioner. Sir Stephen Morell filled in as acting chairman. In the same year W. H. Clarke died after being general manager for twenty-three years. T. V. Millea who had been joint general manager took over the administration. Altogether 880 CUB employees served in the armed forces. Just as the company made up their pay in the First World War, so it did in the Second World War. Then when they returned, all were re-instated with a pay increase of 10s a week. It was a good deal being a brewery worker. The brewery also did its part in actual war work. The engineering workshop produced track driving sprockets for Bren gun carriers. For years one of these steel sprockets hung in the main bar at Carlton. The barman used it as a gong to declare 'Time Please'.

At 9 a.m. on 15 August Prime Minister Ben Chifley announced: 'Fellow citizens, the war is over'. He then declared a two-day holiday. The *Herald* reported:

> Melbourne is boiling over with joy. A quarter of a million people who heard the news just as they started work turned out into the streets as soon as the full truth of it dawned on them.
>
> It took the city a while to realise it was all over. A few who heard the wireless news came to office windows yelling 'Peace' and 'It's finished'.
>
> Here and there handfuls of paper scrap were thrown out. Then the whole city stirred. By 9.10 Collins Street was like a snowstorm with paper falling. 'There go all the boss's engagements for the rest of the year,' said a lass in the Manchester Unity building as she threw all the leaves from his bunch of dates out the window.
>
> Papers falling stuck to the windows of cars moving slowly in the drizzle. Sprinkler alarm bells began to ring and someone hurried up and down pealing an auction bell. By 10.25 Collins Street was packed with an amazing crowd. Someone was 'rolling out the barrel' with a vengeance at the Town Hall intersection, where a big oil drum was being kicked and rolled among the crowd. It broke up several crocodiles and sent hundreds scurrying out of the way.
>
> Revellers could be heard thundering Australia Will be There, Pack Up Your Troubles and Bless 'Em All a quarter of a mile away.[20]

A Carlton Ale label, 1946–47.

One city barmaid, as a patriotic gesture, dyed her hair red, white and blue, which was quite a thing to do in 1945.

The war was over, the troops came home, but it seemed an eternity before anything returned to normal. It took an unconscionable time to get rid of rationing. Sugar rationing ended in 1947, meat and clothing became free in 1948, butter and tea were liberated in 1950. Petrol rationing ended in June 1949 and was incredibly reintroduced in November. This little act, as much as the threat to nationalise the banks, killed the Chifley Labor Government. The new Menzies Government finally released petrol from bondage in February 1952, a grand political gesture.

But for the beer makers it was immensely frustrating. They had been left with the equipment of the 1930s, the population had boomed, and the war years had given Australians a new devotion for beer. But restrictions right through the 1940s were still on. There had to be permits for building, and the material simply was not available. Just before the end of the war CUB bought a series of hotels in the heart of the city, the Cathedral, Hosies, the Kerry Family and the Hotel London, but nothing could be done to renovate them. Then with the end of the war came a change in the hierarchy at CUB. Sir Stephen Morell had died in 1944 to be replaced on the board by his son Major Rodney T. Morell. Brigadier Cohen died in October 1946 and his eldest son Geoffrey became chairman. Amongst the brewery employees there was an extraordinary sense of lineage, son following father, brother joining with brother. And it was exactly the same with the board. The board in 1946 consisted of Geoffrey Cohen as chairman, Norman Carson as vice-chairman, Marshall Baillieu, Maurice Baillieu, Gordon Coulter, Frank Levy, Rodney Telford Morell, Edward

A 1940s label of a famous Richmond brew.

Another very well-known Richmond beer.

Walter Outhwaite and James Richardson. Edward Cohen, Geoffrey's younger brother, joined the board in 1947.

Wartime restrictions on beer ended on 27 December 1945. Selling of bottled beer after 5.30 p.m. on week days and after 2 p.m. on Saturdays had been banned. Liquor near dance halls had been forbidden. It was a law that liquor was not allowed in hotel rooms. Room service had been a sin, and yet another way of helping win the war had been by banning female drinking at racecourse bars. That too came to an end.[21] Now rationing of beer was up to the breweries. CUB had a more benevolent attitude than the government. It was lenient in cases of need. It always listened to appeals in cases of weddings, wakes, twenty-first birthdays and anniversaries. The brewery even sent a special consignment to a funeral directors' convention and received a warm message of thanks: 'When the time comes, if there's anything I can do for you, just let me know'.[22] It must have been nice to be on such good terms with the undertakers.

In 1948 CUB was rationing beer by the month. January was looked upon as a five-week month. February was a four-week month. Inevitably the terrible crises came towards the month's end when the beer ran out. Melbourne was utterly dry on the last days of February and hotel keepers turned on the breweries for their inability to keep the fountain flowing. One licensee said he just couldn't carry on in the face of public abuse. 'The brewery asks us to try to keep open from nine to six,' he said. 'I refuse point blank, because I will not encourage drunkenness and brawls, which invitably follow spirits drinking.' Geoffrey Cohen replied:

My brewery is now producing 30 per cent more beer than before the war. But beer consumption has increased so much it can't meet anything like the demand. Sugar is rationed but that doesn't matter. Malt is the killer at the moment. Also not enough hops are being grown. There aren't enough bottles. Because of a world shortage of soda ash no beer bottles have been made since December.

The chairman added sadly he couldn't even get casks, not enough timber.[23] There was a photograph in the newspapers of barrels of beer being loaded aboard a ship for interstate. This caused an outcry, the equivalent of wheat being exported from starving Ethiopia. The wharf labourers declared a ban on the export of all Carlton & United products and a black ban on the export of malt. The union said specifically the ban did not apply to Richmond beer because this was still being supplied in adequate quantities to hotels. The secretary of the Australian Railways Union, Mr J. J. Brown, announced further that neither would the railway men load any CUB beer for interstate. Actually it was a charming compliment to CUB, because Foster's Lager, Abbots and Melbourne Bitter was infinitely more popular than Richmond. The ban did not last. Geoffrey Cohen explained that if the company's entire export to Tasmania, Queensland and northern Australia came to an end tomorrow, licensees would get less than 4 gallons a week each.[24]

Profits were down in 1946 and down in 1947 by £54 478; the chairman complained the prices of all raw materials had skyrocketed. 'Yet,' said he, 'the return which the company receives for its only product — beer — has not changed since 1920, a position which I do not think obtains for any other industry.'[25] Of course, that story did not apply to excise. It rose very healthily so that the beer drinker would know that every time he lifted his glass he was helping to pay for the war against Hitler. The rise which actually helped the brewers came in 1949. Almost weeping into his beer over the rise of halfpenny a glass, a *Herald* reporter wrote:

> Remember when you could get a pot for sixpence and a glass for fivepence — anywhere, in the public or saloon bar. They were the ruling prices in 1940. You want to remember those figures, you addicts, your glass of beer has gone up 30 per cent in nine years — 50 per cent in saloon bars.

Beer was now 9d a pot and 6½d for a seven-ounce glass.[26] The poor fellow did not know the half. There was much worse to come.

CHAPTER TEN

The New Man: R. F. G. Fogarty

In 1949 Reginald Francis Graham Fogarty became general manager of CUB. He succeeded T. V. Millea who retired to take an interest in the Town Hall Hotel in Swanston Street. Fogarty's rise was extraordinary. He was general manager of a little brewery, Cairns, in north Queensland which was doing well. In the far north Fogarty had proved himself a good administrator, and a tough campaigner. In 1949 Fogarty was exactly the man Carlton & United needed. On one side it was being choked by government restrictions, bound by antique drinking laws which belonged more to a Baptist town in Georgia than modern living, and on the other hand it was under constant assault from an impatient thirsty public that could not get enough beer. Fogarty was on a world tour when the chairman, Geoffrey Cohen, offered him the job. Sir Edward Cohen remembers:

> Absolutely nothing had been done to the brewery since 1939. The board decided he was the man to bring it into the twentieth century. When first he came down there was a press conference at the Hotel Australia; 150 people were there, including me. You would wonder where he was. There would be twenty people standing close around Fogarty. They would be listening, absolutely rapt. It was a tremendous performance he put on.

Fogarty spent a few months surveying the scene, then proceeded to make massive changes. The small bottling plant at Carlton closed and it switched entirely to bulk beer. Abbotsford and Victoria handled all the packaged beer. Stainless steel replaced wood and copper, clean ceramic tiles moved in in place of painted wood. The bottles now came in wire baskets instead of the old boxes, with every bottle in its charming cocoon of straw. Fogarty quickly earned the title of the 'Beer Baron', 'the Earl of Abbotsford', and CUB employees were 'Fogarty's Fusiliers'. He wanted to make the best beer in the world and he would not have any compromises. Furthermore he demanded that it be served correctly. Publicans who failed to meet his high standards, or would not sell the beer at his price were likely to get supplies withdrawn.

Keith Stackpole, ex state cricketer, ex Collingwood footballer, and father of Keith Stackpole the Test cricketer, recalls that one time Fogarty called at the company bar in Abbotsford. He noticed that Keith was using a Pluto tap. He was furious. A Pluto tap is a gun on a long tube which spouts beer instead of bullets, a device of great convenience during a peak rush. But if they are not in constant use the beer lies languid in the tube and goes stale. He told Keith Stackpole he would not have them in the hotels and he was horrified to see them in the company's own bar. There were threats of dismissal if it happened again. Reginald Fogarty was not a man for compromise. Mr Scully, Labor member for Richmond, made a savage attack on him in the Legislative Assembly. He described Fogarty as the arrogant booze baron. He said a notice had gone out from the brewery in his name instructing hotels in the exact manner that they were to serve his beer. The notice carried the warning that if the instruction was not carried out, beer supplies to the hotel would be withheld or restricted.[1]

Fogarty engendered an extraordinary awe and respect amongst CUB staff. He was known generally as 'Foge' or even 'Old Foge', but few would dare to call him anything but Mr Fogarty to his face. Perhaps a select number called him Reg but they were rare indeed. He would listen to the opinions of his experts and he detested yes men. He would put up with errors from staff, but not indecision. Dr Carl Resch said:

> He taught me something and I have never forgotten it. There was a problem in the brewery and Fogarty wanted to know what I planned to do. I said, 'I'd like some time to make a decision on that.'
>
> He replied, 'Resch, even if you make the wrong bloody decision, it is better to make a decision *now*.'

R. F. G. Fogarty in the seat of power.

For the staff, almost all dealings with Mr Fogarty were unusual. Brian Corrigan, who became assistant general manager for properties, was the assistant paymaster in 1956. It was almost the eve of the Melbourne Olympic Games when Fogarty called him to his office and said 'Corrigan, do you know anything about hotels?'

'No,' Corrigan replied.

'That's good, I want you to go down and manage Hosies.'

Hosies was the CUB prestige hotel in Elizabeth Street. It was the first of the hotels to be restored completely to modern postwar standards. It had been open only seven days. The company also restored the Town Hall Hotel and the smooth, new Graham Hotel. The name Graham came from Reginald Francis Graham Fogarty, Graham being the name of R. F. G. Fogarty's mother. Fogarty explained carefully that this was Corrigan's opportunity. He was going to make him understudy to Harry St Leger Byford, the property manager. Byford had been a major in the army and he was due to retire in 1960. Corrigan said:

> I was petrified. I had never been in the pub. I got there bright and early, 7.30 on the Saturday morning. Of course, Foge was already there with the housekeeper. He had instructed the architect, selected all the equipment, plant, furnishings. He did the lot himself. He didn't brook interference with anybody.
>
> We were there together until about 11. He shook my hand, said good luck and added 'Now read this'. He put in my hand a little book, *Message to Garcia*. So I put it in my pocket and got down to work. Every Sunday morning he would ring me at home.
>
> 'Well, son, how did you get on?'
>
> I'd say, we served this many meals, did so many eighteens.
>
> 'Oh great, did you read the book I gave you?'
>
> 'I haven't had time, Sir.'
>
> 'What, haven't had time. About ten bloody pages in it. Read the thing, boy, read it.'

So Brian Corrigan read the little book. *Message to Garcia* came from the Spanish Civil War. Garcia was a runner and he was sent by generals to deliver their instructions. They had no other means of communication. So Garcia would go through hell, fire and brimstone.

> That's what he wanted me to do in the pub, work your guts out, boy. At the end of thirteen weeks, believe it or not, I hadn't had one day off. I was living at Beaumaris. Taxi fares were too great, so they gave me a car. I used to leave at 7 a.m. and I would get home at 1 a.m. the next day. It nearly ruined my life, family, everything. I was buggered so I rang Foge one morning and told his girl I wanted to see him. He came on the line.
>
> 'What do you want?'
>
> 'I'd just like to see you for about fifteen minutes, Sir.'
>
> 'All right, *fifteen* minutes, come in.'
>
> I got there and he said, 'What's the trouble, boy?'
>
> 'I've got a haversack on my back. I've been there for thirteen weeks and I've had only one day off, that's all.'
>
> 'You had a day off? Huh! You can't come back today. All right, you've had a rough spin. You can come back in January and move into the property department.'

Corrigan had another four weeks at Hosies and another four years before he got the job as property manager. It was something to look forward to, because when that happened, at last he would get a company car.

I had been in the job a few weeks. Byford had retired. I was sitting up feeling pretty good. The buzzer went. Mr Fogarty was on the intercom. 'Come down.'

'Yes, Sir.'

He was sitting back in his chair, 'By the way, what happened to that car of Byford's?'

'I've got it, Sir.'

'Where are the keys?'

'In my pocket Sir.'

'Give them to me.'

'Does that mean I don't get the car, Sir?'

'Listen, my boy, the car goes with your increment. Your job. I give the cars out. Not Byford.'

So Fogarty handed back the keys. 'That was another lesson I learned,' said Brian Corrigan. 'He was the boss,' but he was a fantastic man.

There was a strike which went from 13 November to 2 December 1952, which decimated Christmas supplies that year. The company put an advertisement in the newspapers:

> Carlton and United Breweries regret to have to inform their customers, the public, that a strike by *one* of the thirteen Brewery Unions has stopped production, delivery and sale of beer.
>
> The particular issue is the dismissal — in terms of the consent award — of five employees found wilfully absenting themselves from a duty for which they were paid special rates . . . The men were also found drinking unauthorised beer, at an unauthorised time, in an unauthorised place.[2]

The strike was by the Federated Engine Drivers and Firemen's Association and the dismissed men were finally reinstated. R. F. G. Fogarty was much more vocal then than he was to be later. He was proud of the conditions under which his men worked and said so. He told the *Herald* that all tradesmen were paid in excess of the award; that there were penalty rates for shiftwork, overtime and public holidays; that there were three weeks' annual leave on full pay, *plus* two weeks' extra pay, then a week's bonus at Christmas. Keith Stackpole said this revelation in the public press caused a few domestic problems. Not all employees had told their wives about the holiday and Christmas bonuses. Fogarty also revealed the company bar system. There was a free bar at all three breweries, at Carlton, Abbotsford and Victoria, which operated around the clock, twenty-four hours. The men were allowed a free beer, a 10-ounce pot, at morning tea time, lunch time, afternoon tea and knock off. The company still had to pay excise on all this beer given away and it cost £40 000 a year. 'Would Government-controlled breweries give employees similar conditions?' asked Fogarty. 'Does any Government department treat its employees as well?'[3]

In 1951 he launched his own strike. He announced his company would not produce or deliver any more bottled beer until the industry was granted a price increase. The Price Decontrol authorities, he said, had refused the increase. 'At today's prices,' he added, 'we are producing bottles at a loss. There is no authority in the land that can make us produce at a loss.'[4] Mr Fogarty refused all day to see reporters. He just issued a statement: 'Certain assurances have been received from the Prices Decontrol Commission, the production of bottled beer is being resumed. I am not at liberty to amplify this statement.' The Prices Commissioner, Mr Waldon, then put out his

Melbourne Bitter labelled for the forces in Korea, 1951–53.

Used wooden barrels returned for cleaning and refilling.

statement. 'We will not be stamped or pressurised. I have given no assurances to Mr Fogarty.'[5] Mr Fogarty had to wait nearly six weeks for his price increase. Beer went up twopence a bottle on 10 July. [6]

At this time Fogarty was always campaigning and appearing in the newspapers. He demanded to know why Victorians had to put up with ridiculous laws like six o'clock closing. 'Who or what is responsible for our being forced to drink like barbarians?' he said. 'What action is necessary to restore civilised habits to drinking.' He pointed out that the population had increased by 20 per cent since 1939, and beer production had gone up by 170 per cent, but still there were absurd restrictions; building controls did not allow permits for maintenance and repair work.[7]

This was the time that saw the beginning of the end of the wooden barrel. In 1948 CUB had sixty thousand wooden kegs from firkins through kilderkins to hogsheads. Old Emil Resch used to say: 'Give me malt, hops and a good cooper, then I can make beer.' The Coopers' Union was the ultimate power; like the tanker drivers in the oil industry, if they decided to strike, management trembled. It was power of the coopers which helped speed the end of the wooden barrel. Manhandling the old kegs was a work of art. The fillers who wore copper-toed clogs could direct their passage with a beautifully timed kick. Harry Barker, whose father was a brewer before him, began as a cooper in 1928, and he worked at the Abbotsford Brewery.

Early in our apprenticeship they would get us making wooden buckets, because they used them in the tower for malt and grains. Every apprentice was apprenticed to a journeyman. Some were tough. I was apprenticed to old Alf Johnson, he was my boss, one slip up and he'd roar the tripes out of you.

You had to make one barrel or if you were on repairs doing broken casks, two a day. You put a block mark on the end of the barrel. Mine was Z. You'd get a reputation if you sent out a lot of leaks and get blasted for that.

Carlton executives: Gus Cole, George Grant, Harry Pensom, George Gardiner with an unidentified gentleman on left.

Harry said a good barrel would last at least twenty years. By then it wouldn't have many original staves, but it was a remarkable article.

CUB did some experimenting with steel barrels in 1938–39, but the cost of stainless steel was prohibitive. Harold Cole, a member of another of the famous brewery dynasties, worked on stainless steel barrels in the drawing office. His father was Robert K. Cole, brewer and historian, and forty-eight years at the brewery. His uncle was Gus Cole, head brewer at Victoria for fifty years. His cousin Stuart, also a brewer, had fifty years. Harold Cole said T. G. Ferrero, the chief engineer, and F. W. J. Clendinnen, the laborateur, went to the United States and came back with stainless steel barrels made by Firestone. They were 12-gallon and 15-gallon containers which had to be converted to Australian eighteens. They made a wooden mock up; it was a very delicate complex operation to design it so it would hold exactly the right 18 gallons of beer. This was the beginning of the end for the wooden barrel. Dr Carl Resch remembers:

> You can't imagine the fuss, when those steel barrels went out. People were screaming, 'You can taste the metal. Give us back our beautiful beer off the wood'. Of course, it didn't taste of metal and beer never was at any time in its history in contact with wood. The barrels have always had a pitch or resin type of lining. But the publicans would say, 'They'll never drink this stuff off steel'.
>
> But you wouldn't believe the change. Rheem made our steel casks, but we couldn't get enough. The following Christmas we ran out of steel casks and we had to put some woods back on. The publicans started complaining there was never enough beer in the barrels. You see wooden casks vary in size quite considerably. That's a big deal when you are trying to get your last two or three pence out of them.

By 1956 there had been an almost complete rebirth of operations both at Carlton and Abbotsford, an extraordinary metamorphosis which lifted

The Crown Lager label of the early 1950s celebrated the Coronation.

The royal visit of Queen Elizabeth II and Prince Philip in 1954 was commemorated by the Ballarat Brewery.

brewing from the old muscle-heave, gravity operation of the 1930s into a new era of the forklift, the palette, bulk handling, liquid sugar instead of solid, and processes of automation undreamed of twenty years before.

There was a famous and age-old island platform at Carlton, so vast it was known as the Queen Mary. Horse-drawn waggons would enter the brewery at Swanston Street, deposit their empty casks, clip clop their way to the bottling room, load bottles, or maybe go down the other side of the Queen Mary, take on casks of draught beer, then move their way out into Bouverie Street. There was a character who sat in a tiny office at the Swanston Street side of the Queen Mary. In the early days it was Jim Smith, one of the founding fathers of the Liquor Trades Union. By a nod or a gesture he directed traffic to one side or the other of the ship. The drivers would have to stop at the Bouverie Street end to pick up excise duty stamps, have their loads checked and the stamps pasted on to the barrels. Eric Nilan tells the story that on one occasion a driver left his delivery dockets and duty stamps on the edge of the Queen while he filled his pipe. His horse licked a kilderkin stamp from the top of the pile. The driver applied for another stamp. A delivery clerk noticed what had happened but did not realise the gravity of the event, so he said nothing. The Excise department spent four hours overtime trying to balance the number of stamps against the number of barrels until finally they were told what had happened. It was not easy trying to convince the Commonwealth excise officer the truth of the simple entry: 'One excise stamp eaten by horse.'[8]

The old Queen Mary had to go and a whole new string of loading docks took its place. In five years CUB spent $3 million at Carlton. The entire plant was re-built, re-modelled and re-equipped. On the site of the old Carlton bottling room the engineers built a seven storey maturing cellar. Cellar was a charming old-fashioned term for something that was anything but that. Instead of the old style copper and wood there were ten tanks each of two hundred hogshead capacity. They were 7 metres high, 4 metres wide and 6 metres deep. There were new filter rooms, a new refrigeration system and a new bright beer room for the storage of filtered beer. The average output for Carlton in 1946 was two thousand hogsheads a week. Now it was ten thousand, peaking in the summer at thirteen thousand.[9] Back in the 1920s and 1930s, there was a vast difference in the Australian thirst between summer and winter. Come January–February the Melbourne passion for beer could go up 30 or 40 per cent. Now there was little difference. If the Second World War did little else, it taught us to enthuse over beer all the year round.

At Abbotsford the company built an entire new bottling plant. There was a new building, completed in 1956, which was given the august title of 'Bottling Hall'. The bottles were shifted in, soaked, washed, sprayed, cleaned, filled, pasteurised, labelled, all at the rate of a thousand dozen an hour.[10]

In the old days a general manager was rarely seen at the plant. He was not meant to know too much about brewing. R. F. G. Fogarty was always on the move, watching, supervising. He used to urge on his brewers with useful phrases: 'Brewers are just bloody cooks' or 'Brewing! Bloody witchcraft? Any damn fool can do it.' Another famous Fogarty line came out when he had declined to nominate one of his senior brewers for a top administrative job: 'I have technical men on tap, not on top.' This was a shock for some of the brewers. Always they had been regarded as the 'gods' of the industry. He was good at needling his brewers, but then his enthusiasm for the technical side went beyond that of any general manager in the history of the company. In 1958 he installed a research laboratory, which was the best equipped for its time for any Australian brewery. It covered 3500 square feet, the forerunner of the great research centre which was to be opened in 1971. He also established a post graduate fellowship at Melbourne University in honour of F. W. J. Clendinnen of £1600 a year. It was open to graduates who were qualified to study for their PhD degrees for research in the field of natural product chemistry.

Fogarty went to England and in 1952 brought back F. A. Reddish, a top international malting expert. Traditionally malting had been a separate, science, trade, activity, conducted by old and distinguished firms around Melbourne. Fred Reddish described malt as grain which had undergone a process of germination. The classic method for production was to spread it on open floors and laboriously turn it over with wooden shovels in a warm humid atmosphere. Reddish used the beautiful old Yorkshire brew tower in Wellington Street, Collingwood. Since the birth of the combine, Yorkshire had been the empire for the coopers, the home where the barrel was made, repaired and stored. James Wood, architect, son of John Wood, the brewer, built it in 1876. It was supposed to be the marvel of its day; the whole process of brewing was on the gravitation system with the water supplied from the fine new reservoir at Yan Yean.[11] Now the tower was the malt house. The raw barley was taken to the top of the tower, dropped through shutes and conveyors, cleaned, then put in great drums, and slowly rotated at precisely the correct temperature and humidity. According to Reddish, Yorkshire was handling 400 million barley corns every day.[12]

In 1956 CUB decided to build its own brewery in Darwin. This was the end of a long liaison with the Swan Brewery in Perth. One of the founders of Swan was the father of CUB's Montague Cohen. Montague Cohen was chairman of Swan and a director of CUB. Harold Cohen was chairman of the two breweries at the same time, as was Geoffrey Cohen. In 1951 Geoffrey Cohen returned from overseas and for domestic reasons decided his future was in the west. He resigned as chairman and went to Perth to be chairman and executive of the Swan Brewery. Sir Norman Carson, chairman of the Australian Wool Realisation Commission, and former Melbourne manager of the Australian Mercantile Land & Finance Co. Ltd, became chairman of CUB. Sir Edward Cohen, who was a director both of CUB and Swan recalls that his cousin Paul Cullen, a director of Tooth's in Sydney, was keen to start a brewery in Darwin. Neither of the Sydney breweries was interested. He came to Melbourne and put the idea to R. F. G. Fogarty. He had no interest either. Cullen went to Perth and put the idea to Geoffrey Cohen, who said yes. The next move was to get his brother, Edward, also a director of Swan, plus another Swan director, Roy McBride, to go to Darwin to survey the scene. Sir Edward said:

Don't forget Carlton had already turned it down, so there was no bar on me going up there. Ultimately Swan decided they would build the brewery. Paul Cullen by this time had disappeared from the scene too. As soon as Fogarty heard what happened, he decided to move to Darwin as fast as he was able.

Edward Cohen now had a severe conflict of interest. No longer could he serve two breweries. He made his choice, resigned as a director of Swan, and the two breweries virtually declared their trade war. It was a question of territory. Prior to the Second World War almost all the beer sold in Darwin came from Carlton. After the outbreak of war, beer was rationed and areas allocated. The government considered it was easier to supply beer to Darwin from Perth rather than Melbourne, so Swan had all the market. They kept most of it, even after the war ended.

If R. F. G. Fogarty was the beer czar, every year saw him more securely in command of his empire. In 1956 he was appointed a member of the board. It was the first time in the history of the company that an actual employee had become a board member. The comment was 'Mr Fogarty's extensive knowledge of brewery management will undoubtedly prove an asset'.[13] An outsider would wonder why it took the company so long to do this, but all the board members had been appointed as representatives of the original companies — Carlton, Foster's, McCracken's, Victoria, Shamrock and Castlemaine — which, incredibly, were still in existence as paper companies with their own shares and profits, holding their own board meetings.

In late 1956 Fogarty called in Bert Williams, later deputy chief engineer, and told him he had to get to Darwin and, even though Swan had a good start, beat them in the launching of the brewery. Bert Williams' father Jack was with the brewery. So were his two uncles, Bill and Jim. His brother Ted, was a brewer. Bert started at Carlton in 1920 and Ted arrived in 1923. The Williams family between them had more than two hundred years' service. Bert Williams decided speed was everything. He went round all the three plants scrounging redundant equipment. The breweries were just going through their grand reformation, so there was plenty to be had. Even so some of the managers were fearful when they saw him coming, wondering what he was going to steal next. The mash tun and kettle hop back was made by Robinson Brothers in South Melbourne. Bill McLaughlin, the architect, designed a brewery building capable of withstanding a cyclone with winds up to 220 mph, an admirable piece of foresight as the brewery survived Cyclone Tracy in December 1974.

There was no time to send equipment by ship. At the end of June 1957 Bert Williams and his team set out with a Bedford 10-ton truck and a Holden station waggon. There was Keith McDonald from Cairns who was to be the first manager, brewer Maurie Redwood, also from Queensland, and Tom Passmore, engineer. They went by train from Adelaide to Alice Springs, then by road straight to Darwin. They built their brewery. They used three army surplus huts joined together for office and living quarters, and the first brew, fifty hogsheads, went through on 13 October. The Darwin administrator, J. C. Archer, with great ceremony, turned on the flow to rack the precious golden stuff into casks. Carlton Draught it was called, and at least 75 per cent of the population of Darwin was there.

Bert Williams said it was quite a party. The hams, turkeys and other food ironically came up from Perth. Swan did not get their brewery into operation until 1958, a year later. One of the reasons they took so long was the complexity of their operation. They put in a bottling plant, while Carlton went only for draught. All the CUB bottled beer continued to come by ship from Melbourne. Don Watt, an early manager at Darwin, was worried by this. Swan could sell its locally bottled before for 4s 6d a bottle, while the imported Foster's was 5s 2d. Fogarty told him: 'It won't make any bloody difference, Watt.' Don Watt was also concerned about the long voyage the beer had to undertake. By strict brewing standards the locally made Swan was likely to be better than the Carlton product because it was fresher. The local customers, however, were used to the aged Carlton beer; they had developed a taste for it, and they never really took to Swan. Don Watt commented: 'Reg Fogarty was wiser than all his critics. He knew the customers would stay with the beer they were used to.'

CUB Darwin produced only draught beer, but very soon after the opening of the little brewery they had an inspired idea: why not sell the beer in bottles, large bottles. It was expensive getting bottles to Darwin, very expensive putting them in small containers, and expensive recovering them. They chose 80 fluid ounces — 2.25 litres — three times the size of the normal beer bottles. Unquestionably it was the biggest beer bottle in the world, and as Darwin had the reputation of owning the world's greatest thirst, it was appropriate. The *Guinness Book of Records* named West Germany as the world's top beer drinking country, consuming 145.4 litres a head a year, but in the Northern Territory they estimated consumption at 236 litres a head.[14] The big bottles were so popular it was difficult to get them back for refilling, even with a deposit. Every visitor to Darwin wanted to take them away as souvenirs. The US Air Force, for example, was crazy for them. There was a tale about a visiting pilot who was so enchanted with the big bottles that he filled his B29 and took a load of them back home to the USA. Later, when the little stubbies came on the market down south, the Darwin bottles earned the charming title 'Darwin Stubbies' and who would dream of calling them anything else? They are now sold down south at a premium price of over $10.

Lou Mangan, former managing director of CUB, said:

> There's a stockbroker friend of mine in New York. He lives on Long Island, next door to Paul Lohmeyer, who put Foster's on the market in the US. This stockbroker friend loves the Darwin beer so much, every time Lohmeyer comes to Australia he has to take a carton of Darwin stubbies home for him.

Doug Farrell, plant engineer at Darwin, has memories of drinking habits in the old days at Darwin, back in the 1960s:

> The great thing used to be the Saturday night party. Almost every street seemed to have a keg on. We would have about twenty kegs going out. We had a roster system, somebody had to stay on between four and six on Saturday to look after the party trade. We would supply all the dispensing equipment, everything. We had cut down 44-gallon drums, we put the kegs in those and filled them with ice. Then we had handles welded on to the drums, so that they could heave it all off the back of their ute. Oh, yes, it was automatic that you'd get invited and if you did the party went all night.
>
> I remember one time a chap came along dressed in all his finery. He had a tie on which was fancy for Darwin. He wanted two kegs, 18 gallons each. It was normal procedure while attending to customers to give them a beer. Well, this fellow and two others came at four and they were still there at six. The telephone rang, I picked it up, 'Is one of you fellows Mr So and So?' He said,

The famous Darwin stubby.

'Yes, it's me.' He went to the phone and came back and said 'I'll have to go, they're waiting on the beer. It's for a wedding.'

I said, 'Who's getting married?'

He said, 'Me'. Heaven knows what his wife was doing.

Oh yes, we used to have regulars, they would come in every week for their eighteen. One Saturday a particular couple came in and they only wanted a niner. So I said, 'Why only nine this week?' They replied, 'Some of the blokes are away. There are only four of us this weekend.'

By the 1970s Darwin was getting too big. It became too big a task getting the kegs back to the brewery, washing them out and preparing them for the following Saturday so the brewery handed over the service to the hotel trade.

When CUB built its Darwin brewery the local population was only eleven thousand. Even with the splendid northern thirst there was no room for two breweries. Lou Mangan said he went there in January 1959 and stayed a month.

The first Carlton beer cans.

In those days Swan owned all the hotels. They had 85 per cent of the market and we had the rest. At one time we were selling only fifty eighteens a week. But we kept on improving and in the end we had 90 per cent.

In 1973 Lloyd Zampatti telephoned me. He was chief executive at Swan then: 'Look would you give approval for your beer to go into our hotels.' In other words he wanted to free his hotels from having to stock Swan beer exclusively. I said, 'Well I'll think about it' and having thought about it, I said, 'Well, look, I think the best thing to do would be to merge the two companies. Put the breweries, our assets, hotels everything in together. Form another company', which we did. We formed Northern Territory Breweries Pty Ltd, which was jointly owned by Carlton and Swan with CUB holding one extra share giving it the controlling interest.

In 1981 CUB bought out Swan and is now in sole command in Darwin.

If Darwin stubbies were one interesting container, much more dramatic was the move into cans in 1958. Cans for beer were not new. They first appeared in USA in 1936. Some were straight-out cans which had to be opened with a can opener. Others were almost an imitation of a bottle with a crown seal on top. The *Australian Brewing and Wine Journal* commented that clientele was likely to be large in the USA. The American temperament always demanded something new. In the British Isles they were rather more conservative, and there the move could take longer. There were dark thoughts too about cloudiness in the beer, and unfortunate odour.[15] Dr Carl Resch went to the USA in 1957 to investigate can operations and CUB was the first to introduce canned beer to Australia. Acceptance was immediate; over two million cans were sold in the first month.[16] The *Sun News Pictorial* commented:

They look very neat and tidy, half the size of a normal bottle. Roughly they work out at 30 per cent more expensive than bottled beer, but they have some clear advantages: they are perfectly useless as a weapon. They will never cut your feet. They fit easily into a handbag. Then finally if you buy a dozen they give you a free can opener.[17]

The *Sun* also suggested darkly that they were much easier to smuggle into the office. They were precisely the same size as a can of tomato juice. Some citizens who liked a beer with their lunch at the office desk, simply took the paper label off their can of tomato juice and fitted it to their can of Foster's. Cans cooled quicker. They were easy to store in the refrigerator. They were easier to ship interstate and internationally. They were considered more humanitarian when thrown at football umpires. Soon the other large Australian beer companies followed Carlton's lead.

In September 1958 CUB acquired the Ballarat Brewing Company, which owned two breweries, one in Ballarat and the Volum Brewery in Geelong which it had acquired four years earlier. CUB bought the brewing operations but not the 102 hotels which remained with the Ballarat Brewing Company. For many years CUB maintained the Volum Brewery for storage and racking operations using beer tankered from Carlton. In 1986 CUB closed down the Volum brewing operations and turned it into a distribution centre, but they continued to brew beer in bulk in Ballarat and in 1987 began making Guinness under licence. Meanwhile packaged Ballarat Bitter was sent up from Melbourne. Ballarat's ancestry went right back to the days of the gold rush. There was Magill & Coghlans of Warrenheip, founded in 1857 and the Royal Standard Brewery in Armstrong Street, Ballarat.[18] The two breweries combined in 1895 to form the Ballarat Brewing Company.

In Ballarat everybody loves Ballarat Bertie, a product of a smart piece of marketing in 1927. Ballarat Bertie was a silver-haired little character in an apron. In advertisements and posters he was always enthusiastically quaffing a mug of foaming beer. He appeared on the label of every bottle of Ballarat Bitter. When CUB shifted Ballarat bottling operations to the city, it seemed convenient to drop Ballarat Bertie from the label. There was a cry of outrage from Ballarat of such proportions that Bertie had to be returned to the label once again. Lou Mangan said loyalty to the product never quite matched the enthusiasm of the love for Ballarat Bertie. Many a Ballarat citizen was just as happy to drink Foster's Lager or Abbots.

R. F. G. Fogarty continued to be hungry for expansion and the next target was Fiji. CUB frequently had dealings with W. R. Carpenter, one of the oldest shipping and trading companies in the islands. Lou Mangan said:

> In 1957 we heard a whisper that Carpenters were going to put a brewery into Fiji, they were doing it without anyone knowing too much about it. The rumor was correct. They went ahead, acquired brewing plant, but they ran into difficulties. They didn't have the necessary know how. I remember one Saturday morning I was called in by Mr Fogarty. Carpenters' chief executive, Tui Johnson, was there. Tui is the term for King in Fiji.
>
> We sat down, talked about Carlton being involved and that's what happened. We became involved with Carpenters, each owning 50 per cent.

The association continued with Carpenters until 1984 when Carlton took over their share. In 1985 CUB owned 62 per cent of the shares, and the Fiji Development Bank and the public owned 38 per cent. The beer, Fiji Bitter, became famous. It was modelled first on Carlton Draught then Melbourne Bitter. The slogan was 'The Sportsman's Beer'. The half bottles won the name 'Fiji Babies'.

On 13 July 1960, Henry Bolte, later Sir Henry, Premier of Victoria, opened a new block brew house at Carlton, and the brewery moved into

Directors of the Ballarat Brewery, c. 1895. Back row (left to right): Arthur Coghlan, Alex McVitty. Front row: Charles Tulloch, James Coghlan.

Ballarat Bertie in the 1930s: the little man Melbourne couldn't kill.

Ballarat Stout label after the take-over. Those with good eyesight could read Carlton & United Breweries in the small print.

the complete, scientific, automated era. There was a new feature on the skyline, a great rectangular building with vertical louvres which allowed in the light and gave relief from the afternoon sun. The more romantic of the brewers saw beauty in this structure, the geometry, the vertical lines and columns were reminiscent of the Parthenon in Athens. The brewery had created its own Acropolis. Everything was spotless and pure, as if they were refining Chanel No. 5, rather than beer. The first and second floors were all in plain grey laminex, the mash tuns and drainers had moulded fibre glass covers in the correct colour to match and there were tiles on the floor. The beer was still brewed in the classic style, each brew an episode on its own, but the whole process was accelerated; as material evacuated one vessel, more took its place so that the whole of the brewing approached a continuous twenty-four hour evolution, automatically controlled. There was a control room with panels which were reminiscent of the headquarters at the State Electricity Commission. The operation at any time could be switched from manual to automatic.[19]

On the opening day every consultant, every engineer, every man who put in those instruments was on tap like the beer, to make sure that when Henry Bolte pushed that button, the whole marvellous thing worked. It did. There was much agony and many sleepless nights for several years, however, before the block brew house settled down to a comfortable adolescence. The publicity at the time described it as being as modern as anything else in the world.

R. F. G. Fogarty had completed a metamorphosis, the flying insect at last had graduated from the caterpillar. There was only one thing that remained the same from the wartime operation, the beer. Foster's was still Foster's, Abbots was still Abbots, and you could still get your Melbourne Bitter.

Carlton executives in the 1950s (left to right): Brian Breheny, Alf Ran, Carl Resch, R. F. G. Fogarty, George Gardiner.

CHAPTER ELEVEN

The End of Six O'clock

It was hard to keep pace with the expansion in the 1960s. In 1961 CUB acquired the wine and spirit business of Max Cohn Pty Ltd, the Queensland Brewery Ltd in Brisbane, and Thos McLaughlin & Co. Pty Ltd, brewers and hotel owners in Rockhampton. Then in 1962 it took over the Richmond Brewery making Carlton the undisputed king of brewing in Victoria. Of course, CUB had taken over the Cohn Bros Victoria Brewery in Bendigo back in 1925, plus a large number of their hotels. Buying the Melbourne wine and spirit business for cash made a very tidy arrangement. CUB needed to stick to beer no longer. It could give its clients a total service, beer, wine, whisky, gin, vodka, liqueurs, cordials, anything they wished.

Almost at the same time Queensland Brewery Ltd at Bulimba was putting out feelers. The size of their trade was slipping so the makers of Bulimba Gold Top were open to offers. This was the lesser of the two breweries in Brisbane. It would have been interesting had CUB acquired Bulimba's great rival Castlemaine Perkins Ltd as Castlemaine was really a country cousin to CUB; Edward Fitzgerald had first opened the Castlemaine brewery in Castlemaine Victoria in 1857 and had then later launched out with new businesses in Melbourne, Sydney and Brisbane.

Melbourne Bitter, made in Queensland.

Lou Mangan was personal assistant to R. F. G. Fogarty at this time. He recalls there was a chance that they could acquire Castlemaine Perkins, but their bid was never sufficiently attractive. They offered Z shares and Castlemaine 'wouldn't have a bar' of them. (Back in 1951 CUB had issued three million 'Z' shares at £1 each to help finance the great postwar expansion. They had no voting rights, because the original companies, Carlton, Foster, Shamrock and the rest, wanted to keep all the power to themselves.) The CUB offer to Queensland Brewery Ltd was worth £7.8 million with one Z share for four of Queensland Brewery's 5s ordinary shares. Castlemaine Perkins Ltd countered with an offer of a 10s ordinary stock unit for every two Queensland shares, worth £7.1 million.[1] There was much talk about the Z shares. The Castlemaine board said the Z shares were not officially listed, they did not carry voting rights on the stock exchange, and they would not be worth more than a pound in a wind up. CUB fought back. The Z shares were traded just like ordinary shares, they received the same dividends, the same bonuses. And the profit was stunning, £1.9 million in 1960, 19 per cent on paid capital with a guaranteed

The old Richmond Tiger Beer before it perished in 1962.

Richmond label of the 1950s.

dividend of 12 per cent.[2] Actually it turned out to be 13 per cent. CUB won the contest and bought the Queensland Brewery.

Six days later CUB bought the old brewery of Thomas McLaughlin and Co. in Rockhampton for an undisclosed number of Z shares. The brewery dated from 1881 when Thomas McLaughlin and William Higson bought all their machinery, plant and stock at auction for £450. It was known everywhere as 'Macs Beer'. Eight years later CUB opened a new $2 million brewery; by then it was one of Queensland's biggest manufacturing industries.

By 1962 the Richmond brewery was deeply ailing and but for its tied hotels it would have sold almost no beer. There were utterly faithful devotees of the Tiger brand, which had its own distinctive well-hopped bitter taste, who would drink nothing else. Yet in the war years those who served in New Guinea, Morotai, Borneo, recalled that Richmond Bitter was so unpopular the trading rate was two Richmond for one Foster's. Apart from tight little areas around Swan Street and Bridge Road, Richmond, the Richmond citadel was Mildura. The three clubs, the Working Men's Club, the Settlers' and the RSL, with combined membership of six thousand, served nothing else but Richmond. The Working Men's Club had the longest bar in the world, served by thirty-two pumps. The bar was so immense it even had five fireplaces.[3] In 1957, in the days of desperate bottle shortages, the clubs had started bottling their own beer, using Carlton draught under pressure. R. F. G. Fogarty believed this was lowering the standards of the product and had threatened that if they did not stop there would be no more CUB beer from Melbourne. The clubs had given in. Three months later Carlton had told them that they must put up their prices by a penny a glass to bring them into line with the hotels. The Working Men's Club had switched to Richmond, and soon the other clubs had followed their lead.[4]

In August 1961 there were rumours that Charrington and Co., the big British brewing combine, was negotiating to buy the Richmond Brewery for £1 million. What's more Charrington's would spend another £2 million expanding plant and buying hotels. Newspapers reported that John Charrington, chairman of Charrington's, was seen at the races with Sir Rupert Clarke, director of Richmond and son-in-law of its founder, Mr P. Grant Hay. Sir Rupert Clarke said Mr Charrington's visit was just a courtesy call. It was always his policy to meet rival brewers. *Truth* commented: 'It was significant that he did not see Mr R. F. G. Fogarty, chairman of the Associated Brewers of Australia and general manager of Carlton & United Breweries.'[5]

There were more visits by Charrington executives in November, and in January 1962 there were stories that the Charrington board was considering an offer of £1 800 000, but Mrs Peter Grant Hay, widow of the former chairman, said she knew nothing about it.[6] On 10 January Australian Associated Press reported from London that Charrington's would make their decision within thirty-six hours. Whether they made a decision nobody ever found out. On 16 January R. F. G. Fogarty told the press that CUB had bought the brewing assets and twenty-five hotel freeholds from Richmond. He would not say anything about price. It was not a share deal, but he made the picture very clear. In 1961 CUB had brewed sixty-nine million gallons; Richmond had brewed only three. In reply to questions about CUB now owning all the beer and all the hotels, he replied it was not true. There were 1581 hotels in Victoria and CUB owned only 139 of them.[7]

The Richmond Brewery was in Church Street, close to the spot where the Belvedere Hotel stands now. Its full title was Richmond Nathan System Brewing Co. Pty Ltd. Dr Nathan, a German, invented the system. At the time most brewing had been in open vats and Nathan had gone for fermentation in closed vessels with conical bottoms like the deep fermentation vessels which came later. Richmond, with its Nathan system, produced Richmond Pilsener, Richmond Bitter, Richmond Lager, Richmond Draught, and Kentdale Lager in honour of Peter Grant Hay's hop property. Animal heads glared from their colourful labels. Richmond Special Lager had a snarling tiger, Richmond Special Export Lager had an elephant's head with a long curling trunk. At its peak, production was five million gallons a year.

Another Richmond label in use in the years before 1962.

There were some tearful stories in the newspapers. The *Sun* reported that passionate Richmond enthusiasts came from as far off as Glen Waverley and Ashburton to drink at Ron Richards' pub, the Prince Alfred, opposite the brewery. One employee at the brewery had been so worried about his future supplies he had been building 'a cache' at his home. He was caught going off with two bottles that he had 'borrowed'. This cost him his job.[8] On the final day the 120 workers at Richmond received half an hour's free beer at the Prince Alfred. One prankster ran up a white flag on the brewery flagpole and some coined a little verse:

> The Game is Lost,
> The Battle's O'er,
> They're knocking on our bloody door,
> We tried our best to win the day,
> But lost our mate in P. G. Hay.[9]

Richmond labels became collectors' items and many sentimentalists kept full bottles of Richmond for future drinking. It wasn't always a good idea: good beer tastes best when it is younger than six months.

Right at this time hairdresser Lillian Frank was causing a mild sensation at her salon in Collins Street. Just when bottles had been scarce over Christmas Lillian was using beer to set hair, saying

Special Bulimba Draught to celebrate CUB's million dollar extensions to the Toowoomba Maltings in 1968.

> The malt gives the hair body. It comes up well and looks better. There is no beery smell. The beer evaporates completely under the drier. But the cost! Every day we use up to two dozen, sometimes more. And on Saturday mornings, when everybody wants party style settings, we go through at least three dozen.

She was getting her beer at a hotel down the street. She didn't reveal which beer gave the most wholesome hair styles, Carlton or Richmond.[10]

Producing good beer has always been a question of finding the right ingredients. R. F. G. Fogarty wanted the best malt, so in 1952 he bought the defunct Toowoomba Maltings in Queensland and revitalised the barley growing industry on the Darling Downs. Legend has it that back in 1926 Peter Grant Hay, who had large hop fields on the Derwent Valley in Tasmania, couldn't sell his hops to Montague Cohen, so he said: 'All right,

OPPOSITE PAGE:
*Hop harvesting in the Ovens
Valley, Victoria.*

if you don't want to buy my hops, I'll start a brewery of my own.' Finding high quality hops has been an eternal problem. Brewers imported it from England, they brought it from Tasmania, and one of the prime crops of the north-east of Victoria has been hops. It is a member of the vine family, and it grows on strings between tall poles to a height of 4 or 5 metres. God seems to have given it to mankind for no other reason except to provide that marvellous bitter taste in beer. Some people, however, have thought of other interesting uses for it: at one time it was said to induce sleep and cure 'hysterical affections'; the demented King George III used to sleep on a pillow stuffed with hops.

The English were slow in discovering the wonders of hops. In medieval times ale, made of malt and water, was the natural drink of Englishmen, while beer, composed of malt, hops and water, was the natural drink of the Dutchman. Henry VIII did not like it and he warned the Royal Brewer of Eltham that he wanted neither hops nor brimstone in ale. Some ripe English verse of the day went like this:

> And in very deed, the hops but a weed
> Brought over 'gainst the law, and here set to sale,
> Would the law were removed, and no more Beer brewed,
> But all good men betake them to a pot of good ale.[11]

For a weed the hops caused a devil of a problem. High quality clusters from Britain and America were expensive and by the time they arrived in Melbourne they were aged and stale, too bitter. Clusters from the Ovens and King Valley were not exactly superior. Tasmanian hops definitely were the best to be had, but prone to disease and often in short supply.

*Harvested hops on the way to
the drying kilns.*

Immediately after the harvest in February and March, as if they were apples or pears, the cones, a tight little group of female flowers which imparts all the flavour, had to go into cold storage. Cold storage space, too, was scarce because so much fruit was in harvest. By the time the hops had come by boat to Melbourne and had been left on the wharves, the hops were more than a week old. In 1952 Dr Carl Resch tried bringing them over by night-flying aircraft, twenty 63-kilogram bales to each plane.

It was like finding a better sheep, a better apple, a faster racehorse, the perfect breed that would grow locally. In 1950 the company brought to Melbourne A. S. Nash, a New Zealander, a man whose work on hop research had an international reputation. He set up a research station at Ringwood and started the laborious job of raising thousands of seedlings, cross breeding to find an ideal hardy, high-yield variety, the super hop. The best of them he planted out at the company's own hop station, 25 acres at Myrtleford. The best of the new breed, an early ripening variety called Ringwood Special, went out to growers in 1955. Then came a late maturing variety, Pride of Ringwood, which took over in 1958. Pride of Ringwood was such a champion it became the Victorian classic. It also transformed the industry. A. S. Nash reported that when he arrived Victoria had only 278 acres of hops, by 1969 this had jumped to 700 acres, almost all due to Pride of Ringwood.

Neville Wigan, who became head brewer at Carlton in 1953, says that those who live along the Yarra often talked of the magic smells emanating from the brewery at Carlton and Abbotsford. Maybe they nosed the whiff of malt from the malt house on Victoria Street, a biscuity sweet smell, but not the hops. Hops did have some smell, but certainly not in the past twenty years. Until the early 1960s the hopping of beer was all done by a slow muscle heaving process and was not always exact. Mr Wigan said:

CUB research team (left to right): Peter Murray, Stan Morieson, Brian Clarke, Peter Hildebrand and Frank Harold.

'We weighed the full cones in canvas bags. When boiling the malt extract we would tip these bags into the boiling kettle and then boil for about an hour and a half. That gave the hops flavour.'

There had to be a better, more scientific approach to hopping beer. Starting in 1960, a laboratory team, R. P. Hildebrand, P. J. Murray, A. S. Morieson, B. J. Clarke and Frank Harold as chief chemist, went to work to create a hop extract. Frank Harold said:

> The actual idea of extracting hops with an organic solvent goes back to the turn of the century, but nobody had found the right way. What we wanted to do was to remove from the initial extract, the actual precursor. The alpha acids in hops are not bitter. When you boil the hops in wort the alpha acids chemically re-arrange and form a bittering material. It is a very wasteful process. In actual practice using hops and simple extracts, utilisation, return of bittering material as related to initial alpha acids is only about 30 per cent. You have a wastage of 70 per cent of potential bittering material.
>
> Now what we did was take that initial extract, selectively remove from it the alpha acid, leaving all the other flavouring materials behind which we put in the boiling kettle in the normal way. We add the converted alpha acid at the end of the fermentation and achieve 95 per cent utilisation. We had a world first. We won the plant of the year award. We have exported the extract around the world. We still do.

The hop flower Pride of Ringwood strain developed by CUB.

Frank Harold said the laboratory had an even bigger breakthrough in 1979.

> The use of solvents seemed to be a disadvantage. When you use a solvent you always have to evaporate the solvent off. We picked up the idea of using liquid carbon dioxide. We built a pilot plant and within eighteen months we had the first commercial plant in the world. It has had world acclaim and the process is not only used for extracting hops but all kinds of plants.

For a moment he sounded faintly nostalgic. 'You never see hop leaves in the brewery any more. You know, some of our younger brewers are around for a year or two before they see any hops.'

Victoria was leading the world in processes for the production of beer, but it was also unique in its strange drinking habits. Six o'clock closing for hotels came in as a temporary measure to help defeat the Kaiser during the First World War. Tasmania got rid of it in 1937, New South Wales in 1954, and South Australia in 1967. Naturally Victoria was not going to be led by anything done in New South Wales. In 1956 there was a referendum on 24 March, one of the objects being to give Melbourne ten o'clock closing in time for the Olympic Games to be held there that year. The Victorian Local Option Alliance fought on the slogan 'Stick to Six'. One advertisement read:

WOMEN OF VICTORIA
YOUR TOTAL VOTE WILL DECIDE WHETHER LIQUOR BARS STAY OPEN AT NIGHT

Later closing will mean
1. More liquor consumed at night in bars and beer gardens.
2. More drunken men roaming the street at night.
3. More dangerous drunken brawls.
4. More drinking motorists at night — more road deaths.
5. More assaults on women and girls at night.

6. Young people lured from career studies, cultural activities and encouraged to drink at night in bars and lounges.
7. More of the family income spent on liquor — less on necessities.
8. More broken homes — more neglected children.[12]

Only six of Victoria's sixty-six electorates voted for ten o'clock closing and they were Albert Park, Carlton, Melbourne, Port Melbourne, St Kilda and Toorak. The dry areas in Balwyn, Burwood, Box Hill, Camberwell and Kew had easy 'no' wins. The final figures were 804 875 for six o'clock closing and 529 951 for ten o'clock closing. As a serial it was better than the *Perils of Pauline*. Towards the end of 1953, the Victorian Government sent Judge Fraser on what many considered a dream assignment. This was to spend four months browsing round the pubs of the world inspecting the way others imbibed alcohol. The judge returned and came out for ten o'clock closing, but the government accepted few of his recommendations.

In 1963 the government decided to hold yet another Royal Commission, this time under Mr P. D. Phillips QC, one of the most brilliant and lively wigs at the Victorian bar. The Commission sat for eighty-five days and heard two-and-a-half million words, enough to fill forty-one novels. Cohorts of people lined up to give evidence: brewers, vignerons, grocers, theatre owners, police and temperance workers unlimited.[13]

One of the principal witnesses was R. F. G. Fogarty. He immediately baffled the Commission by refusing to make any recommendation as to whether there should be six, nine or ten o'clock closing. He was concerned that the brewery would be looked upon as a hungry monster. No amount of continuing cross examination could extract a word out of CUB's chairman, R. F. G. Fogarty. He told them the brewery would make no more money whether the hotels remained open until ten, even though Mr Phillips QC, raised a skeptical eyebrow. He was in the witness box for three days, and at times took an unnerving battering. John Thomas Rowan, who owned the Jindera Hotel near Albury called him an 'irascible, pedantic, dictator'.[13] Rowan told the commission that the brewery insisted he provide a guarantee of £325. His beer would be delivered on Friday, payment would have to be made by the following Wednesday and if he didn't do that there would be no more supplies. 'I spent six years of my life fighting one dictatorship and I don't want to spend the rest of it under another,' said Rowan.[14]

P. D. Phillips questioned Mr Fogarty about the way he told hotels what to do. This was one of the replies:

In 1951–52 when we were the first brewery to emerge from rationing . . . the hotels were opening from half past eleven to one or half past and then reopening at half past four until six. My aim when I first came here was to get them open from nine in the morning until six at night, and give them enough beer to achieve that. I was sorry I did, because I was inundated with calls about the hotels that were closed, asking me about this hotel and that hotel. I had to take some disciplinary actions, Sir, which are so abhorrent to most hotel keepers. I had to withdraw supplies from hotels that did not open from nine until six and keep open all day.

Mr Phillips was startled. He said surely if hotels didn't stay open that was their problem. If they were inefficient and badly run they would go out of business. It had nothing to do with the brewery. But Mr Fogarty disagreed. The brewery always got the blame for everything, particularly when the hotels did not provide quality beer at the right time. Mr Phillips kept tackling him about how he only liked to have the hotels open for long hours so the brewery could make bigger profits. Fogarty replied coldly, 'In the first place, Sir, I would like to correct the impression, which you seem to have . . . with respect . . . that we are doing nothing else but making money. We have got some principle in regard to certain things we do.'[15]

Mr Phillips always provided great copy for the newspapers. His most original performance was a special dinner party designed to prove that it was wise to take food with alcohol. It took place at University House, Melbourne University. Among those invited were Mr Kevin Coleman, assisting the Commission, and Mrs Coleman, Mr. R. F. G. Fogarty, Mr W. S. Johnson, senior lecturer in criminology, Mr S. E. Sharp of the Wine and Brandy Producers Association, and the Reverend D. Hurse of the Presbyterian Church. Before dinner there was a choice of martinis or Rhine Castle's Rameda extra dry sherry. At dinner the first course was a choice of consomme or spaghetti marinara. The next course was fresh water trout, which was served with Rhine Castle Victorian Bin 92 moselle. This done there was filet mignon and what was described as a rather lovely Coolalta Hunter River hermitage, vintage 1958. Finally with the coffee there was Cockburn's port from Portugal, Remy Martin Cognac VSOP, Drambuie or Benedictine; as Mr Phillips put it: 'a very enjoyable party'. Everything was scientifically recorded under the eyes of the pathology expert, Dr Norman McCallum, and the Police Surgeon, Dr John Birrell. The star performer of the evening, and the deliberate test case, had two martinis, one dry sherry, two white wines, one red wine, two ports and one liqueur. His breathalyser reading was .053. The police regarded .050 as the plimsoll mark.[16]

Mr Phillips was pleased. Everyone drank varying amounts, but no more than the equivalent of nine and a half seven-ounce beers. So it proved that if liquor was consumed slowly in relaxed conditions in not unreasonable quantities, one would not come to any harm. As Mr Phillips put it: 'It seems that people who show a reading of more than one per cent in police tests must be having one hell of a time'.

On 14 October 1963, Mr Phillips, later to be Sir Phillip Phillips, produced his report calling for ten o'clock closing and the government accepted it — an unusual fate for the recommendations of royal commissions particularly those concerned with the liquor trade. Ten o'clock closing came to Victoria in February 1966. Contrary to the terrible warnings, there was no carnage on the roads, no ten o'clock swill. Indeed the hotels were half dead in the evening. One reporter wrote:

> The city was so empty it was frightening. I looked in at the Cathedral Hotel at 9 p.m. There was only one other person in the bar, and we experienced the sort of pure happiness of Crusoe when he discovered Friday.[17]

The Kaiser had been defeated. The lights in the bars were on again in Victoria.

Sir Norman Carson died on 20 January 1964. He had been on the CUB board since 1925 and he was chairman until he retired in November 1963.

He was chairman of the Wool Realisation Commission and he controlled the disposal of £90 million worth of surplus wool carried over from stocks acquired by the government during the Second World War. He received his knighthood for this. He was a gentle, kindly man with an incredible devotion to the brewery. He presented himself at Bouverie Street almost every day. He was a Rotarian of extraordinary devotion. It was said of him that he had 100 per cent attendance. If he missed his lunch meeting at Melbourne, then he would make it up at Collingwood Rotary the next day, or Northcote the day before.

The new chairman was R. F. G. Fogarty. He won a CBE in 1959 for his work as chairman of the City Development Association and a knighthood in 1966. Yet a grateful government in Australia so often is tardy in awarding its honours. There was little time left to enjoy the title Sir Reginald. He died at his home in Toorak, 66 Clendon Road, on 27 February 1967.[18] He was a huge personality and almost every executive had his favourite story. Brian Corrigan, who was assistant general manager properties, said he had fond memories of him, but one needed to hone one's wits to keep pace. In the late 1950s and early 1960s the company was expanding, improving hotels all over the state. 'I was working eight days a week,' said Corrigan. R. F. G. Fogarty never wanted to miss anything. As general manager he would demand to see the new hotels himself.

One time they went to Horsham to look at a hotel. Mr Fogarty called in Brian Corrigan and told him that the following morning they would leave together. It was explained to the general manager, very delicately, that Corrigan's car was four years old, it had done 80 000 miles and he would not be very comfortable.

'All right, you can take my Buick. You were in the Transport Unit during the war, weren't you?'

'Yes, Sir, I've driven tanks and most vehicles.'

'Good. You be at my house at 8.30 in the morning.'

'I'll be there at 8.15.'

'No, you won't. You'll be there at 8.30,' Fogarty corrected.

Brian Corrigan said early next morning he hid around the corner from Clendon Road until the tick of 8.30. Sure enough there he was outside waiting. Corrigan parked his Holden in Fogarty's garage then went to inspect a distinguished but ancient Buick, which was waiting on the apron. Corrigan explained:

The Buick was a 1946 model. It was in the books at £15. He kept it to teach his executives a lesson. 'Why do you all want big cars, new cars?' he would say, 'Look at mine, it's a 1946 model'. So I got into the Buick. On each side of the steering wheel there were eight white buttons. 'Oh Geez,' I said to myself, 'which is the starter?' I was looking, looking, getting hotter. Suddenly Foge puts his head in the cabin, 'Huh, you've driven tanks and transports. It's easy to see you've never driven a Buick. Where's your right foot?'

'My right foot?'

'Yes, your right foot.'

'It's on the accelerator.'

'Well, press the bloody thing.'

Of course, it had a solonoid to start the electric motor, the accelerator would push the solonoid to activate the starter motor. The car was 17 or 18 years old. I remember we got to the first staging spot where we needed some petrol. He's watching me like a cat. Where's the bonnet catch? There's nothing under the dashboard. It's all right. It lifts from one side. But where's the petrol cap? He's still watching.

Corrigan managed to save face this time. He got the tip from the garage mechanic. The petrol cap was hidden under the number plate. When they got to Horsham, rain was falling, there was a camber on the road and the Buick was not happy. Corrigan said:

> The clutch was making awful noises, going shudder, shudder. I said to the boss, 'Somebody driving this car must be driving the clutch'.
> 'Whatdya mean somebody's driving the clutch. I'm the one who drives this car.'
> 'I beg your pardon.'
> We got home all right. The next day his own driver, Norm Ruddick, had to take it to get it serviced. On the way back the tail shaft dropped out. He got a new car after that.

After this things began to improve with company vehicles. Corrigan's own driving in the early days was in an unadorned Holden.

> In 1957 I was out on my first trip. I was on the Calder Highway. It was raining cats and dogs and there was so much mud I had to clean it off the windscreen with brown paper. When I got back I said to my boss, it would be nice to have a windscreen washer for the car. He said, 'You write a memo and I'll take it to Fogarty'. At the appropriate time Fogarty got me and said, 'Listen, my boy, if the car maker felt there was a need for a windscreen washer it would have been on the vehicle'.

'An amazing man with an extraordinary memory,' said Brian Corrigan. 'He never forgot anything. He expected his executives to perform and if they didn't, they wouldn't be there.'

Eric Thomson, who was company secretary from 1956 to 1975 and chief accountant when he arrived in 1949, knew him as well as anybody.

> It was amazing the way he controlled Board meetings. I don't think any director at any meeting objected to anything he put up to the Board. You could write your minutes out before the meeting started — everything would be approved. I don't think the staff was frightened of him. Respect was more the word. He didn't mind people arguing. You could put your point of view. Usually you finished up doing things his way.

Eric Thomson, company secretary 1956–75.

Fred Coulstock, former group executive director of CUB, was in charge of production at Abbotsford in 1962. He made the dramatic move of switching the bottling line to twenty-four-hour production. High speed bottling lines are the agony of all brewers, one hitch, one recalcitrant bottle can cause a jumbled nightmare, and all production would stop. Keith Stackpole remembers that when this happened sometimes it would be good for the workers. The foreman would declare 'Bar-oh' and the men would go for an early drink while the engineers straightened it out. Fred Coulstock said:

> When we started twenty-four-hour production I went to Fogarty and begged him to let me go to America where I knew they had been running twenty-four-hour bottling lines, but he wouldn't let me do it. It took me about five months

Leonard 'Fred' Coulstock, brewing division head in the early 1980s.

before I wrecked the whole bottling line. I was about 34 then, a youthful enthusiast. He sent for me. 'Well, you realise what you've bloody well done?'

'No Sir, I haven't done anything, it's the company that has done it.'

'What do you bloody well mean by that?'

'It's the policy of the company. You expect me to be able to do this. We have one engineer, one foreman. We pump up forklift tyres with a hand pump. We don't have lathes, but I still believe the concept is sound and it ought to work.'

'All right, what do you need to make it work?'

'You let me do it my way, give me the organisation. Don't let anybody from head office interfere and I'll make it work.'

'Done,' he said.

In nine months the whole operation at Abbotsford was refined, working smoothly, and by 1964 bottles were being filled at the rate of 525 a minute, but Coulstock still needed to go to the US. They were having trouble with the filtration equipment and it was important to visit the Tommy Manville diatemaceous earth mines near Santa Barbara, California.

'I want to go to America,' he said.

'Do you indeed,' replied Fogarty. 'What do you know about filtration?'

'Not very much, but neither does anyone else either.'

'All right, you can go for a fortnight.'

Fred Coulstock said that after a fortnight he went to Fogarty and said: 'I'm leaving, Sir, for America.'

'Who the hell said you could go to America?'

'You did, Sir.'

'All right, you can go for a week.'

'A week's no good, I won't go.'

Fred Coulstock said that he walked out. Fogarty shouted: 'Come back here. All right you go for a fortnight'.

So he went to California for a fortnight and solved all the filtration problems. Later he made history by sending his foreman, Ian Coutts, to study in America with the biggest brewer in the world, Anheuser Busch. Coulstock said:

Foster's Lager in the late 1950s and early 1960s, labelled to meet the maze of United States regulations.

Coutts would have been a first class honours engineering graduate had he been given the chance. I thought he could sell the new techniques to the blokes on the line at a level I never could. It was the best thing I did. That was the turning point at Abbotsford.

Fogarty was a close friend of R. G. Menzies and Sir Arthur Fadden. He was said to be a great raconteur. He hardly ever drank beer, mostly whisky. In 1964 he was guest of honour at the Melbourne Beefsteak and Burgundy Club. He listened for some time to rhapsodic comments from members on the sherries, the rieslings and the clarets. When they asked for his comments he said that all his life he had been a beer man. He couldn't tell the difference between a claret, a burgundy, or anything else.

'But ah,' said he, 'put in front of me a beer from Brisbane, from Perth and from Melbourne . . .'

The club members waited eagerly for him to continue.

'And I wouldn't be able to tell you the difference either.'

For most of his career he suffered from drinking bouts. These did not in any way affect the sharpness of his mind or his extraordinary skills. One executive said:

> A bout would be like a thunderstorm. He would see it coming from far off, something one would have to live with while it was there. There would be the downpour, the claps of thunder and suddenly it would be all gone. He would drink orange juice for six months.

Eric Thomson said:

> His magnetic personality would inspire loyalty in the staff. On some occasions he would say, 'Eric we will go up to the brewers' room'. He didn't really drink beer, but on the way out he'd be in a very mellow mood, and he would pass through all the departments. He'd meet someone. He'd see the Credit Manager, say, 'How much do you get a year? Seven thousand pounds? Eric, that's bloody disgraceful. Give him five hundred extra tomorrow'. I'd have to go round later and say, 'Don't take any notice of that, he won't remember it tomorrow'. He was an amazing man. He would have his drinking bouts but still he commanded the admiration of everybody.

According to one board member there was a move at one stage to get rid of Fogarty and there was a meeting to discuss it. However Fogarty knew what was afoot. He sealed off all the departments in Queensland so that only he knew what was going on. It was impossible to get rid of him. Fogarty was an institution. It would have been easier to remove the Shrine of Remembrance. In his later years he was an old man on the job. He ruled the Victorian beer scene for almost twenty years although he had not come to Melbourne until he was 55. He once told his personal assistant, Lou Mangan, that he was reluctant to come to Melbourne because he believed he was too old.

Fogarty's law was complete and utter. The ultimate Fogarty crime was to sell interstate beer during a strike or, almost as bad, stock Richmond. Douglas Crittenden, a licensed grocer who had branches in several suburbs, recalled that one time they wanted a price increase.

> I was vice-president of the Licensed Grocers' Association. We were a sort of rebel group. We wanted to raise the price of beer from 2s 6d to 2s 7d a bottle. Most of the grocers went along with this and we got the hotels on our side too. In those days the price was known as 'Fogarty's Law'. It was Fogarty who decided when the price went up. It was Fogarty who decided on your profit margin. I mean, if beer went up 12d a dozen he might decide your profit was 8d. Break Fogarty's Law and he'd cut off your beer.
>
> Well, we decided we wanted another penny. There was a call from Fogarty, 'Hello Critt, what's this I hear about you joining the rebels?'
>
> 'Well, yes,' I told him, 'we can't make a profit on the present margin'.
>
> He replied, 'I tell you what the price of beer is. I tell you what margin you can have. You don't set it'.
>
> I explained to him that most of the hotels were on our side and if he refused to sell them beer, would he mind if we put in a bit of Richmond. I didn't realise that was absolutely red rag to a bull. If you put in any Richmond any time, he'd cut off your beer. We upped our price and sure as his word he cut off our beer. He did it to all the rebels and, of course, we had no choice. We backed down and sold at the old price. Everybody was forgiven, except me. I still didn't get any deliveries. Immediately I got on to George Dally, sales manager

at the brewery. I said, 'What's going on, George? Why don't I get any beer?'

He said, 'The old man's pretty upset with you. You sold Richmond beer. The word has gone down that you are cut off permanently'.

What could I do? I had to consider my fellow directors. I got in the car and went straight in to see Fogarty. I had to go down virtually on bended knee and beg forgiveness and promise never to misbehave in the future. He replied, 'All right, you'll get your beer, but you keep your promise and don't ever step out of line again'. He was a tough operator. He'd do the same to you over Ballarat beer. Ballarat used to have a depot in the city, but when CUB took over the Ballarat brewery, he stopped the beer from coming to the city and sold it only in the Ballarat area. Fogarty's Law was not to be denied.

His trading terms were seven days. If they did not pay that was the end of their beer supplies. Breweries have always been strict because they are in the unenviable position of being a tax gatherer. The excise has to be paid before the beer leaves the brewery. Now the terms are fourteen days and a hotel is unlikely to be cut adrift under twenty-one days. But Fogarty was famous for being ruthless and many hotel keepers resented him bitterly. Always they were looking for a new opposition. They made moves in the hope of persuading Charrington's of UK to take over the Richmond Brewery. Fogarty got there first. They thought some brewer might move into the Ballarat Brewery. Fogarty got there first. Ultimately the hotel keepers persuaded the great English brewing combine, Courage, to come to Melbourne. Had Fogarty handled the hotel trade with just a little more tact and diplomacy the hotel keepers would never have been interested in talking to Courage and there is no doubt the English would never have started in Melbourne. It was a battle which was to last ten years and cost CUB countless millions of dollars. Sir Reginald Fogarty was a great administrator, but he made the mistake of having too much power as chairman and managing director and staying on the job too long. Fogarty died on 27 February 1967, aged 74. It was really the end of one-man rule at Bouverie Street. Maybe it was the end of the days when Carlton & United was an old-fashioned family club.

And it was like a club. Keith Stackpole said it was extraordinary how CUB attracted sporting people, Collingwood footballers in particular.

> We had Harry Collier, captain of Collingwood. He played in six premiership teams. We had Albert Collier, Marcus Whelan, Perc Bowyer, Jackie Ross, Jack Carmody, Vin Doherty, Albie Pannam, Leo Morgan, Harry Lambert, Frank Kelly, Terry Waters, Cyril Kent, Charlie Brown . . .
>
> Leo Morgan, Jackie Ross, Jack Carmody and Marcus Whelan, all got jobs on the one day and the other clubs went crook. They said, 'How come they all get jobs with the brewery and other clubs can't?' Of course, Jock McHale, coach of Collingwood was a foreman there, worked there all his life.

Keith Stackpole said he came at a time when there was a ban on Collingwood players, so he had to put in time first with Vacuum Oil and then the City Council. 'However,' he continued,

> I went to see old Bill Raabe, a one-eyed Collingwood man, foreman at the Abbotsford plant. He said, 'You come and see me, I'll see Jock'. So between the two I had to go and see the personnel manager, who was really a red hot Fitzroy lover. I was playing with Fitzroy at the time. I played five years with Fitzroy and five with Collingwood. I got the job.

EMPLOYEES OF BREWERIES VFL & VFA PLAYERS 1938

CUB any time in the 1930s could have fielded a mighty football team. Top row (left to right): R. Price (Brunswick), F. Kelly (Essendon), S. Vaughan (Brunswick), R. Pratt (vice-captain, South Melbourne), V. Doherty (Collingwood), J. Doherty (Preston), L. Morgan (Collingwood). Middle row: M. Whelan (Collingwood), W. Lock (Melbourne), F. Froude (Collingwood), A. Knott (Fitzroy), J. McHale (coach, Collingwood), J. Austin (South Melbourne), P. Bowyer (Collingwood), J. Carmody (Collingwood). Bottom row: W. Mitchell (vice-captain, Sandringham), L. Monaghan (Fitzroy), A. Hender (St Kilda), B. Diggins (captain, Carlton), R. Goullet (captain, Brighton), H. Collier (captain, Collingwood), P. McNamara (Melbourne).

But the brewery was not entirely Collingwood. Keith Stackpole listed other players: George Smeaton and George Rudolph of Richmond; Mick Grambeau, Glen Wigraft, Leo Monaghan, Archie Knott, Dick Saunders of Fitzroy; Les Hill, Collingwood and Fitzroy; Wally Lock, Melbourne; Bob Pratt, South Melbourne; Alan Hender, St Kilda; Leo Brereton, Carlton; and Dodger Ryan, North Melbourne.

Another interesting feature of the brewery was that everybody had a nickname. As soon as you started there, they'd give you a name based on some personal feature. I don't know half their real names. I never worked in a place like it. My wife would say, 'What's his name?' I'd have to say, 'Awww, that's Sparrow.' She'd say, 'What an odd name!' 'Well, everyone calls him that.'

Apart from Sparrow we had Golden Boy, Whiskers, Spy — he knew everything — Mongrel, Porridge, Stalky — big feller he was   Jocky, Scxy Rexy, Banjo, Penguin, Spider — he was a fitter, used to climb all over the place — Baldy Bill and Baldy Jack, Ocker, Roughhead, Chops, Bye-Bye Birdie — he used to nick off on his own, always had a full bottle hidden behind a downpipe — Knackers, Crazy Horse, Podgy, Cakes, Dogs, Bugs, The Whip, The Wombat — Oh I tell you, I could go on for ever.

CHAPTER TWELVE

The Battle of Courage

Just three days after the death of Sir Reginald Fogarty a new age began at Carlton & United Breweries Ltd. Edward Cohen became chairman of the board and Brian J. Breheny became general manager. As the newspapers put it, Edward Cohen had a fine quiver of directorships. He was chairman of E. Z. Industries, chairman of the Emu Bay Railway Co., chairman of Commercial Union Assurance, chairman of Derwent Metals, director of Associated Pulp & Paper Mills, director of Pelaco, director of Glazebrooks Paints, director of Michaelis Bayley, director of Standard Mutual Building Society and, of course, director of CUB since 1947. His father, Harold Cohen, and Montague Cohen had been on the board at the same time, and his brother Geoffrey was a former chairman.

Edward Cohen was born in 1912, went to school at Scotch College, Melbourne, and just possibly he was the first chairman of a brewery to be an exhibitioner in Greek and Roman history. Sir Edward explained:

> There used to be a master at Scotch called 'Forty-Five' Clayton. We called him 'Forty-five' because he walked like this, his shoulders at an angle of forty-five degrees. It was a tradition that every year he won an exhibition in one of the histories for one of his students. In my year it looked as if he was going to miss out. I actually came second to Chester Wilmot, the writer. He was at Melbourne Grammar, but Chester was over age, so I won the exhibition. I got first class honours in the three histories, Greek and Roman, European and British and in economics. I took the line of least resistance, followed the family footsteps into law. I wouldn't have wanted to be a doctor because I hated getting my hands dirty.

Sir Edward Cohen, chairman of CUB 1967–84.

In 1930 Edward Cohen won the senior government scholarship to Melbourne University. This was an embarrassment because his father, Harold Cohen, was Minister for Education. 'What was he to do?' said Sir Edward.

> He didn't think that the State should pay for my education, but he wanted me to have the honour and glory, as he put it. So he let me keep the scholarship, but he gave a scholarship of equal value to be won by some other person. I was at university from 1931 to 1934.

Immediately he went into the old family firm of Pavey, Wilson & Cohen. CUB was one of its clients, so his work for the brewery began almost at once.

Cohen was 54 when he became chairman and Brian Breheny 55 when he became general manager. The Breheny tradition went back just as far as the Cohens. Brian Breheny's father, James Patrick Breheny, was head brewer at the old Barley Sheaf Brewery in Ballarat, and in 1904 became first head brewer at the Melbourne Co-operative Brewery. James' brother Peter was also a brewer at Abbotsford. Brian Breheny went to school at Xavier College and started work at Carlton as a trainee brewer on £1 a week with one penny deducted for tax.[1] He became technical assistant to R. F. G. Fogarty in 1949, personal assistant in 1950, and assistant general manager in 1950. In *Who's Who* he listed his recreations as working and reading in that order.[2]

The difference between Breheny and his predecessor was like that between Disraeli and Gladstone. Breheny had a greying Ronald Coleman moustache, charm and style. Suddenly all the doors were open at CUB.

> The spartan bareness of Carlton and United executive suites has been banished by redecoration [said the *Age*]. The old Bush Inn has gone for ever. Gone are the days when the publican waited in ill-lit ante rooms in fear of what was awaiting him.[3]

> It's when you get inside that you notice the change [said John Sorell of the *Herald*]. It hits you like a smack in the eye. No bouncers, plain teak desk with an attractive young girl in a Pierre Cardin dress. She smiles, you smile, people shuffling through the thick pile carpet smile too. Mr Brian Breheny apologises for keeping you waiting three minutes.[4]

There was an instant attempt to create a new image. The 130 brewery trucks received new paint. Instead of the old dull red, they were now white and brown. The drivers were be-decked in new uniforms, grey tailor-made trousers and jackets with the CUB emblem on the pocket. The first dramatic public relations move was the launching of 'stubbies'. The stubbies were 13⅓ ounce and a revolution almost as big as the departure of the Clydesdale. They were throwaways, not refillable, and the days of the old bottle-o seemed over. What's more a new word came into the language, the six-pack. The bottles came in a handy cardboard container of six. The labels, too, were new. Not the classic old labels with the fine print and memories of medals won in famous exhibitions gone by. They were bright, rounded at the edges, sporting big letters 'F', 'M' or 'VB'.

Brian Breheny, general manager of CUB 1967–72.

Brian Breheny created history by giving a lunch at the brewery. Almost every senior journalist, radio and TV man was invited. Few of them had ever been inside the brewery. There were questions about what would happen to the stubbies. Would they lie at the side of the road forever? Brian Breheny said it was true that stubbies were filled only once but they were very much sought after by the glass companies, because they were melted down and turned into bottles again. One lady had assured him that stubbies made particularly attractive flower vases.[5] As the journalists departed Brian Breheny handed each one a case of stubbies. He looked at one journalist who had been on the Fogarty 'banned' list, smiled and said: 'I think you deserve two cases'.

The Cohen–Breheny team took over just in time for the great new battle against Courage. In November 1966 a consortium of Courage, Barclay & Simonds Ltd, British Tobacco Company (Aust.) and a group of Victorian hoteliers announced that they would build a new $8 million brewery at

Broadmeadows in Victoria. The challenge sounded formidable enough. Courage had assets of $250 million in Britain and owned more than five thousand hotels. The sign of the rooster and the slogans 'Take Courage', and 'John Courage, the best beer of our time' had been well seared on the brains of Englishmen through blanket advertising.[6] It was a battle Sir Reginald Fogarty would have loved but he was not to be in it. In one of his last statements he said: 'Past experience has clearly demonstrated that our general efficiency, continuous research and development and the high quality of our product will find us well geared to meet the challenge of yet one more competitor.'[7] He was right, warfare was not new to CUB. When he came from Queensland in 1949 the group profit was $1.1 million with assets of $10 million. Now they were $90 million with profits of $7 million a year or more than 20 per cent on capital.[8]

It was a fascinating battle. As the *Australian* put it the CUB board was heavily oriented to Melbourne Grammar School, Melbourne University, Oxford, Cambridge, marriages with heiresses, Toorak and the best clubs in several cities. Directorships were as thick as autumn leaves. On the other hand Courage had chosen Sir Maurice Nathan as their front man. He was rich, very successful, managing director of Patersons chain of furniture stores, founder of the Moomba festival, and a former Lord Mayor. He knew everybody, was excitable, impulsive, loquacious, shrewd, and into everything boots and all — a doer.[9]

Courage built their brewery at Broadmeadows with extraordinary speed. The first announcement was on 2 November 1966 and from then on everything was top secret until the publicity tide broke on Tuesday 8 October 1968. On that day, Sir Maurice Nathan, as Courage chairman, took delivery of twenty-five red-and-gold International trucks bearing the Courage emblem from International Harvester at Geelong. Next they drove them to Melbourne in military convoy and straight up Swanston Street towards the Carlton Brewery. It was the finest example of raw power since the Germans moved into Sudetenland. Some felt Carlton should have had twenty-five Foster's Lager and Melbourne Bitter trucks moving back the other way in an act of confrontation, but this did not come to pass.

Wednesday 9 October had been declared C-day. First deliveries of the new beer were made to hotels at 5 a.m. and truly devoted radio roundsmen were on the job at 5.30 a.m., giving on-the-spot 'I was there' accounts of tastings of Courage. The press invitations for C-day were for 10.30 a.m. out at the brand new $8 million brewery. Not only did the newspapers send full teams, but there were TV editors, editors of agricultural journals, sporting editors, real-estate writers, social writers, cartoonists, and proprietors of trade papers. Brewery openings receive better all-round attendance than other dull functions.

The Courage men were lined up, most of them very well English-suited, all of them with the golden cockerel on their lapels. The most impressive was the managing director of Courage, Barclay & Simonds from London. He was slim, grey haired and had a magnificent name — Mr Hereward Swallow. Sir Maurice Nathan did all the talking. He never actually mentioned Carlton. It was always 'the opposition' or 'the other brewery'. He was most poetic. When he talked of their secrecy period, they had 'hooded the cockerel', and he even broke into verse:

Life is mostly froth and bubble,
Two things stand like stone,
Any beer in any glass,
But always Courage in your own.

There was a forty-five-minute tour of the brewery. The various areas had imposing names — 'Brew House', 'Bottling Hall' — and all was clinical and automated; the tanks were painted a pale green, the pumps were in sweet lolly pink and the pipes were stainless steel. Sir Maurice claimed it was 'the trend-setter for all breweries in Australia to come'.[10]

Every commentator, both amateur and professional, was keen to pass opinion on the new beer. Nearly all thought the same. One columnist said: 'Frankly, it looks like Carlton, tastes like Carlton, turn me round, blindfold me, and I'd swear until the roof fell in that I was drinking Carlton.'[11] A television station, HSV7, interviewed Bernard Heath, a consulting chemist and beer connoisseur. He said scientific analysis of the two beers showed that the chemical difference between them was minimal. He found that Courage contained 4.85 per cent alcohol compared with Carlton which had an average of 4.75 per cent. The hops were the same and the sugar and the protein content of the two beers were almost identical. He had tested the taste differences with a panel of five scientists, trained in beer tasting. Only one out of the five was able to pick the difference.[12] Why then did Courage set out to make almost a Xerox copy of CUB? Why did they not stick to a classic English Courage style? It was never admitted, but clearly the feeling was that a taste is something which is cultivated and grows in a community until it becomes a great tradition. They knew Melbourne loved their Foster's and their Abbots. It was too dangerous to experiment with a new taste. It would be like trying to convert Chinese to hot dogs.

Sir Maurice said he was looking for 10 per cent of the Victorian market, but he was so pleased with the reaction he planned to grab a much larger slice.[13] Had he been a Roman Emperor he might have been more suspicious; some of the omens were not all that rosy. Melbourne's La Trobe Library found an old Troedel poster for Elliott's brewery at Echuca, which started in 1883 and supplied most of the beer for the Riverina. Its emblem was a golden cockerel. 'What happened to Elliott's brewery?' asked the *Bulletin*. 'It was swallowed by Carlton some time around 1922.'[14]

Courage never achieved anything like the 10 per cent share so enthusiastically claimed by Sir Maurice. In the first year Courage Breweries Ltd declared a loss of $1.7 million. The *Australian* commented: 'It is thought that the company captured between six and eight per cent shortly after launching in October last year, but the figure steadily fell to around the three and a half to four per cent level'.[15] Unquestionably the beer was too lacking in its own definitive flavour. The Victorian beer drinker was so ingrained in a habit that there was no point in switching over. Courage also had to contend with the laziness of a busy barman. If he had two taps and nine out of ten customers were drinking Carlton, it was a nuisance going for the Courage. If both were similar in taste often the fellow who asked for Courage received Carlton anyway. As well, the Courage that had been languishing too long untapped in the pipelines tasted flat and stale when it reached the glass.

*Courage: the First
Anniversary Brew, 1969.*

Sales did not improve and Sir Maurice Nathan became progressively more angry. He accused CUB of monopolising beer sales through tied hotels. It all came to a head in March 1970 when the Commodore hotel chain decided to deal exclusively in Carlton products because of the 'lack of demand' for Courage. Sir Maurice was angry. He issued a press statement saying Commodore's decision to have CUB as its exclusive supplier had nothing to do with lack of demand for Courage. 'Commodore's only existing outlet worth mentioning is the Village Green Hotel at Glen Waverley,' said Sir Maurice. 'All their other major hotels are sheep in wolves' clothing. That is to say they are operated by Commodore on lease from CUB and Courage products have never been nor ever will be, available through them.'[16]

Edward Cohen waited a little time before he replied. He was now Sir Edward, having been knighted by the Queen in the New Year's honours. On 19 November he made a supplementary statement at the annual meeting:

In the light of recent publicity to statements in respect to tied houses it seems desirable that I should say something to put the record straight . . . Of almost fifteen hundred hotels in Victoria, a smaller proportion is owned and tied to our company than is the situation in any other State in Australia. Of the many hundreds of hotels in Victoria not in any way tied to us, over five hundred do not choose to sell our competitor's bulk beer and over two hundred and fifty do not handle any of its products, presumably due to lack of demand.

It is true that we enter into arrangements for people to sell only beer produced by us and everyone that does so does it by his own free choice and free will. No one is compelled to borrow from us.

It is quite remarkable that Sir Maurice Nathan should be quoted as saying that his company is a little one and cannot meet requests for loans by hotels. In fact, his company is 75 per cent owned by two huge, enormously powerful and financially strong overseas controlled companies, each far larger than us.

Courage Limited in England has assets totalling $A280 million ... British Tobacco has $233 million in assets.

I would point out that our competitor should have known the conditions in Victoria when it came here. As in every industry, there is intense competition in ours. As President Truman once said, 'If he doesn't like the heat, why doesn't he stay out of the kitchen'.

The heat was most severe. CUB had not been doing a great deal of advertising; it had been kept to a minimum with billboards proclaiming: 'Good beer is good for you'. There had been almost no television advertising as R. F. G. Fogarty had thought it unnecessary, a waste of good brewery money. Brian Breheny, however, wanted immediately to change the company's image. He went to the biggest advertising agency, George Patterson Pty Ltd, which had done good work for the company in Queensland. Dick Cudlipp, the Victorian manager, and Colin Fraser, the creative director, called at Bouverie Street. Fraser remembers, 'We had six story boards of commercials that we might run. Looking back they were adventurous, but they were a mile away from what the industry eventually proved to need. Yet they were sufficiently exciting for Breheny to say we had the account.' It was a decision that was to run into an annual expenditure of millions. There was much work to be done. It was a campaign that had to be very subtle and precise, an intense research programme. 'We had a Goliath coming against a David,' said Fraser, 'and the David was not liked by the public.'

This was the result of the research:

1 Melbourne beer, they said, was widely acknowledged as the best beer in Australia. No doubt about it, because even Sydney people (who didn't think much of anything in Melbourne) agreed.

2 Probably, they believed the difference came from Melbourne's excellent soft water.

3 Hotel keepers and drinkers alike agreed that the Carlton Brewery had been notoriously arrogant and high-handed over the years. For instance, it was widely held that the brewery provoked strikes every Christmas to create a shortage and so artificially stimulate demand.

4 But everyone agreed that the brewery did know how to make great beer.

5 English beer, they thought, was weak, warm and flat and Courage, even modified, probably wouldn't suit the Australian taste.

6 Nevertheless, they recognised Courage as a big, successful English brewery. Maybe they could be big enough and good enough to do what, over the years, nobody else had been able to do.

7 And finally, there was an enormous public curiosity about the way Carlton would react to the Courage challenge. It was common knowledge, they said, that Carlton had always refused to advertise on television. If Carlton started advertising now, it would be a sure sign that Courage really had them worried. On the run.

Then CUB, as client, laid down a few thoughts of its own. There would be:

• No competitive claims.
• No too positive statements, or specifics.
• No reference to alcoholic strength, colour, sweetness, bitterness
• No reference to price.

- No suggestion that they were seeking to sell more beer.
- No obvious urge to action.
- And no suggestion whatever that CUB was worried by the competitor's impending launch.

Colin Fraser said: 'It fell to me to write the first commercials. I well remember the feeling of having been left alone in the middle of a particularly lethal minefield'. There was another problem. The brewery had hired the McKinsey management consultancy to overhaul its marketing operations. McKinsey was a big international organisation of great prestige and it recommended that Carlton should forget all its multifarious products and concentrate on a single fighting brand.

Dick Cudlipp, being very brave, took the opposite view. Sure, the big battle for the drinkers' minds was going to be fought over the draught beer served in the pubs, but the packaged section of the market was certain to be the growth area. Why not exploit the difference in all the Carlton products? Why not give each of them a different character? Courage could only start with one or two labels. Crowd them off the shelves. CUB agreed with Cudlipp rather than McKinsey and Courage was crowded out of the bottle shop.

Another thing they learned from research was the extraordinarily conservative nature of the beer drinker. In studies of other markets Patterson's found that in the retail store field routinely 60 per cent of people buy a brand or go to a store because of past satisfactory experience, or because they are influenced by word of mouth recommendation. That leaves a healthy 40 per cent to influence by advertising. The beer trade they found was different. The stream of confirmed, satisfied users was 80 or 90 per cent. Word of mouth was more potent than in any product they had ever looked at. Researchers discovered that Melbourne Bitter was more in demand in the country than in the metropolitan area. In some suburbs the demand for Abbots Lager was greater than in others, and some suburbs preferred Victoria Bitter. Abbots Lager was more popular with white collar beer drinkers and those in higher income groups. On the other hand women liked Foster's Lager. They thought it lighter and less filling and the best beer to drink with food. City manual workers thought Victoria Bitter was the most satisfying after a hard day's work.

So they went to work on the labels. Abbots Lager needed something that was restrained, more subtle, the name of the beer in red on a white background. For Foster's Lager royal blue was the choice, something with feminine appeal. As for the two bitters, the emphasis was red, with a green centre for Victoria and light blue for Melbourne. In each case the background was gold. All the labels had to be rounded because corners lift off too easily. The length had to be greater than the width to lessen the risk of their being placed sideways on the bottle. It was important that they should have an easily distinguished top and bottom; nobody wanted those labels upside down.

Everything was top secret. Working for the advertising agency, according to journalist Laurie Oakes, was like working for MI5.

> You are not permitted to breathe a word about your job to an outsider. Even when Carlton scripts were sent out for quotes to film production houses, they were doctored. They didn't mention the real names of the products they were

dealing with — code names like 'Special Beer' and 'Zippedy Doo-Dah' were mentioned instead.[17]

So Fraser produced his first commercial and this was the script:

> This city.
> This sprawling,
> striving,
> restless,
> crowded city.
> This busy city,
> so often beautiful,
> so often tough.
> There's a beer here that the city
> earned itself,
> CARLTON.
> For a hundred years as the city
> grew, a great taste was perfected.
> A big
> satisfying
> beer that's rewarded
> honest work for
> generations, Carlton,
> as cool and delicious as it looks,
> a fresh smooth beer
> that starts with soft
> trickling on cool mountains,
> that's full of the rich goodness of
> Australian barley,
> the heady taste of
> Australian hops.
> Carlton,
> the beer that began a century ago
> in Bouverie Street,
> now one of the world's
> great beers.
> Your beer, from
> CARLTON.

There were elegant shots of busy Melbourne: a Clydesdale and a dray going down Bouverie Street, a shot of the brewery, good citizens enjoying their beer, mountain streams, hops growing, and a splendid triumphant musical theme adapted from the 'Magnificent Seven'. 'What was that about?' said Fraser,

> Well, first of all pride in the city, pride in the product, emphasising the fact that the beer had grown up with the city, that it had Melbourne water in it and that its ingredients were Australian. The theme, the beer you had earned, was designed to legitimise the desire for a grog and that has survived in our advertising right up until now.

Carlton Draught was presented as a reward for hard work. Foster's Lager was the beer with the distinctive taste. Victoria Bitter was the man's beer. Melbourne Bitter was depicted with rural settings and Abbots was the beer for the fellow with the discriminating taste. Then there were the songs, the jingles. They became so well known they almost ate into the brain and were hummed more than the songs at the top of the charts. This was one of the most popular:

> If he's a man who knows the best time of day,
> If he's a man who knows the right thing to say,
>   If he has an ear,
>   And a taste for a beer,
> He's the man who asks for Abbots.

Many people noticed the similarity between a Carlton 'Carry-Cans' jingle and 'Cinderella Rockefeller', which was riding triumphantly at the top of the hit parades. This was hardly surprising, both were sung by the same people, Johnny and Anne Hawker. Johnny Hawker also arranged the music for the commercial. The cost of the commercials of course was enormous. Infinitely more time, effort, and care per second went into those commercials than any feature movie. Laurie Oakes reported that if producers of television programmes worked in the same way it would have taken six months to make one episode of a one-hour television programme like *Homicide*. Patterson's hired the best talent. For example, they had John Dixon, director of Cambridge Films, the same man who co-directed and wrote the script for *Anzacs* and was scriptwriter for *The Man From Snowy River*. Casting for commercials was as serious as casting for *The Man From Snowy River*; voices, faces, mannerisms, all had to be authentic. John Meillon, maybe Australia's best character actor, was the narrator for the Vic Bitter ads. No voice was more authentically Australian. The scenes for the commercials had to be just right as well. They did one at the Patchewollock Hotel for Carlton Draught and the 'tired red-dust-stained men' who raised their foaming glasses after a hard day's work were genuine characters from the Mallee.

One commercial, a Foster's beach barbecue scene, won an award at a film congress in Singapore. It involved six male models and eight bikini-clad girls, plus production crew, all on location at Waratah Bay near Wilson's Promontory and it took four days to shoot. It was some barbecue. Patterson's hired the chef from one of Melbourne's leading restaurants to prepare and lay out the food. Then they had refrigerated trucks to chill the beer and keep everything sparkling fresh.

> Simultaneously with the release of Courage [Fraser said] a rumour flew round the pubs that the Courage beer was green, green in terms of immature. Where that came from we don't know, but it had a devastating effect. Whether it was planted or just the way the seasoned drinkers felt about it, the discussion that went on in the pubs was enormous. There were lots of suggestions, too, about beers being switched and whether you were getting what you asked for. Dick Cudlipp recommended that Carlton identify their taps so that there was absolutely no confusion about which product they were drinking.

The commercials always had to be very pure. The industry had to set its own standards. There were no guidelines. Unlike the soft drink commercials they could not fill the screen with sex, muscled young men and bouncing girls in bikinis. Indeed they had to be careful not to have anyone in a commercial who looked too young. The message that you could get

One of Foster's greatest advocates, John Meillon, at the John Meillon Bar, Oaks Hotel, Neutral Bay, Sydney.

your girl through alcohol was a no with a capital N. Furthermore the beer drinker must never be seen driving a car or a boat.

Fraser said proudly that the whole campaign worked exactly as they hoped. It was vital to win that battle right in the first round.

> In the beginning hotel keepers everywhere wanted to sell Courage. Many of them felt that Carlton had given them a hard time and this was a way to even the score. But putting in the second brand means that you double your work. You've got two deliveries interrupting your day, and twice the number of barrels to handle in the taproom. So eventually inertia takes over. The strong tendency is to toss out the brand that doesn't catch on. That happened in our market, until the pubs were cancelling Courage orders in droves.

Colin Fraser said that over the years they searched the nation for the right, rugged outback scenes.

> We wanted locations where there were real men, dust, sunshine, real stockmen, a feeling of thirst and reward. Finding the right places to do that was a nightmare. I had the idea of cattle coming into a railway station, then being driven off a barge into water. Oh yes, we got complaints about being cruel to cattle but we got assurances from the RSPCA that no harm was being done. So we had

this wonderful outback scene, stockwhips cracking, stockmen and horses plunging into the water. David Kirkcaldie, a great writer did the words.

This was the script, slow, melancholy, sung in the Simon and Garfunkel style:

> And he'll tell you
> He likes the kind of
> life he leads
> He's glad that he was born.
> And he likes the taste
> of real draught beer
> When his time's his own.
> And this man earns his pay twice over
> By putting first things first.
> There's nothing like
> a long cold beer
> to satisfy a thirst.
> If you want the taste
> of real draught beer
> Only Carlton Draught will do.
> When the taste you want
> And the taste you get
> Is the taste that's right for you
> 'Cos it's brewed with care
> And mellowed so
> The flavour's there
> And don't you know
> there's nothin' beats a
> long cold Carlton Draught.

That commercial was so sentimental it almost brought tears to the eyes and it ran for many years.

The late 1960s through the 1970s saw the biggest change in drinking habits in Australia's history. Until then the suburban and even the city hotels were horrors. They had a cold, lavatory-like atmosphere. The outside of the hotel, inevitably, was coated with lavatory tiles. Inside it was dung coloured, with dung coloured linoleum on the floor and matching lino on the top of the bar. There were no seats, no tables, no stools, no clutter that might interfere with high-speed action. With six o'clock closing and the desperate 5.30 p.m. rush a bar had to be like below decks in a naval battle, everything had to be clear for the war. Brian Corrigan, who was assistant general manager properties, recalls:

The peak period was 1968 to 1972, a five year pressure pipe. I had to go round looking at sites, recommending sites for hotels. Jim Sadler was the architect. We hardly ever stopped, working eight days a week. We built hotels like the Bayswater, the Croydon, the Keysborough, the Frankston. We had 64 major projects going at the one time. Can you imagine the paper work, the problems with the liquor commission.

The change was breathtaking for drinkers. For the first time in history there were public bars with carpet on the floor. Some drinkers found it inhibiting. They wondered if they even dared go inside. The Tavern Bar in the Graham Hotel had sporting prints on the wall and Hosie's had its intimate Polo Bar with red carpet on the floor and comfy stools so that one could sit up at the bar, nose to nose to the barman. The Summerhill Hotel at Preston had an hexagonal-shaped lounge with a high vaulted ceiling, just like a modern church, enough to give one prayerful thoughts. The Sportsman's Bar at the Council Club in Preston had comfortable chairs and tables, a lovely polished timber bar rail and bar with prints of old time boxers on the walls.[18]

An even more dramatic change was the tavern licence, introduced in 1970. Until then all hotels, by law, had to provide accommodation. So frequently there were six to a dozen rooms upstairs all with beds nicely made which had not been used since Queen Victoria was on the throne. The first of the new licences went to the old Mitre in Bank Place, a pub which had hardly changed since it began in 1868.[19] Next came Matilda's in the Victoria Club building and then the Eureka Stockade in Bourke Street, which was a surprising title, considering that the major event at the Eureka uprising was the burning down of a hotel. The taverns brought with them the greatest breakthrough yet for the feminists. Women for the first time actually entered public bars. Until modern times our pubs had a monastic quality, so monastic they did not have female lavatories. In the Royal Commission on Employees of Shops 1883 this was cited as an excuse for the abolition of barmaids. A girl of 20 had died of 'haemorrhage of the stomach' brought on by constipation and long working hours. For periods of up to eight days 'she had been unable to move her bowels'. There was no lavatory for women in the hotel.[20]

It was social ruin for a lady even to be seen entering a hotel, but slowly this stain disappeared, and the 'Ladies Lounge' appeared. Here a lady,

A new era comes to the hotel industry: the main bar of the Bush Inn, Toorak, in the late 1960s.

A Carlton Pilsener label, 1966.

properly escorted, could be taken for a drink, albeit one paid for at a higher price than in the public bar. Even as late as 1969 the unescorted lady was something to be feared. When granting a licence for a new St Kilda cabaret, Judge O'Driscoll warned the nominee: 'The commission will not tolerate women attending without an escort'. He talked, too, about girls with 'very doubtful objects' in hotel lounges.[21] But all this ended with the coming of the Mitre, Matilda's and the Eureka Stockade taverns. All the bars were open to women and unescorted they could buy their beer at public bar prices. The lavatories were there too. At the Eureka Stockade they were labelled 'Gentlemen' and 'Gentlewomen'.

There were new beers as well. Crown Lager was named in honour of the Queen and was the premium Carlton beer, served in half-size bottles with a gold label and a long elegant neck. Beer had to compete with wine in restaurants so it needed to look just as elegant. Dietale was developed specially for diabetics. Then came Carlton Pilsener. Leslie Jordan, CUB's marketing manager, reported that the company spent hundreds of thousands of dollars and a year of research to produce it. Pilsener came as a result of the Liquor Royal Commission; it was a drink to tie in with later closing hours, a beer with 12 per cent less alcohol with the blessing of the police surgeon, Dr Birrell. George Patterson's produced two 60-second commercials, one at Hunter's Lodge, Croydon, with people dancing in Bavarian costumes, and another at the Dorchester by the Yarra. The jingle which would have had some doubtful connotations a decade later went:

> Keep it light,
> Keep it bright,
> Keep it young,
> Keep it gay,
> If you like it light,
> Pour a Carlton Pilsener.

It was all kept top secret until launching day. The bottles went unlabelled with plain crown seals and the beer just had the name 'Special Brew No 1'. Only the board knew of the plans and only after the name was revealed did the labels go to the printers.[22]

Unfortunately Pilsener was a decade ahead of its time. There was something not manly enough, something which did not fit the Australian image about drinking a low alcohol beer. The CUB Annual Report of 1973 confessed the failure. It was the least popular of all the company beers and despite big promotion it did not sell. So the marketing department changed the name to Light Ale and somewhat sadly the annual report added: 'We are persisting on a national basis to cater for the minority who prefer such a beer'.

While CUB was going lighter, Courage was going stronger. Simon Whitmore, Courage general manager, announced Tankard, a darker, more flavoursome, slower-maturing beer.[23] It caused a furore. Not only did the name suggest that one would drink it in large quantities but the alcohol content was the highest on the market. Courage countered the criticism by saying it wasn't an average beer, to be drunk by the fellow in the pub, but a premium, sophisticated beer which sold for a cent more than other beers. But the battle was on. CUB issued a statement to prove that by world standards its beers were not over strong. Carlton beers ranged from

A 1972 Carlton Light Ale label.

THE BATTLE OF COURAGE 141

4.25 per cent by volume for Pilsener to 5 per cent for Carlton Draught. 'The CUB strengths are in line with all recognised beer drinking countries,' said Hugh Bingham, spokesman for the company. In Denmark Carlsberg was 5.55, Tuborg 5. In Germany, Lowenbrau was 5.5; in Holland Amstel was 5.1, in the US Schlitz was 4.7, Michelob 4.95, Miller's High Life 4.65; in England Bass Pale was 4.45, Allsop's Lager 4.75, Whitbread's Brewmaster 5.4; in the Philippines San Miguel was 5.00 and in New Zealand Leopard Lager was 4.6, DB Export 5 and Steinlager was the strongest of all with 5.85. As for Courage Tankard it scored 5.6. The *Financial Review* commented: 'CUB must be annoyed at Courage for bringing the product on to the market at a time when Victoria's road toll is creating a delicate socio-political situation for the liquor industry'.[24] If Carlton Pilsener had failed because of too little muscle, Tankard also failed, perhaps through having too much. The tastes of Victorians were hard to change.

Habits were changing though, ten o'clock closing had seen to that. Hotels like Young & Jackson's in the heart of the city had been the top of the pile. Now the biggest drinking wells were way out in the suburbs, the Matthew Flinders at Chadstone, or Sandown Park or Sandringham. Once draught beer had been the big seller by far, but now packaged beers, bottles, cans and stubbies, were well in front. People were starting to drink at home.

Nor was Carlton the big brewery any more. Abbotsford was the giant, the monster, the biggest brewery in the country. Sir Edward Cohen announced plans to spend $30 million at Abbotsford to make it one of the largest beer-packaging plants in the world. Already the company had spent $3.5 million on a new wort production complex. The new plan was to build eight stainless steel fermenting tanks, the first of twenty-four which would give a fermentable capacity of three million gallons a week.[25] These new tanks seemed nigh beyond belief. Each one had a capacity of 64 800 gallons and was 60 feet high with a diameter of 16 feet 4 inches. They were the tallest fermenters in use in any brewery in the world. The total

New fermentation vessels under construction at Abbotsford. Each one holds the equivalent of three-quarters of a million cans of beer.

capacity was half a million gallons, or 110 million seven-ounce glasses of beer. They should be well able to cope with the summer thirst.

The building of these fermenters with their conical bottoms was an act of extraordinary courage. Was yeast really a deep water creature? Would it still work at depths of 80 feet or more? The responsibility fell on Fred Coulstock.

> We had a technical committee and in the finish everybody backed off because there was no proof around the world or at Carlton that the yeast cells would tolerate this depth of fermentation, constantly moving in heat cycles.
>
> Well, we made the final decision and it went against me. I forced it to the Board. Then I was told, 'Well, what are you going to do if it doesn't work?' I said, 'We'll just cut the top off and make it part of a second vessel'. That wasn't quite as silly as it sounds. The tanks were built in sections, in tiers. It would have been easy to make two out of one. You make them in sections, 10 feet high, weld it, jack them up in the air, then jack up some more.
>
> But I was convinced that it really would work. I had a small advantage. I had graduated in two majors, chemistry and botany, so instinctively I felt that yeast was more precocious than most people imagined. He wasn't going to be down there all the time. He was in convection. We had all the configurations or cyclical movements and convections worked out. The laboratory was in it. The brewers were in it. And it worked. It really did.

It was a world first, giving a whole new economic edge to beer production and the idea was copied everywhere. It couldn't have been tested first with a small pilot programme, because the whole point, the whole worry, the area of the unknown was the size of the operation; a pilot programme would have proved nothing. The 100-foot stainless steel fermenters were merely the beginning, much bigger structures were yet to come.

In November 1972 a complicated plan went before the Supreme Court. All those companies which had amalgamated in 1907 were to be merged into one. Actually, the situation was ridiculous. Carlton Brewery Ltd, Melbourne Co-operative Brewery Ltd, Foster Brewing Co. Ltd, Shamrock Brewing Co. Ltd and Castlemaine Brewery Co. Ltd had not made a drop of beer for many many decades, yet they still had their annual meetings, still appeared on the stock lists and their directors controlled Carlton & United Breweries Ltd. There was an excellent reason for winding up those small companies. According to Sir Edward Cohen a group had tried to buy a controlling interest in one of the ancient, now non-existing breweries. As the little companies held the original A shares, all they had to do was to circle the corral, shoot down a few of the holding companies, and all CUB would fall with them. So shareholders in the holding companies were allotted new Z shares for each share, and at last, sixty-five years after the birth of the union, the famous old names disappeared for ever.[26]

A person not present for this announcement, nor at the last annual meeting was Brian Breheny, the general manager. He had gone into hospital. Breheny was a chain cigarette smoker, nearly always with cigarette and elegant white cigarette holder. He had cancer of the oesophagus and died on 11 December 1972, aged 60. He had been general manager for only five years. The *Herald* commented that he, probably more than any other person, had been responsible for the improvement in eating and drinking conditions in Victorian hotels. Breheny's comment had been: 'I'm a bit of a frustrated architect'.[27]

CHAPTER THIRTEEN

The Cyclonic Seventies

Brian Breheny, although general manager of CUB, never became a director. Unquestionably the directors did not wish to repeat their experience with R. F. G. Fogarty who had wielded awesome power, not only as a general manager, but as director and company chairman. Fogarty had become a law unto himself, almost the sole arbiter of policy, and had been immovable, remaining until he died in office at 74.

The new general manager, appointed in 1973, was Louis Joseph Mangan. He served four years' apprenticeship and became a director in 1977. Not as flamboyant as Brian Breheny, he was nevertheless one of the new breed. He was the first cost accountant in the company's history. Lou Mangan was born in 1922. He went to school at Christian Brothers College in Middle Park, Melbourne. In 1942 he joined the air force and trained as a navigator, but he injured his knee, suffered serious cartilage problems, and had to remuster into administration. After the war he did a four-year course in commerce at Melbourne University under the re-construction scheme. After graduation he worked for two years with a friend who was an accountant. Then in 1951 he applied for the job as cost accountant with Carlton through the University Appointments Board. He arrived just at the right time. The huge postwar expansion was taking place. He became personal assistant to Fogarty and was in all the big deals, the Richmond Brewery take-over, the Ballarat take-over, and the great drive into Queensland.

As the new general manager he inherited a company that was in good shape. There was a new $2 million brewery to replace the old Mac's brewery at Rockhampton, the Cairns Brewery had started packaging and producing Carlton Draught, there was a new 26-ounce rip-top can on the market, and the company was making more beer than ever before. The battle against Courage was virtually over. Sir Maurice Nathan resigned as both chairman and a director on 10 November 1972. He told the Courage annual meeting that because of the brewery's decision to obtain retail outlets he was in a position of conflict with his own company, Patersons, which had joined with the Great Universal Stores of England. 'I judge it to be my responsibility to devote the whole of my business activities to Patersons,' said he.[1] It was a decision that convinced no one. Had Courage been the conqueror a team of forty Clydesdales would not have removed the ebul-

L. J. (Lou) Mangan, managing director of CUB 1981–85.

Tom Williams in the first laboratory established at Carlton Brewery, c. 1925.

Inside CUB's modern technical centre. Every brew at each stage of production goes through laboratory tests.

lient Sir Maurice from his chairman's seat. Clearly this was the beginning of the end.

Over the road from the brewery in Bouverie Street a magnificent technical centre was built. Four storeys high, it was the finest thing of its kind in the country. Originally on the site there had been an old foundry with a branch of the State Savings Bank at the corner of Victoria and Bouverie Streets. The bank was rebuilt into the corner of the new building. Assistant general manager Frank Harold could well remember the old lab in the heart of the brewery building. Back in 1950 there were two other graduates apart from himself, and two assistants. It was a classic, dimly lit laboratory complete with Bunsen burners.

In the new building there was a staff of seventy-six, enough manpower to run several entire breweries back in the 1880s. Among them were twenty-five professional scientists. The laboratories were all earthed and the foundations were such that it was vibration free. The difficulties there must have been in the old building, trying to conduct sensitive scientific tests with pounding machinery operating only metres away, are unimaginable. And it must have been almost impossible to get antiseptic cleanliness for microbiology tests.

Dr Peter Hildebrand.

Dr Peter Hildebrand, formerly of Queensland University, was research manager. He died in 1976. The current research chief is Brian Clarke. The technical centre has many functions. Pure research is one, care and propagation of the strains of yeast is another. Tests for quality control, raw materials and all stages of beer production go on constantly. The centre uses its computer to gather an enormous quantity of scientific data on beer production, but one of the most fascinating activities is that of profiling or 'fingerprinting' a beer. This began back in Frank Harold's day. The scientists analyse a beer and reproduce its exact profile on a chart, enabling the brewers to reproduce a beer and maintain a consistent quality. 'What we have,' said Brian Clarke, 'is a big data bank which enables us to produce Foster's Lager, if you like, wherever you want to have it and make sure it is still Foster's Lager.' The mysteries of how to take a famous brew and reproduce it in another city still baffles many famous brewers around the world. It certainly baffled Emil Resch when Foster's stopped brewing at its original brewery in Rokeby Street, Collingwood. He was amazed how you could make a beer in one brewery, then move no more than one or two kilometres to another brewery, use the same ingredients, same water, everything, yet incredibly the beer wasn't the same. Precise methods of 'fingerprinting' solved all that.

Normally it takes a trained palate to tell the difference. Tasters are on the job almost every day at the technical centre. They are given a course, and instructed on the composition of beer, and the tastes to look for. The tasting room is divided down the centre. The glasses are filled in one section and then passed through little windows into booths where the devoted tasters go to work. They get three glasses. Two have the same beer and they have to pick which is the odd glass and analyse the difference. All the results are charted and catalogued and quickly they discover which tasters know their business.

The year 1975 was historic for the beer drinker. It was difficult to imagine how beer consumption could ever decline in Australia. Right back to 1890 various governments have looked upon beer as an extension of the taxation department. There was outrage and horror when the Victorian Government first imposed a tax of 3d a gallon back in 1890. The breweries then claimed it was a crushing burden which would drive them all to ruin. At the turn of the century most Australian states were paying 3d and since then it has gone for ever upwards until it reached the stage that when a man downed a glass he knew always that the government was an equal partner, except that the government never paid the next shout. The taxpayer could console himself with the thought that when he drank beer he was doing his patriotic duty. Every time he lifted his glass he was paying for a member of the armed forces, supporting a public servant, keeping an RAAF fighter in the air, or perhaps even contributing to the support of an old age pensioner.

Both beer and tobacco were prime government targets because taxing them was easy and convenient — the breweries and the tobacco companies were unpaid tax gatherers. Rarely a Federal Budget went by without another increase.

In 1969 Cyril Pearl gave the breakdown in Victoria. If you spent 13 cents on a glass of beer, the publican did best with 6.2 cents, Commonwealth scored 5 cents, the brewery 1.4 cents and the state 0.4 cents. So the tax authorities were getting very nearly four times more out of it than the people who made the stuff.[2]

On the night of 19 August 1975, the Federal Treasurer, Mr Hayden, on behalf of the Labor Government, brought down what was called the 'Give-and-Take' Budget. There was much more take than give. There was an extra 6 cents on the average packet of cigarettes, and beer went up 11 cents a bottle, bringing the price to 70 cents. The federal tax went up 11 cents to 30 cents, which, with the 4 cent state tax, brought it to 34 cents. On draught beer an 18-gallon kilderkin, which used to cost hotels $30.76 wholesale, now cost $41.92 with excise rising from $19.97 to $31.13.[3] Mr Hayden's reasoning was this: the government *take* for the previous financial year was $480 million; next year the beer drinkers would *give* him $740 million. There were cries of pain everywhere. A spokesman for the Australian Associated Brewers said:

> This tax increase is a body blow to beer drinkers. They have to pay this enormous, scandalous tax while wine and brandy drinkers get off scot free. A flagon of wine which has two and a half times more alcohol now costs 40 cents less than the equivalent volume of beer.[4]

Particularly eloquent was a letter writer to the *Australian*.

> During the Kaiser's war our Federal pollies imposed a special tax against beer drinkers 'for the duration of the emergency'.
> During the Depression the Federal pollies increased the special tax against beer drinkers 'for the duration of the emergency'.
> During Hitler's war the Federal pollies increased the special tax against beer drinkers 'for the duration of the emergency'. Now they are at it again with no pretence about duration. May I invite Federal pollies of all parties to explain in your columns the reason for their special hatred of beer drinkers.
> The Kaiser is dead but his work goes on in Canberra.[5]

In his annual report for 1975, Sir Edward Cohen made much of 'the incredible Budget'. He said it had

> hit the beer drinker with the ruthless power of unassailable authority . . . Only in topsy turvy Australia is beer, the least alcoholic of such beverages, taxed the most. The wine drinker pays neither excise nor sales tax while even the young child buying his lemonade pays 15 per cent sales tax. It is astonishing that the wine industry can maintain such a cherished position. This high rate is direct encouragement to people to drink tax free beverages of much higher alcohol content than beer.

This was the first time that a brewer had recognised the infant rival. In the old days the wine drinker had been divided into two classes. He was either the port drinker, the alcoholic who haunted the once infamous wine bars, or he was your higher income, upper middle class connoisseur who liked a glass of wine with his meals. Consumption was low; merciless liquor laws discouraged drinking with meals. The tax hit so hard in this Budget that it was a trigger, a turning point in the habits of the Australian drinker. Except during depression years consumption of beer had gone for ever upwards; beer was an article of faith as necessary as bread or milk. Now all this was changed. The wine industry produced the cask, the plastic bladder with the tap attached; something that could sit on the sideboard, as easily available as instant coffee. A new style of restaurant came into being, the BYO licence. Robert Carrier on a tour looking at Melbourne was astonished at the sight of gourmets labouring under their heavy loads, carry-all bags filled with bottles to consume with their dinner. Something, he said, that didn't go on anywhere else in the world. But the BYOs contributed to wine consumption, and the Budget helped even further. Hotels started putting wine casks on their bars. In the 1950s or 1960s this would have been considered a move beyond belief; the drinking of a riesling in a public bar would have been practically un-Australian; but not any more. This was the new era, and besides, the out-of-the-bladder riesling was easily the cheapest drink around.

So if the beer makers had not noticed before, now they had cause to worry. In 1970–71 beer consumption was 123.8 litres a head and wine was 8.5 litres. Both continued to rise steadily. The peak year for beer was the year of the horror Budget, 1974–75, when Australians drank 139.6 litres a head, and wine consumption had gone up more than 30 per cent to 12.5 litres. The effect of that Budget was immediate, and unquestionably damaged the nation's finest taxing machine. In 1975–76 beer consumption dropped to 138.8 litres, and wine continued its climb to 12.5. litres. The following year beer was 135.4 litres and wine was 13 litres. A steady graph was traced, the beer line going slowly but steadily down, wine going sharply up. For 1984–85, beer consumption was 115 litres a head and wine was 21.4 litres, a dizzy climb from the 8.5 litres of 1970–71.

Even though the brewers were majestically serving their country by being almost the top tax gatherers, they were not loved. CUB had a delicate and difficult battle with the Queensland Government. In the old days there was at least an unwritten law, if not a gentleman's agreement, that brewers kept within in their own states. That started to break down when Carlton faced Swan in the Northern Territory. Then the niceties ended for ever when CUB beat Castlemaine Perkins in a financial tussle and bought the Queensland Brewery in 1961. Raiders from the south were never popular in Brisbane where the entire world was divided into Queenslanders and southerners, so the battle commenced. CUB poured out huge sums into Queensland hotels, so that from Thursday Island to the Gold Coast there were 190 CUB-financed hotels. The object was to tie them financially so that they would sell their Melbourne beer, Brisbane Bitter and Bulimba Gold Top. It was never actually said that Carlton should not be there, but in February 1974 the Queensland Government brought down multi-brand legislation. This meant hotels had to stock a complete range of beers. Furthermore it meant that Carlton had spent its money in vain on those Queensland hotels. They couldn't be just Foster's houses any more because Premier Joh Bjelke-Petersen had made sure they also stocked Castlemaine Fourex.

A Carlton Lager label from the Queensland Brewery, Toowoomba, in the late 1960s.

Sir Edward Cohen had some bitter comments.

It is difficult to understand the Liberal–National Party Government legislating in such a way that a Brisbane-based company without any plant investment in north Queensland can be given privileged access to the northern market to the detriment of existing de-centralised industry.[6]

Worse was to come for decentralisation. At the end of March 1976 CUB closed down its Toowoomba and Rockhampton breweries. Both produced bulk beer, but the modern trend was towards cans and bottles. Distances in Queensland were huge and the government would give no help whatever in easing costs. The Toowoomba Brewery was old and inefficient but the end at Rockhampton was a sad one. Lou Mangan commented:

We felt we had done something in decentralising. The old McLachlin Brewery was flood prone through the Fitzroy River. We sought out a brand new site and spent about $1.5 million on the new brewery which was quite a bit of money at the time. Very modern, very well equipped but within just a few years we had to close it.
   Rail freights ex-Brisbane for Fourex beer became so cheap they could land their brand in Rockhampton virtually below our cost. Was that deliberate? You ask yourself. They had a lot of political persuasion.

Lou Mangan said he called on the minister responsible concerning the closure. 'He almost said, "What are you here for? Why are you telling me about it?". '

There were all sorts of ingenious ways for tackling the breweries. In June 1975 the Trade Practices Commission found that the tied house arrangement between New South Wales brewers and hotels was a breach of the Trade Practices Act and gave them thirty days to clean up their operations. The ruling rocked the entire industry and what with appeals and counter claims between breweries it was to keep lawyers happily busy for the next decade. Tied hotels was a tradition that went back to the birth of the industry. Back in the 1870s and 1880s many a small brewery could not have survived without its tied hotels. The hotels that sold their beer were their only outlets. The breweries always claimed there were other very real reasons for owning their own hotels: they could make sure they were properly run, that the pipes were clean, that the beer was pure and not watered. Every brewer could tell stories of the hideous unsavoury things that were done to their product.

New South Wales was the most utterly tied state. Tooth had 933 tied hotels and Toohey's had 318, a total of 1251 hotels out of 2030. In other words 62 per cent of all hotels in NSW were tied.[7] By contrast CUB in Victoria had 350 tied hotels out of 1440, and with around 95 per cent of sales the ruling did not cause the same concern.

The Commission stated its feeling about tied houses: they tied up a quarter of total beer sales; they made it difficult for another brewer or wholesale supplier to break into the market; they ensured that licensees of tied houses didn't have to compete with each other and, of course, in a tied house the consumer had no choice, but had to drink the tied house beer or go elsewhere.[8] It was several years before the Commission's ruling actually came into force, and the biggest sufferer was Tooth & Co. It had three times as many hotels as Toohey's and it meant that now Toohey's could get into all its 933 hotels. It was one of several cuts that was causing the old company to bleed to death. As far as the brewing industry was concerned it was the end of a long era. Always it would be interested in hotel ownership, but never again would CUB show the passion for building fine hotels that it did in the 1950s and the 1960s. There were far more interesting avenues for capital development.

The brewing industry did not suffer only from government in the 1970s. On Christmas Eve 1974 Cyclone Tracy hit Darwin in perhaps the most devastating assault by the elements ever suffered by an Australian town. The Carlton Brewery did not suffer badly, but the little brewery was hit with damage which cost $1 million. When Swan and Carlton had merged their Darwin operations in June 1973 it had seemed logical to concentrate all the brewing at the Swan plant and to use the Carlton brewery as a warehouse for beer, wine and spirits distribution. It was ironical that the old Carlton plant was barely damaged. Had the company remained there they could have started brewing operations again almost on the following morning. The late Swan brewery where they were now was devastated. Whether it was due to the quirks of Cyclone Tracy or the Carlton building being more solidly constructed of galvanised iron, is anyone's guess. Lloyd Annets, transport foreman was there:

> I remember, Nick Norgard, the brewery manager, came round about two o'clock on December 24. We had some bikkies and cheese and he talked to the boys about the year's work. Thanked them, that sort of thing. He claims he said, 'We'll do better next year unless we have a cyclone'. So we knocked off around 2 p.m. Of course, it was raining. It had been raining for days, then we started to get messages that the cyclone was changing course.
>
> I had to get my boys back to work, putting everything under cover, including the vehicles. Didn't do much good as it turned out. At four or five the boys left to look after their own houses. At that time the cyclone was heading close to Darwin, but hadn't turned straight across. I went down the track about 16 miles to a friend's place at Howard Springs to give them a hand.

Cyclone Tracy's devastation to the cold room at Carlton's Bishop Street plant, Darwin.

We tried to tie the roof down with a piece of cable. We attached one end to the axle of his car and the other to a steel stanchion. The cyclone hit at about 10 p.m. It was a fibro house and it just blew apart. The whole place came to bits except for three walls. My mate's wife and three kids hid under beds and under the table. We propped ourselves against the remaining wall. Scared? You bet I was. Meanwhile the dog had pups on the bed, in the last remaining room, all the rest had gone.

Actually the wreckage wasn't so bad, the first part. Then came the centre of the cyclone, the eye, you understand. It was absolutely dead calm for about half an hour. I'd read about it and knew what was going to happen next. It was about one o'clock when it turned around. The noise was incredible. You could hear it coming like a bloody express train. Everything that had been loosened in the first blast came off in the second. At six when it got light we went outside and checked things out. The cable which we used to hold the roof on pulled the axle clean out of the car.

We were supposed to be having Christmas dinner at a friend's place in Darwin. It was still raining and blowing but not real bad. On the way we met the person who was supposed to be having the Christmas dinner. He said, 'There's no use going on. There's no Darwin left'. It was true, the more we went along the Sturt Highway the worse it got.

I went straight in to the brewery. No roofs, no louvres, and the great stack of beer in the store had entirely collapsed into an enormous pile of broken bottles and spewed beer. Except on one side there was a stack of Victoria Bitter cans, right up to the roof that once was. The cyclone had stripped away all the cardboard, but still perfectly symmetrical, all standing and clean, was this pile of bright green VB cans.

Oh what a mess, flies, maggots, everything got in. It took us three weeks with front end loaders and semi trailer tippers to cart it all down to the tip. Make me want to leave? It did to some, but not to me. This is my place and I wouldn't leave it for the world.

Doug Farrell, plant engineer, remembers:

The roof came off our place at midnight and then the house started to disintegrate. It was one of those houses on stilts and even the floorboards were going. It was obvious we had to move. Our brewer, John Moffat, lived in the next street, so I thought we would go there. Probably a silly thing to do. I got out the car, took my wife Natalie and our boy, Paul, aged nine. It was only a few hundred yards, but the air was full of flying debris and I couldn't see a thing. When we got to John's place his roof was coming off too. He had four children and he herded the lot into a wardrobe. They all survived. His place wasn't as badly damaged as mine. We went back to my neighbour's place. His roof and part of the walls went, but at least it was made of concrete.

We sat in one of the bedrooms all night, rain drenching down. Heart breaking for the women seeing everything destroyed. In the morning I got in touch with John Moffat and some of the brewery people. You couldn't really drive anywhere. There was so much debris, so many powerlines on the road. We moved into the local school, a two storey building. The top section was demolished but underneath was quite good. We lived in there for a week. We had mattresses, plenty of food. The super markets just opened their doors, go for your life, help yourselves. We got a barbecue going and bathed down in the local creek. Terry Tweddell was manager of the wine and spirits side. His house wasn't so badly damaged, partly livable. He didn't move into the school.

Doug Farrell said all the wives and children were air-lifted out of Darwin and they were away for a month until the electric power came on.

Melbourne sent up their top brewing man, Wal Fisher, and engineer, Jack Kelaher. They came up to do an assessment to decide whether Carlton should pull out altogether or decide whether we would repair the place and get going on. There was doubt then whether even Darwin would continue. There were even rumours that another cyclone was on its way. They decided we would rebuild. The pair worked on the job, physically, for a week, cleaning up. Actually I was very grateful to them. I was so shocked I guess I lost all sense of values.

They said to me, 'What are you going to do on Sunday?' I said. 'I guess I'll go to my house. There's a catamaran out there.' So I went out to my place. The catamaran was in a shed, undamaged. But Jack and Wally said, 'What are you going to do with all of this?' Amongst the ruins there was a fridge, shovel, spade, garden gear . . . 'Not worth worrying about,' I replied. 'It'll go to the tip.' Well, they came back, filled a seven tonne truck and it all went into the new place when I eventually re-built. Even rescued the garbage bin.

Where did we live? We were in the school for a week. The company owned the Don Hotel in Darwin. We all moved in there. For a time there was no power but there were a couple of generators and there was a gas stove. We survived. Our families returned, they moved in with us. So the whole Carlton team was there for about four months. It took us three months to get the brewery going again.

So Northern Territory draught came on stream again. But oddly enough Victoria Bitter remained the champion in the Northern Territory and in north Queensland and still is. Maybe it is just that extra taste of bitterness that appeals to the more rugged northern taste. Not so everywhere else; Foster's Lager was the new champion.

Some cartoon characters, originally minor figures to their creators, develop such huge personalities that they take over the whole strip. This happened with Foster's Lager in the mid 1970s. In 1977 Foster's headed Carlton Draught as the brand leader for the first time.[9] It was the unquestioned champion in Australia and it was making its presence felt in forty different countries, in New York, Katmandu, New Delhi, Barbados, the United Kingdom, Hong Kong, even Heard Island in the Antarctic.[10] The *Financial Review* reported from London in 1976 that no longer was Foster's just a drink for the devoted Australian bigots in Earl's Court. It was suddenly the in thing in darkest Brixton. London's West Indian, Pakistan, Indian and African populations developed a taste for the Australian amber fluid during the long hot summer of 1975 while watching cricket.[11] There was more to it than that though; CUB had an extraordinary ally in the Australian satirist Barry Humphries.

In the 1960s Humphries created a comic strip, *The Wonderful World of Barry McKenzie*, for an English magazine. McKenzie had a big shovel jaw, a broad-brimmed hat and the sweet naive innocence of the visiting colonial. He had an exotic, earthy Ocker line of talk, created entirely by Humphries, and he was always being treated mercilessly by rapacious, crafty Poms. Above all Bazza McKenzie had a huge insatiable desire for the amber fluid, the chilled article. He couldn't drink the warm, flat English stuff. Always he was yearning for an ice-cold Foster's.

The *Adventures of Barry McKenzie* came out as a comic book and for three years it was banned by the Commonwealth Government. It was too obscene for tender Australian minds.[12] But then the very government that banned the book as an obscenity put up $250 000 through the Common-wealth Film Development Corporation and Barry Humphries went to London with director Bruce Beresford to make the film version. Barry Crocker, who had a chin exquisitely designed for the part, played Bazza, and there were many interesting minor roles such as Spike Milligan as the repulsive concierge of the Kangaroo Valley Hotel and Dennis Price as Mr Gort, who had a penchant for dressing up as a schoolboy and being thrashed. Carlton provided unlimited stocks of blue-label Foster's for the film and although CUB directors winced over the Ocker Bazza behaviour it was extraordinary publicity. Bazza rarely had a can of the chilled article out of his grip. He could open his Foster's with superb elegance with one hand. The movie was a sensation in Australia. It received punishing reviews in Britain, but people still went to see it. In 1971 people in Britain might have wondered at the name Foster, but by the end of 1973, thanks to Bazza, it was a household word. In 1975 Foster's Lager made up 80 per cent of the million gallons of Australian beer that went to Britian.[13]

Even more remarkable things happened in the United States, without the help of Bazza McKenzie. All Brand Importers Inc., with some trepi-dation, started importing in 1972 and incredibly sales doubled every year. It gained notoriety with the Australians when they challenged for the America's Cup at Newport. It was exported to the US in the 26-ounce can which caused some interest. Tennis players Fred Stolle and John New-combe were photographed drinking from the big blue and white can. Soon the big can began to appear on the supermarket shelves right across the US. It stood out amongst all the little cans and bottles of US and European beers. 'They used to mistake the beer cans for motor oil,' said Ed Smythe who ran a grocery store near the United Nations in New York. 'They'd say "Why the hell are you chilling oil along with the Budweiser?" ' One Chicago bar-owner who sold a lot of Foster's swore that women partic-ularly loved the big cans. 'They drink the beer and take the cans home,' he said. 'I think they cut the tops off and grow plants and stuff in 'em.'[14]

Sales went up and up. In July 1976 there was a shipment of a million cans of Foster's, which won the accolade for the largest single consignment of foreign beer to enter the port of New York. There was some very useful promotion. Brandishing a Foster's can John Newcombe told an interviewer that he 'drank five of these after every five-set match'. Robert Redford gave the word to an interviewer he had been drinking Coors, but because he didn't like the brewer's right-wing politics he had changed to Foster's. Paul Newman and Billy Carter, the president's brother, were also photo-graphed with Foster's.[15]

By 1978 Foster's was well up on the charts for imported beers in the US behind Heineken and Carlsberg. The company introduced a new look Foster's Lager stubby, designed to meet American standards with 12 fluid ounces. The advertising agencies plotted their publicity to provoke nos-talgia amongst US servicemen who had been to Australia during the Second World War, the Korean and Vietnam wars. One poster showed an Aus-tralian soldier, digger hat and all, holding his can of Foster's with the message 'A Taste of Australia'. The figures for 1977 were 10 million litres of Australia beer to the US, almost all of it Foster's Lager.[16]

The Carlton group of companies made a profit of $21.1 million in 1977–78, but it sounds tiny when compared with the tax. CUB paid $257.6

John Newcombe, showing his patriotic fervour as an Australian 'ambassador' to the United States.

million to various governments in that year. Government won twelve times more money than the shareholders. If this wasn't enough, the August budget brought in another 32 per cent hike in the tax rate. This meant 52 cents tax a litre. Canberra now expected drinkers to provide a $1000 million a year. No beer drinkers on earth worked as devotedly for their government as Australians.[17] To survive such taxation savagery a company had to be extraordinarily efficient and successful. The pattern continued, every year there were fewer breweries. Courage succumbed on 26 May 1978 when Tooth & Co. in New South Wales took over the Courage brewery for 11.4 million. It brought back memories. On a happy optimistic October day in 1968 Sir Maurice Nathan, the chairman, had smashed a celebratory bottle of Courage across a delivery truck, tasted a sample drop and pronounced it 'delicious'. The estimated share of the market was 10 per cent. 'But I know it will be more than that,' said he. Ten years later it was under 5 per cent and going down. The brewery had never paid a dividend and it had lost $8 million. Eric Beecher in the *Age* commented, 'The great master plan to knock Carlton & United off its pedestal has not worked ... Not surprisingly the two major shareholders, the giant Amatil group (British Tobacco, food products) and Courage UK have had enough'.[18]

A dramatically successful poster for the promotion of Foster's in the United States.

In the final year Courage had done everything to lift its game: it stopped copying the Carlton product; it brought out a high alcohol beer, Tankard; it launched a beer called Flinders designed to appeal to younger people who had been brought up on spirits and wine; it tried Ace, a low calorie beer, also aimed at the younger drinker; but nothing had worked. Courage's general manager, David Angus, blamed their failure on the conservatism of Victorian drinkers. 'It's very hard to make a better beer than our competitor makes,' he said.[19]

Courage had only one real triumph, football. For any company which wants to achieve glory in Melbourne it is almost compulsory to sponsor an Australian Rules Football team. Between March and November all serious thoughts are devoted to this subject. Courage had the good fortune to be sponsor of North Melbourne when it appeared in four Grand Finals. North Melbourne won the Australian Rules premiership in 1975. It didn't win in 1976, but it was there in the Grand Final. In 1977 there was a tie, so there had to be a replay, which North Melbourne won. The TV companies estimated at least four million Australians watched the game on television, so Courage was never out of sight. There was a Courage logo on the chest of every North Melbourne footballer. Whether this inspired many people to 'Take Courage' is open to conjecture, but sponsorship does not come cheaply. It cost Courage $44 000 for the year 1977. Meanwhile CUB, which was scoring rather better with sales, backed Richmond which finished down the ladder.[20]

Tooth & Co. bought 30.6 million shares at 32 cents each which gave it 87.5 per cent of the capital. Finance writers generally described the purchase as a bargain and a very sound move for Tooth. Tooth already had lost 10 per cent of its NSW market to Toohey's. The company had been very slow in reforming after the Second World War and was burdened with two old breweries. Their decision was to close down the old Waverley Brewery and completely modernise the Broadway plant. All this reconstruction left them short of capacity and they hoped that Courage at Broadmeadows, Victoria, would fill the gap. Tooth's managing director,

Mr H. T. Alce, said not only would they continue to produce Courage and confront CUB, but they would use Broadmeadows to produce KB Lager and Reschs to supply the NSW market.[21]

There was all sorts of speculation on what this meant for CUB. The *Financial Review* said Trade Practices Act or not, it could never have happened in Sir Reginald Fogarty's day. The enterprising Sir Reg would have found some way to acquire Courage before Tooth came to town. 'The monopoly of Bouverie Street is broken for ever,' said the *Financial Review*, and it saw open warfare ahead between Sydney and Melbourne.[22] James McCausland of the *Age* thought there would be sighs of relief in Bouverie Street. There had been rumours that Toohey's, coupled with Philip Morris were moving in. Philip Morris was the huge tobacco group that had acquired America's Miller brewing company. It could have been an awesome combination.[23] There were, however, no obvious signs of shivering or fear inside the bluestone at Bouverie Street. 'We're not losing any sleep about it,' said the CUB general manager, Lou Mangan. 'We've won the first battle,' he said, and he doubted whether Tooth could be any more aggressive than Courage. Their products KB and Reschs were virtually unknown in Victoria, but Foster's was known everywhere.[24]

If there was to be aggression maybe the worst came on 2 November when bandits robbed the $109 000 payroll from Carlton & United's Abbotsford plant. The bandits drove a white van through the South Audley Street gate at 12.30 p.m. and pulled up outside the personnel time-keeper's pay office. A Mayne Nickless guard standing in the trucking yard at the entrance to the building had a sawn-off shot gun pushed in his back. A bandit told him: 'Turn around and I'll blow your head off'. Then the bandit grabbed a .32 calibre pistol from the guard's pistol holder. One bandit stayed in the van and another covered the guard while another two men went into the time-keeper's office. They told four people inside to lie down on the floor. A CUB watchman tried to close the gate on the van but they told him to back off or he would be shot. CUB forklift driver, John Halos, said the raid was over in a minute. Some men had already been paid when the van pulled up. 'One bandit kept watch at the door with his gun pointed at the guard,' John Halos said. 'He also pointed the gun at me and other blokes in the yard. I saw the gun and got out of the way ... blokes were going everywhere.' The bandits wore beanies and rubber gloves. About eighty-five pay packets had been distributed when they struck. After grabbing the money they drove off quickly. Police found the van abandoned near the corner of Victoria Parade and Grosvenor Street.[25]

Meanwhile there were troubles in Queensland. CUB conquered north Queensland back in the days of Edward VII and that situation never changed, but southern Queensland was a different tale. Queensland considers itself the most Australian of states, and is not too sure about the others; it worries about creatures who come across the border and is sensitive to the interloper, to the take-over from outside. Brisbane had seen almost all its big stores and many of its firms taken over from the south and now the manager of local business tended to be a pink-cheeked young fellow from Melbourne on trial before he went on to greater things with the parent company. Brisbane was the testing and training ground for the young. So Melbourne beer was only just tolerated. Melbourne

Bitter and Victoria Bitter were ugly names because they were reminiscent of the south. There was intense loyalty to the local brand, Castlemaine Fourex. It mattered little that it was a Victorian name and had its origins in Castlemaine, Victoria, it was as much Queensland as were mud crabs and Moreton Bay figs. CUB was bashing hard against this competition and not even gaining 10 per cent of the market.

Then came the strike. It has always been the tradition in Australia to have beer strikes at Christmas. Christmas means heat, warmth, relaxation, and even as far back as 1890 when Foster's was struggling for survival consumption would double at Yuletide. Summers may have been warmer then, but it was the Melbournian Christmas heat that saved the company from penury. So the unions right through to the 1970s would save their grievances for mid-December, the time of maximum twisting power.

Cairns Bitter Ale, 1971–72.

The nation's worst beer strike, however, hit Queensland on 7 September 1978. It began with Castlemaine Perkins Ltd, then Carlton & United five days later. The combined brewery unions were claiming a $25 a week wage increase, disability payments of $12 a week, increased penalty rates and increased benefits for long service leave, penalty rates, Christmas bonus, sick leave, annual leave plus a thirty-five hour week.[26] Immediately semi-trailer loads of bottled beer trundled across the border from New South Wales, but the operations had to be delicate and clandestine. Like the smuggling of heroin, trucks came by night. The Transport Workers Union went on strike and declared a ban on the shipment of beer into Queensland.[27] Furthermore, it was not done for one brewery to appear to be profiting too openly from the misery of another. Strikes are most contagious. Carlton & United could not supply beer from Melbourne for fear of spreading the damage to Bouverie Street. The strike did not affect CUB's brewery in Cairns. The Cairns Brewery maintained a level of production agreed between the combined brewery unions and the management. There were no extra bottles on the line, so north Queensland remained happy and sated while the south became increasingly parched and desperate.[28]

One reporter, Max Jessop, recorded on September 27 that Brisbane was lonesome, morbid and dreary: ' "Even the fish look as if they've had it," groaned one drinker as he mumbled into his Scotch and looked into the pub's mini aquarium.' Some hoteliers were air-freighting beer from Papua New Guinea, but many hotels were closing their doors, the night trade was disappearing and hundreds of barmen and barmaids were being laid off.[29] Ultimately most of the beer during the strike came from Toohey's brewery at Grafton, Tooth's in Sydney and Tooth's Courage brewery at Broadmeadows.[30] There were all sorts of side effects. Brisbane barmaids reported constant broken fingernails from rip-top cans. Packaged beer only was available in most clubs and bars. Then truck hi-jacking was the new crime. Just like the days of the nineteenth-century highwayman two 20-tonne truckloads of Brisbane-bound southern beer were held up on the road. The rewards were high: a load of beer was worth $20 000 and the commodity was as saleable as cool drinks in the Sahara.[31]

A Brisbane Bitter label of the late 1970s.

Queensland chauvinism became more and more intense. The Liberal member for Merthyr, Don Lane, claimed that Queensland hoteliers were spending $5 million a week buying beer interstate. Furthermore there were terrible suggestions that Queenslanders were becoming accustomed to the taste of southern beer. Perhaps the most curious story, complete with picture, appeared in Brisbane's *Telegraph*. The Queensland racehorse, Charlton Boy, was retired and living at a dairy near Nambour. Charlton Boy was used to drinking regular stubbies of Fourex. According to the Suncoast Dairy managing director, Des Scanlan, he wouldn't drink southern beer. 'Charlie's jacked up completely. He won't touch the southern stuff and now he's getting cranky.'[32] The next day Mr and Mrs J. Carlisle read of Charlton Boy's awful plight. They bought a carton of Fourex in Sydney and had it air-freighted to the Suncoast Dairy. Once again Charlie was consuming two stubbies daily. Similar consideration was not shown to humans.[33]

The strike finally came to an end on 28 November. The breweries' compromise offer was accepted. The new deal was $8 more a week. Beer allowances were up 25 cents to $2.75; meal allowance up 25 cents to $2.75; laundry allowances increased from $2.50 to $3.50; accumulated sick leave increased to seventy-five days after fifteen years' service and to 120 days after twenty years; long service leave was eight weeks after ten years and thirteen weeks after fifteen years; week-end penalty rates were up from time-and-a-half to double-time; an additional set of clothing was awarded, to be replaced if damaged at work, and two pairs of socks were awarded for employees in cold cellars.[34]

The *Financial Review* estimated that Castlemaine Perkins and Carlton had lost the profits on the retail sales of over $50 million worth of beer. A spokesman for CUB commented: 'We're glad it's over. We don't think anyone won.'

CHAPTER FOURTEEN

Who is John Elliott?

The 1980s was the era of the python: it was the age of the merger, the take-over, of one company swallowing the other. The python, being a remarkably elastic creature, could frequently swallow a company infinitely larger than itself. Much depended on the tastiness of the morsel to be devoured. Often the richer, the more successful the morsel, the better the prospect. If it was well run, making profits, free of debt with lots of tangible assets, then swallowing was inevitable. It was a like a plump young rabbit waiting to be eaten.

A new word had come into the language, 'gearing'. You needed to be highly geared, have friendly bankers, and borrow to the limit of your assets. Some operators had more gears than a 20-tonne truck.

In November 1979 Castlemaine Perkins of Brisbane merged with Toohey's of Sydney. It was a $215 million union. Castlemaine offered three shares plus cash for every five Toohey's shares. Castlemaine claimed 75 per cent of the Queensland market and Toohey's 43 per cent of New South Wales, but who swallowed whom was a matter of debate. It was well known that one always had to tread carefully in Brisbane. The Queensland Government was eternally sensitive about predatory southerners, so matters had to be arranged with much delicacy. It was even-handed on paper, with five representatives from each company on the Castlemaine–Toohey's board and Mr E. J. Stewart, formerly of Castlemaine was the chairman. Sir Edward Cohen, chairman of CUB, saw it as a reverse take-over, however. He said 54.5 per cent of the shares were owned by former Toohey's shareholders.[1] The *Age* described it as the biggest merger in the history of Australian brewing but Sir Edward claimed Carlton was still number one.[2]

The whole brewing industry was tense with rumours. CUB was doing very well with a $23.8 million profit to 30 June 1979. Tooth, by tradition the giant of New South Wales, was not performing well. It had been losing ground to the smaller, more aggressive Toohey's. The Tooth profit was $16.3 million, while Toohey's declared $12.5 million. The marriage of Castlemaine–Toohey altered the scene altogether. Apart from making a weight-for-age rival for CUB, it put the final end to the charming old arrangement which went something like 'you stay in your backyard and I'll stay in mine'. There had been a gentlemen's agreement that New South Wales beer would not go into Queensland and vice versa, that Melbourne wouldn't advance into New South Wales beyond the Riverina and vice versa, and that Swan would stay in the far west. Such niceties now were gone for ever.

What would be the next take-over? The *Financial Review* thought Tooth could merge with Swan, South Australian Brewing or Tasmania's Cascade. CUB could take over or merge with Tooth. The *Review* quoted Carlton's general manager, Lou Mangan, however, saying that CUB was not interested in taking over or merging with any other brewer, including Tooth & Co. CUB would stick with what it had always done, making beer in Victoria and Queensland. Valerie Lawson of the *Review* commented that clearly Lou Mangan wouldn't want to be the loser in a battle for Sydney. After all, he had 150 hotels in Victoria, 163 in Queensland and none in Sydney.[3]

There was an eight-week beer strike in Sydney and Tooth's performance went flatter than ever. Its profit for the six months ending 15 September 1980 was down $4.73 million and everybody was saying it was on the market. Yet CUB went in a different direction and bought 33 per cent of Henry Jones on 7 December 1980. The *Financial Review* commented:

> The eventual consequences of sitting on a very large cash flow with no growth were obvious to all at Carlton and United Breweries. Indeed the search for growth at Bouverie Street has so far been like King Arthur and the Holy Grail . . . this was the answer to a brewer's prayers.[4]

Almost everyone applauded the move. It was wise. Henry Jones had taken over Barrett Burston the same year and was the largest producer of malt and hops in Australia. Furthermore Henry Jones was in a joint hop venture with CUB in north-eastern Victoria. *Business Review Weekly* came forward with a remarkable prophecy which hardly anyone noticed:

> Just as John Elliott must now trust Lou Mangan, one day the boot may be on the other foot. For while acquisition of about one third of Henry Jones might greatly increase Carlton's earnings per share after equity accounting and therefore improve the share price, the company must be said to be even more vulnerable . . . Provided Carlton does not increase its interest in Henry Jones above 50 per cent, if there is any strange Carlton buying, Henry Jones can quickly raise the cash and move into the Carlton market. One can assume the buyer is very friendly to John Elliott. And Lou Mangan trusts John Elliott.[5]

There was a fascinating trio involved here, Lou Mangan, John Elliott and John Madden Baillieu. And who was John Elliott? He was almost unknown to the general public, but the *Financial Review* already had produced the headline: 'The Jones Boy is Growing into a Big Lad'.[6]

In 1980 John Elliott was still only 39. He kept on playing football until he was 34, and even though he had several years in the United States he scored 247 games for Carey Grammar Old Boys. His father worked in the ES&A Bank. One son became a doctor, another an accountant and John went to Melbourne University on a BHP scholarship and did an honours commerce degree. It was not easy for the Elliotts. When John Elliott was a teenager his mother and father ran a milk bar so that they could keep the boys at Carey. His mother worked there during the day and his father at night. After he left the university he took a scholarship with Broken Hill Proprietary Limited, a move he would have cause to

John D. Elliott, the Elders IXL head, who led the take-over of CUB in 1983.

remember many years later. He spent two years in their purchasing department, felt he was not moving fast enough, and joined a small accounting company while he was doing his Master of Business Administration. Rod Carnegie was one of the guest speakers while he was doing his MBA. Carnegie at the time was running McKinsey's, the international management consultants. McKinsey's took on Elliott for six years and he spent two years in Chicago problem-solving for big American corporations. At 30 he decided to go out on his own and he convinced Carnegie, the CRA Bank, National Mutual, Baillieu Myer, the Kimpton and Darling families that they should back him for $30 million in a take-over bid for Henry Jones IXL. Just as he had been as a footballer, Elliott was an irresistible force; his powers of persuasion must have been enormous.

The more John Elliott learned about Henry Jones the more he admired him. Sir Henry Jones died of a heart attack, aged 64, in 1926. His famous trade mark was IXL, his abbreviation for 'I Excel'. Elliott admired that line so much he determined never to get rid of it and it is still there in the masthead of Elders IXL. John Elliott commented

The amazing thing is Henry Jones never learned to read or write. We still have some of his original share scrip. He signed his name with an X. But he did know XL and that's why he called it IXL. He was responsible for forming the jam business in Australia, also the fruit canning. He went overseas and started the canned fruit business in South Africa and the United States, both of which until the European community started giving subsidies, were the major canned fruit countries a hundred years later. He was the first to export hops. He started the apple industry in Australia. He tried to convince the apple growers to let him take their apples on consignment to England. They wouldn't, so he bought all their apples, hired a ship, went over there, made a fortune, then all the growers got upset. He was quite a staggering fellow.

By 1972 Henry Jones IXL was asset rich but run down and Elliott reasoned that even if he sold off its assets he would come out in front. He was 31 when he moved in as managing director. The shock in the old firm must have been profound. 'I guess I found it as hard as they did,' Elliot said later.

It took me eighteen months to realise they weren't all my friends — they were the people who reported to me. They had a very old management. There hadn't been a chairman under 65 since the war. One had been 77 and another 82. We reversed the decline in the company.

In eight years he took Henry Jones from a turnover of $40 million to $400 million.

The discussions about the move into Henry Jones were between Elliott, Lou Mangan and John Baillieu. John Baillieu was a typical Baillieu, athletic figure, grey hair, sun-tanned face, good-looking; his wife a collector of art and fine antiques. Like most of the older Baillieus he preferred it when his name did not appear in the newspapers. He grew up in Toorak, went to school at Melbourne Grammar, then on to Trinity College, Melbourne University, then Magdalen College, Oxford, for his MA. In 1936 he was a barrister at the Inner Temple.

There were two dynasties involved in the Carlton Brewery, the Baillieu and the Cohen families. The chairman was nearly always a Cohen and the deputy-chairman was nearly always a Baillieu. The Baillieu tradition began with William Lawrence Baillieu who married Bertha, daughter of Edward Latham, founder of Carlton Brewery Ltd. W. L. Baillieu started as a bank teller and he used to crew on Edward Latham's yacht. Latham was not impressed when romance blossomed between young Baillieu and his daughter, so he did what fathers are still doing today and took his daughter on a world trip. It did not work; when he returned W. L. was still waiting and in their absence he had left the bank, gone into real estate and was on his way to making one of his several fortunes. So W. L. became chairman of the Carlton Brewery. Meanwhile Montague Cohen was chairman of the Foster Brewery and between them they masterminded the great merger which created Carlton & United Breweries in 1907. W. L. Baillieu did not remain a director for long, he was too busy. He was succeeded on the board in 1908 by Richard Percy Clive Baillieu, his younger brother. He was the C. in the firm of E. L. & C. Baillieu sharebrokers. E. L. and C. were W. L.'s second and third oldest brothers. Clive was succeeded by son Marshall Lawrence Baillieu, who was chairman of North Broken Hill Holdings, and then John Madden Baillieu, son of Maurice Howard Baillieu, another of W. L.'s brothers, took over from him in 1946. M. H. Baillieu was on the board from 1931 until he died in 1961.

John Baillieu recalls that he and Edward Cohen both joined the board at the same time when they came out of the army after the Second World War. 'It's remarkable,' he said,

> We used to run against each other. I was at Melbourne Grammar and he was at Scotch College. Eddie held the public school record for the 100 yards for many years. He was a very good sprinter. I remember when we were about 10 years of age, my father arranged for us to run off to see who was the fastest. So we were taken to a paddock and the race was set up. Funny, neither of us can remember now who won. We raced again at University. I represented Trinity and he was running for Ormond. There was no doubt who won that time. Eddie was the University champion.

John Baillieu was to be involved in far more dramatic board decisions than those of the previous Baillieu generations. He says Charles Goode, senior partner of Potter Partners came to him.

> He had the selling of the Commercial Bank's holding in Henry Jones IXL. They wanted to get out. 'Do you think the brewery would be interested?' he said. Lou Mangan had heard about it and he had expressed an interest. We thought we would be less vulnerable to take-overs if we expanded and got into other areas. So we put it to the board and it was accepted.

This was the start of a new era of diversification. John Baillieu remembers:

> Until we went into Henry Jones the company had never extended itself or borrowed anything significantly. They didn't believe in that. That was the old fashioned argument, never spend what you don't own. When I came back from the war we bought a place in the country. I bought it, then went to my father and said, 'I've finalised it. They will take 50 per cent down and the balance in six months'. Dad said, 'You tell them that unless they take the lot now I will

not go on with the deal'. That's the way it was. He never owed a penny in his life. Dad had been through the land boom and bust and had seen too much of the sufferings caused by over-borrowing.

But if CUB was ungeared, like a vintage bicycle, very rapidly it was to become a 10-speed. On 6 March 1981, the company spent $2.4 million on 750 000 shares in Tasmania's Cascade brewery. This raised its stake from 8.7 per cent to 17.85. Lou Mangan told reporters: 'We want to preserve Cascade's independence'.[7] He was just being the general protecting his rear flank. He did not want Castlemaine–Toohey or anybody else establishing a nice handy base just across the water. The next move was to buy 2 408 000 shares in South Australia Brewing to increase the company holding to 22.7 per cent. Lou Mangan wanted to protect the company flank there also. Lou Mangan in one of his rare private interviews told the *Australian* the company was now adopting a role of not putting all its eggs in one basket. It had chosen Henry Jones because it was a growth company with good earnings, a good record and very good management. 'To think that John Elliott or somebody else is going to come into this organisation and run it would be the furthest thing from our mind.'[8]

If gearing was to be had now the predators were working in overdrive. Soon CUB was to be associated with Henry Jones far more closely than the Carlton directors ever anticipated. Just a month later on 31 March 1981 the morning newspapers had big headlines. The *Age* called it 'The Billion Dollar Day'. There was a formal announcement that Elder Smith Goldsbrough Mort and Henry Jones IXL would merge to create a $500 million pastoral and food business. Under the deal Elders would offer one share or $4.40 cash for each Jones share and Carlton & United Breweries would buy 12.6 million shares offered by BT Australia, a merchant bank. After converting its Jones scrip to Elders scrip and buying the BT parcel, CUB expected to hold 35.4 per cent of Elders. On the surface it appeared that Elders was taking over Henry Jones, but it did not work that way. It was part of the deal that John Elliott would be chief executive of the new company. The chairman of Elders, Sir Norman Young, now 70, would step down, and the new chairman would be a Henry Jones nominee. The *Age* commented:

> John Elliott has come a long way since he arrived back in Australia from America ten years ago looking for something to do . . . he has achieved more in that time than many do in a lifetime and it appears what has happened so far may be only the first chapter in a tale of business success built on an eye for opportunity.[9]

The whole deal was complicated, full of secret moves, and lightning forays. It was to be many months before the public and even the share market fully understood what was going on. It had begun the previous year when Robert Holmes à Court began a sortie into Elders. Holmes à Court was the chief executive of the Bell Group, a South African born maverick entrepreneur, a master take-over expert, and destined to be the richest man in Australia. As soon as Elders came under threat from Holmes à Court, John Elliott called Sir Norman Young and asked if he needed help. The answer was no. But the following March Holmes à Court stepped up his buying, increasing his interest to nigh on 20 per cent. Sir Norman Young and the Elders board became alarmed, some say even panicked, and started looking round for help. Help came from the merchant bankers BT Australia under Chris Corrigan. BT acted for a number of unnamed buyers. The first offer to Holmes à Court was for $4 a share but eventually the market went to $5.

On the Tuesday John Elliott was in Hong Kong, but he returned on the Wednesday morning. Sir Norman Young flew to Melbourne and there were some intense days of negotiation. The price for the 20 per cent of Elders held by BT Australia was $65 million. Elliott did not want to be a mere white knight, the saviour of Elders. If he was putting up the money he wanted to be in control and according to Robert Gottliebsen of *Business Review Weekly*, he was encouraged by his directors, Baillieu Myer and his old colleague Bob Cowper, the former Test cricketer, who had been with him almost from the beginning.[10]

Elliott had a number of options. At one stage he was planning to raise the money himself in America, but then he made the offer on the Saturday morning to Lou Mangan. There were discussions with directors, Sir Edward Cohen, David Darling, John Baillieu, and an emergency meeting of the board on the Sunday. The conservative board was hardly used to such dramatic stuff, and it had only twenty-four hours to make up its mind. As Robert Gottliebsen pointed out this was a dream deal and the whole thing was settled before nightfall.[11] It was all very ironic. When CUB had first started courting Henry Jones and bought the stake from the CBA bank it also bought 8 per cent from Elders. Now it was buying Elders. These were times when it was difficult at any time to know who owned whom, but if there was any winner in the affair, unquestionably it was Robert Holmes à Court. According to those who were good at figures he made a tax free profit of $16.5 million.[12] Both Henry Jones and Elders were suspended from listing on the Melbourne and Adelaide Stock Exchanges. The Adelaide exchange wanted to know the names of the BT clients. After a week Henry Jones and Elders were re-instated, but few people were any wiser as to what had happened. It was to be months before the marriage between Henry Jones and Elders was consummated.

The next move came in mid May. The South Australian Attorney General was not satisfied with the deal. When Holmes à Court originally bought into Elders he gave an undertaking that he would extend the bid to Elders shareholders. Even though he had sold his stock to BT, the Attorney General said he should honour that undertaking. Holmes à Court's Bell Group took legal advice and prepared to renew its offer for 50 per cent of Elders at $5.10 a share. BT Australia mounted an immediate legal challenge and obtained an injunction restraining Bell from proceeding. It was a good time to be in the legal business. But what was CUB to do? If they went into retreat, pulled out, and Holmes à Court moved in, it would be like a game of bridge, they would be extremely vulnerable. Holmes à Court would be poised to take Elders, then CUB as well. The nice little decision to take a third of Henry Jones was now becoming enormous. On 19 May 1981 CUB decided to counter-attack and launched a $139 million bid for 50 per cent of Elders. They offered $5.15. Holmes à Court, no doubt, could have come back with a $6 offer, but he made no move. The acceptance rate was staggering. Carlton was actually offered far more shares than it could handle. In the end CUB acquired 25 500 000 shares and in the annual report the brewery was able to announce that it held 60 per cent of the issued ordinary capital of Elders.

Again, the question was who owned whom. The merger between Elders and Henry Jones still was not complete, but for a short time the runs were on the board. Robert Gottliebsen said:

> Carlton and United Breweries now owns 61 per cent of Australia's largest pastoral company, Elders GM, yet not one of its senior management people has any detailed knowledge of the pastoral industry.[13]

CUB stated very clearly, however, that once the merger went through the CUB holding in Elders/Henry Jones would be 49 per cent. The figure of 49 per cent was extremely sensitive. Gottliebsen said provocatively:

> While Carlton might at present deny any intention of it, once they have 48 per cent of Elders, it would make sense to increase the holding to 51 per cent and make Elders a Carlton subsidiary.[14]

That was not ever part of the agreement. John Elliott wanted to remain in command. He would have tolerated no minority situation. Had CUB done that, unquestionably he would have left and taken his talents elsewhere. In its annual report of 1982 CUB reported that on 17 July 1981 its holding in Elder Smith Goldsbrough Mort Ltd was 61.3 per cent at a price of $184.4 million. Before the end of 1981, however, the wedding of Elders and Henry Jones was consummated and the CUB shareholding shrank back to a tactfully poised 49.4 per cent.[15]

Just keeping up with what was going on in the brewing industry would have left anyone's head reeling. On 5 September 1981 the Bond Corporation, 52 per cent owned by Alan Bond and his family, made a $150 million dollar bid for the Swan Brewery Company. The *Business Review Weekly* described Bond as a very rich man, possibly Australia's richest, the head of a conglomerate which spread across oil, gas, the media, gold and coal mining, property and retail. Swan was renowned for being one of Australia's most modern and efficient breweries run by Lloyd Zampatti, also a famous Perth personality. Like Bob Hawke and the Treasury's John Stone he had been educated at Perth Modern School. And like Alan Bond, Robert Holmes à Court and Garrick Agnew, according to the *Review*, he was a Perth institution. His chauffeur trips home for lunch were part of Perth's character. Zampatti, although an extremely good administrator, had chosen the wrong protector in Holmes à Court; he should have chosen Alan Bond.[16] By October 26 Bond was declaring victory and within a week Zampatti had resigned. After Christmas there was the formal announcement that Lloyd Zampatti, chief executive at Swan for more than ten years, would join Castlemaine–Toohey on 2 March as deputy managing director and on 31 July would succeed Mr Lloyd Hartigan as managing director. 'I have not accepted the new job because of any ill feeling at Swan,' said Zampatti, 'in fact Mr Bond has asked me to stay.'[17]

Meanwhile CUB was making equally remarkable moves. On 25 August, Lou Mangan announced that CUB had made a deal with Watney, Mann & Truman Brewers Ltd to make Foster's Draught under licence in Britain and that it would be on tap in a thousand London pubs by October. It was a logical move; excise was too high in Australia and beer consumption was stagnant, not moving with the rise of population. The way to expand was to make Foster's an international beer. Frank Harold, assistant general manager brewing, said: 'Watney's came to us. We didn't approach them and at first we were a bit sceptical. They wanted a product which wouldn't be confused with all the other European lagers on the UK market'.

The operation had a secret code name, Phoenix, and so as not to attract attention the first meetings between the CUB and Watney's men took place in Singapore. The big problem was the yeast. The quality is fundamental and vital to beer, and the Foster's yeast, of course, was historic. It had gone through countless generations of brews since the first cultures came to Carlton from Professor Jorgensen in Denmark back in 1923, but it was still the same yeast, and considered priceless by the company. As Frank Harold said, it made even gold seem worthless. So the yeast was really the heart and soul of the beer and had to be protected. Frank Harold gave the impression that he would give away the yeast as readily as he would hand over the key to a national treasury. The decision about the yeast had to go all the way to the board and the chairman. Finally a little phial, 56.7 grams, in a briefcase went safe-hand to London. The operation almost had the atmosphere of a John Le Carre mystery.

Australians in London were startled to discover that the Foster's Draught was not the same as Foster's Lager back home. 'It had to be different,' said Frank Harold,

> for two reasons. First Watney's wanted a draught beer, and all draught beers in England are lower gravity beers and lower in alcohol. Then excise in the UK is determined by the gravity. Standard Foster's would rate so high in excise you wouldn't be able to sell it in competition with other draught beers. And you see, in England they drink beer by the pint, you'd have difficulty in drinking Foster's by the pint.

Ted Kunkel, who was superintendent brewing for Victoria, was one of the Carlton team.

> Foster's Draught was just a slightly lower gravity beer than Foster's Lager. We picked a gravity slot we thought would produce a high quality lager beer and went to bat with that. We did a lot of laboratory work in Melbourne before we left for London. Then at Watney, Mann & Truman they undertook a lot of research under our supervision. A tremendous number of flavour parameters were measured and we were bringing samples of trial brews back home for testing. The build up took five or six months. The next step was to produce trial batches on a large scale.

Frank Harold flew to London for the launching of Foster's Draught on 25 August. It was his fourth trip associated with Operation Phoenix. At Australia House in the company of the Australian High Commissioner, Mr R. V. Garland, the Victorian Agent-General, Mr J. A. Rafferty, and Mr Robin Soames, chairman of Watney's, he said:

> My presence here today is unique on at least two counts. Firstly, I am possibly the first man in history to have travelled some 12 000 miles to have a glass of beer. I had that glass of beer last week, gave it my fullest approval and that of my company, and hence we are today to launch Foster's Draught in Britain. Secondly for an Australian brewer to be in England associated with the brewing of an Australian type beer is a full turn of the wheel of history.

He explained that Australia learned its beer drinking habits from England and also how to make it. In our early days we imported English ales and when we started brewing we imported English malt and hops. What's more, they were genuine ales, top-fermented beers, often heavy, warm and sweet. But Foster's was the pioneer, a bottom-fermented lager, made in the German style and served ice cold. Here was a country with a burning summer heat. The lagers served ice cold were what the people wanted and the style swept across the continent. There were some ales brewed, and still are, such as Tooth's Old in Sydney, but they were a very small percentage of the market. England remained the home of ale, the home of top-fermented beer, but in the 1980s Britain started to develop a taste for the lagers of Europe, just as Australia had almost a hundred years ago. So why not Foster's Draught? For ten years now it had been known the length of Britain as Foster's Lager in the can. The logic was there, but would it work? Frank Harold said Watney's launched a $3 million advertising campaign and the result was astonishing. Even though they had fifteen competitors, within two years they had 6 per cent of the UK draught beer market. The share in southern England was 10 per cent.

The success of the campaign had much to do with the remarkable personality of the Australian actor comedian, Paul Hogan. Bruce Siney, marketing director for CUB, recalls that Watney's advertising agency origi-

OPPOSITE PAGE:
Foster's overseas success reaches Scotland. This piper holds a bottle of refreshing Foster's in front of Edinburgh Castle.

The dinkum touch of Paul Hogan was magic for selling Australia and Foster's.

nally wanted to use an English comedian with lots of jokes about Australians. Frank Harold remembers the pilot versions. 'They were awful,' he said, 'Ocker in the extreme'. Bruce Siney said, 'We decided that the man to do it was Paul Hogan. After all he had his own reputation to put on the line. The Australian humour could be double-edged. Very nearly a million Australians pass through London every year. We were very concerned that it could damage us if they got it wrong.' Hoges, the ex-Sydney Harbour Bridge rigger, the ex-plugger for Winfield cigarettes on television, was just as he has always been, Hoges. The first commercial had Hoges saying these words:

> G'day. They've asked me over from Oz to introduce youse all to Foster's Draught, here it is. Cripes! I'd better start with the basics. It's a light, golden liquid, like, except for the white bit on top, the head, and it's brewed from malt, yeast and hops. Technical term is Lager. That's L-a-g-e-r. But everyone calls it Foster's. Ahhh, ripper! Tastes like an angel cryin' on your tongue. Foster's.

In the next advertisement Hoges is outside a London pub in a deluge of rain. The rain had to be turned on for Hogan by courtesy of the local fire brigade. A curious country is England. As it was likely to rain anyway the producers also took out a policy to insure against rain disrupting filming. This time Hoges says:

'Foster's — Australian for Lager' was the key message in taking Foster's to the world.

G'day. You know I can't help thinkin' of Oz and that dry thirst outback. We'd sit there month after month prayin' for rain. When the drought finally broke we had our own special way of celebratin' with a drop or two of the amber nectar. You too can celebrate now that the drought has finally broken.

The advertisement ended with a voice rather more upper crust even than Prince Charles', 'Foster's, the Australian for Lager'. The commercials went through a whole range of very English settings. Hoges is seen at the hunt. 'Reminds me of the days when we chased packs of wild dingoes through the scrub.' And as the hounds set off he remarks: 'It won't take long to catch them pack of funny-looking dingoes'. He goes to a royal garden party, can't find his Foster's, and describes his throat as drier than a drain pipe in a drought. Then he gets into the stalls at the ballet. 'This is just like the dances at home. The girls had to dance with each other too while the boys nicked out for a drop of the amber nectar. Struth! There's a bloke down there with no strides on.' Hoges was so popular the commercials made him a cult figure and Peter Smark, London correspondent for the *Age*, described it as the marketing sensation of the decade.[18]

Promotion was now the story everywhere. Sales doubled in Japan and Carlton beers were selling to sixty-five countries around the world. One columnist reported with deep nostalgia the finding of an empty can on a lonely road in Wyoming. Foster's was going to Abu Dhabi in the United Arab Emirates, to Dubai on the Persian Gulf, to Yap a tiny Pacific island in the Caroline group. Foster's was at the Down Under Club at the Australian Embassy in Moscow and diplomats reported often it had to be kept warm just so that it could be drunk. An Australian nine-man army team took CUB beer to the Himalayas and when they reached the top of 6333-metre Mt Tseringma they downed a can of Foster's. They had to wrap cloth around the can so that the cold metal would not stick to their hands.[19] The world-wide activities won CUB an Australian Government export award in 1980. The strangest place for a CUB product, however, was perhaps this. Alphonse Tobin, one of the founders of Tobin Brothers funeral directors was talking about his thirty-nine years in the business.

It was a hot summer's day in the days when we still wore long coats, top hats and starched collars. We had made a quick dash from Fawkner to Keilor to bury a hotelkeeper. We were about to screw down when in rushed the head barman. He was clasping a cold bottle of Melbourne Bitter. We looked at him gratefully . . . until he explained that his boss wanted to be buried with a bottle of the best. So in went the bottle and on went the lid.[20]

For promotion, the badge, emblem, the symbol for CUB was always a beautifully groomed team of Clydesdales pulling a brewery waggon. Even when horses had long since ceased to deliver beer, the brewery always kept a few teams of horses for promotion work. If anyone could be called Mr Clydesdale it was Paddy Ryan, who retired from the brewery in 1987 after forty-five years. Paddy Ryan used an old brewery truck and trailer, big enough to carry four horses, waggon, plus feed, and he would use his outfit to visit country shows, fairs and festivals from South Australia across to New South Wales. In 1980 he took his Clydesdales to the Sydney Show for the first time. 'The idea, of course,' said Paddy,

was to promote Melbourne beer and we actually delivered beer around Sydney in the grand old style. We went to licensed grocers and pubs in the main streets,

George Street, Kent Street and all around the metropolitan area. In the Clydesdale events at the Show there were only two classes, the fours and the pairs and we got firsts in both. We have won prizes there ever since.

Amongst the horses taken to Sydney was old Lager, aged 29. 'We had to take him,' said Paddy. 'He would have fretted if we had left him home. He won a third prize in the single horse show. The judge said, "He'll be better when he settles down. He's a flighty young thing". That's how good he was, flighty at 29.'

Paddy said the horse era with the brewery came to an end in 1952. They were being phased out progressively for trucks, but 1952 was the finish. At the peak of operations the brewery had two hundred horses; it was part of Melbourne life seeing the brewery waggons rumbling down Flinders Street towards the docks. The stables were on the present site of the hop extractor plant in Ballarat Street, Carlton. 'They were amazing,' he said.

Carlton's Black Bess, winner of the first prize at the 1928 Royal Melbourne Show. Bill Murphy, at the reins, and George Barker, standing, were in charge of the Carlton Clydesdales.

In the old days the horse would go all the way to Frankston [41 km] with their loads of beer, all the way through St Kilda Junction, out along the Nepean Highway. They didn't change horses. They'd go down and back. When trucks came in they would go as far as Moorabbin and contractors would take over from there. Traffic never worried them. The fellow coming back from Frankston, could be drunk, or he could be sound asleep simply from fatigue, but the horses would know the way back to the brewery. The stablemen would be there to greet them, unharness them, have their feed ready, put their beds down and put them away.

In Paddy's opinion the horses have always been smart, just as smart as their drivers. He said he used to go to the city every Friday on promotion work.

> If we didn't stop at the Melrose Hotel opposite Royal Park in Flemington Road, Flash, the end horse, would prop and refuse to move. The publican used to feed him apples, spearmints and Steam Rollers. One day at the Fox & Hounds Hotel in Flinders Street, they filled him up with buckets of beer. Got him drunk. He still wouldn't go past the Melrose on his way home. He wanted his spearmints and Steam Rollers.

Both horses and men had to be powerful creatures. They used to have teams of fours and pairs, but mostly pairs. They could pull a load of forty-one 18-gallon barrels. One man would be expected to drive the waggon, unload the barrels. 'To get the kegs off,' said Paddy,

> they used skids and they would roll them onto a bag of corks. Then putting them into the cellar they lowered them with ropes. Strong? They were all big fellers. I knew one feller in particular, Joe Bretherton at the Abbots brewery. They used to have bets. One day I saw him pick up a 36 gallon keg, just like that, and put in on the back of a truck.

By tradition the horses are all named after the product. In Paddy's team there was the leader, Victor, show name Victoria Bitter. The other leader was Michael, show name Abbots Lager. Prince was Crown Lager, 19-year-old Flash was Melbourne Bitter and Herbie was Foster's Lager.

Paddy stopped going to Sydney in 1983. CUB needed its own team to step up promotion in New South Wales, and it wanted something more imposing, a shift from four-horse to six-horse teams. The headquarters for the team was in Taree. So Terry Goodear took over. Terry was born in 1953 and grew up at rural Mt Macedon in Victoria. Always he was fascinated by horses. He used to sneak into local riding schools or pony shows in the hope of getting a ride. He used to ride, too, with the local milkman and that caused a disaster when he tripped, and fell under the milk cart. The wheels went over him and broke both his legs. Terry says he was so obsessed with horses his father used to dock his pocket money to bring him into line. When he was 16 he moved to Melbourne and worked at Flemington Racetrack. For several years he did everything. He was a strapper, a work rider. He owned, trained and drove trotters, and made the simple discovery, like many before him, that horse racing is not always the path to fortune. So he joined the transport division at CUB, drove trucks, and for a time he even chauffeured the chairman, Sir Edward Cohen. But Terry would go to the Showgrounds, sit up in the stand and admire those horses. His interest was more in four hoofs than four wheels, so the company asked him if he would form the Clydesdale team in New South Wales.

Terry went to stud breeders throughout Victoria and NSW, selecting horses for size, deep bay colour, matching legs and blazes on the face. Then CUB bought a special float, 12.5 metres long, fitted with padded berths for each horse. At the time it was the biggest float in Australia. Not only did it carry the horses, but the waggon too. The waggon was beautiful, rebuilt from three old original beer waggons used for deliveries

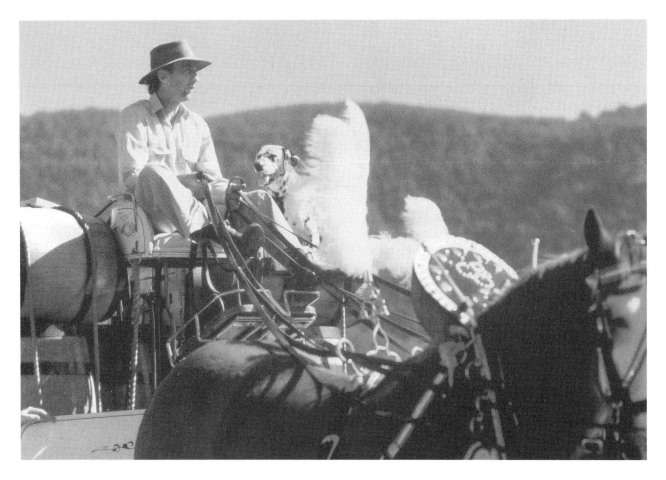

Terry Goodear with his mate, Carlton, the Dalmatian.

back in the early 1900s. It was luxury accommodation. There was even a small dining space for the grooms.

Terry had to start from the beginning. Many people told him it could not be done. No one could handle a six-in-hand into the Showgrounds and it would be absurd to try in city streets. But he did it, training, training, training, often still worrying over his horses at midnight. His horses had all the classic brand names, but there was a ring-in, Carlton, a Dalmatian bitch. Terry found Carlton on the way to work. She was starving, covered in eczema and savage. He nursed her back to health, and trained her to sit up beside him and bark the command to set the team in action. It was a nice turn of events because Dalmatians, by tradition, have a natural affinity with horses. Back in the nineteenth century they used to run with the waggons, the coaches and the fire engines, diving around and under the horses, keeping predatory dogs at bay. After the success at Taree, the Victorian team was also expanded from four to six with Mike Thill in charge. Mike was also an experienced horseman. He spent time in Britain handling Prince Philip's famous coach horses and he drove the Queen's horses at a show in Windsor Great Park.

Paddy Ryan, as he went to retirement, was still heavily biassed in favour of the horse. He felt still that it was a better deal and more economical to use horses on runs up to 7 or 8 kilometres around the city. Difficult to manoeuvre? 'Certainly not,' he says.

You can train them to back, go forward, go anywhere. And a good horse will last you twice as long as a truck. What's more, they are mates. Big though they are, they love to be petted. They snuggle up to you. I talk to them all the time. Start talking to a truck and they'll think you're out of your mind.

Meanwhile, the rest of the brewery seemed to be winding up like a rotary motor, going faster and faster. In August 1981 there were reports that the great Dutch brewing company Heineken was about to buy the Courage brewery at Broadmeadows. Tooth & Co. had taken over the Courage brewery for $12 million in 1979 and had been using it both to try to break into Victoria and supplement its Sydney market. As the finance writers put it, sales had been less than exciting. Maybe Heineken was deterred by the Courage experience, maybe it was deterred by the almost fanatical chauvinism and loyalty of the Melbournian drinker but it made no move. Tooth was said to be offering a half share for $12 million.[21] In 1982 Tooth & Co., now owned by Adelaide Steamship Co., was advertising the Courage plant all around the world. CUB did not need another plant at Broadmeadows but it was too good, too modern to be left there, idle, waiting to be picked up by a competitor. The company bought it for $20 million, almost three times the plant's written-down book value. John Spalvins of Adelaide Steam and chairman of Tooth & Co. said he was 'quite satisfied' with the price.[22] Lou Mangan said the brewery would become a regional warehouse. As for Heineken, there was just a touch of irony that CUB became the Australian agent for Heineken beers. Lou Mangan said the next time he visited Amsterdam he reminded the Heineken directors how easily it could have been the other way round.

Just before Christmas there was a sad end to the chapter. Sir Maurice Nathan, the man who turned the first sod with such optimism and ebullience at the Courage brewery in 1968, died aged 68. Obituary writers recalled how Sir Maurice, when he was invited to turn the first sod, scorned the shiny shovel offered to him and unnerved both officials and pressmen by climbing on to a bulldozer. Thereupon he thundered towards the ceremonial site and gouged out some sod, leaving a giant-sized cavity.[23]

As if 1982 had not already been filled with sufficient beer-laden shocks, in October the Government of Victoria announced it would allow hotel bars to trade on Sundays. One of the first to get a trading licence the following year was the Princes Bridge Hotel, better known as Young & Jackson's. Not only was it operating on a Sunday, right opposite St Paul's Cathedral, but it was the home of the famous nude, *Chloe*, generally considered to be on a par with the stuffed effigy of the horse Phar Lap as Melbourne's greatest tourist attraction. *Chloe*, painted by Jules Lefebvre of Paris came to Melbourne for the International Exhibition of 1880 and caused a regrettable fuss when she was offered on loan to the National Gallery. *Chloe* of course was utterly naked, but what really outraged respectable citizens was that the gallery was showing her to the public on a Sunday. 'Can it be right,' said one letter writer to the newspapers, 'that a mother cannot take her young daughter to a public gallery, never to speak of her sons, without her cheeks tingling with shame?'[24] Heaven knows what mother and sons would have thought had they entered Young & Jackson's after matins on a Sunday in 1983.

CHAPTER FIFTEEN

Elders IXL – CUB

The history of Australia is tied up with maintaining a sweet balance of power between Melbourne and Sydney. Prime ministers with their cabinets have had to be careful to maintain not only a sensible stratum of Protestants as opposed to Catholics, but also not too many Victorians over New South Wales people or vice versa. Royal and political visitors have had to be careful not to show too great a love for either city and they have had to be careful not to prefer one to the other. The best example of this was the visit of the US President, Mr L. B. Johnson, in 1966. The programme was arranged carefully, four hours for the President in Sydney and four hours in Melbourne. The *Bulletin* in Sydney commented, 'No doubt the discussions took place at the highest level on the fearful dangers of one city getting one second more than the other. The high office of the President of the United States simply could not afford to get involved'.[1] There was something of a non-aggression pact between the two cities. Melbourne newspapers did not invade Sydney although they made their assaults in every other city, and neither did Sydney papers invade Melbourne. The brewers also kept their distance. The cities viewed each other with respectful contempt. There was an old saying in Sydney: only two good things ever came out of Melbourne — the beer and the Hume Highway to Sydney. This, of course, was not quite a true statement. On the first Tuesday in November they did have a certain admiration for the Melbourne Cup and they would willingly have transferred it to Randwick.

From the beginning of the 1980s CUB was seriously trying to build its market in Sydney, and in February 1982 the *Age* stated:

> In less than six months CUB has won about $12 million in retail sales with Foster's, Victoria Bitter and Carlton Draught in Sydney alone, which brings its share of the total NSW market to just over 10 per cent. CUB's public affairs General Manager, Paul Ormonde, said: 'There does seem to be developing a certain prestige attached to drinking a Victorian beer with a reputation for quality in New South Wales. Research shows that our average Sydney drinker is under 35, a white collar worker with a middle to high income who lives in the better suburbs.'

At trendy oases like the Royal Hotel in Paddington, Carlton drinkers were outnumbering Tooth drinkers two to one.[2] Tooth was the vulnerable brewery in New South Wales. The business journals for the past year had been writing that it was in trouble, losing money, with an astonishing down-curve in sales. Foster's was doing well as a newcomer, but Toohey's was doing even better. So the finance journalists were speculating who would be the buyer — Castlemaine–Toohey's, Alan Bond, CUB? Tooth & Co. had always been the big one in New South Wales, the brewery with the undisputed lion share of the market. A Holmes à Court with the cash flow of Tooth's in the early 1960s could have bought anything. The Kent Brewery on Broadway, just beyond Central Station, is the oldest mainland brewery in Australia. Only Cascade in Hobart is older.

John Tooth, late of Kent, a general merchant and commission agent, and his brother-in-law, Charles Newnham, a brewer, founded Tooth & Co. They bought 4½ acres at the head of Black Wattle Creek in 1834. It was a lovely spot for a brewery, hardly any houses and a splendid supply of good water. They started trading on 5 October 1835 and products for sale were X, XX and XXX ale. Tooth was the first brewery in Australia to use crosses, thus indicating the strength and quality of their various beers. The prices were 1s for single X, 1s 6d for double X and 2s 6d a gallon for triple X.[3] Tooth's Single X appeared on some noble occasions; take, for example, this 1851 advertisement in the *Sydney Morning Herald*:

> Grand Civic Feast — Required on 1st proximo on which date the Right Worshipful the Mayor retires from office: 30 ham sandwiches, 30 ox tongue sandwiches, with 30 pints of the best Cape (decanted) and 30 pints in pewter of Tooth's single X, for use of the Mayor, Aldermen, and councillors of the body incorporate . . . The contractor will be obliged to serve up the repast in a similar elegance and splendour as the celebrated and much admired Dejeuners a la Flood during the Mayoralty of 1849. The Aldermen and councillors are required to appear in civic costume. For particulars inquire at the Town Hall. God Save the Queen.[4]

Tooth's took over Resch's Brewery in 1929 and so the giant became larger and larger. It was responsible for the marvellous mirrors that appeared inside and outside New South Wales hotels. They depicted sporting and social scenes. It was always nice to see sporting heroes triumphing never with a hair out of place. Many reasons have been given for the decline of Tooth & Co. Lou Mangan said in its earlier days Tooth was bigger than CUB. Until 1970 it had 75 per cent of the New South Wales trade, which was by far the biggest market for beer in Australia. Postwar they were too slow to modernise and when the time came to rebuild the Kent Brewery it was too late. They had to split their activities, brewing at Waverley, Lismore and Broadmeadows. The quality of their product went down and so the number of their customers decreased. Then Tooth always had a stranglehold on New South Wales; it felt it didn't have to do anything because it owned or controlled most of the hotels. Toohey's made their first breakthrough when New South Wales created registered clubs in 1956. Toohey's went on tap in all the poker machine boosted Leagues clubs. Then came the removal of the tied house system under the Trade Practices Act in 1979. This was the beginning of the end.

There were other reasons. According to David Austin, CUB's Sydney marketing manager, Toohey's advertising was so much better.

When we were looking at penetration of the Sydney market, we did our research

Resch's Special Export Pilsener, 1971.

and we were confronted by two things, Toohey's had a good product and their imagery was very strong. For six years they had been working on a campaign, based on winners, winners in sport with a catchline 'I feel like a Tooheys or two'.

He cited one commercial which depicted Dennis Lillee standing alone in the centre of the Sydney Cricket Ground, shots taken upwards depicting Lillee looking very tall and heroic with the stands in the background.

> You've earned it D. K. Lillee.
> You've given it your best.
> You've shown us you're a champion
> Over 70 great Tests.
> You've been an inspiration
> To Australia and your mates
> And you've written verse and chapter
> In the cricket book of greats.

The tale continues becoming progressively more deeply moving, ultimately ending with the message that all this Lillee achievement makes you feel like a Toohey's. David Austin said that while Toohey's was on winners Tooth's was actually on losers. The Tooth advertisements were fun and amusing. They had one which depicted a character building a house. Everybody tried to chip in, tried to help each other build a fence, but palings fell off and things kept going awry. After these mishaps, presumably you needed a Tooth's KB to overcome your frustration. It was the wrong approach.

Discussions between Tooth and CUB began in earnest in March 1983. Pat Stone, CUB's executive director, southern region, said Lou Mangan and George Haines, managing director of Tooth, were old friends, and knew each other's breweries. At one stage they even discussed the possibility of a joint Tooth–Carlton venture at the new brewery. There were worries that a CUB take-over might infringe the Trade Practices Act. The move when it did come, as it often happens, was very sudden. Ted Kunkel, who was to be the future New South Wales executive director, said he was having a holiday on the Gold Coast at the time. The date was 9 August and he was the superintending brewer for CUB's Victorian operations. 'I got a message', he said,

> from Fred Coulstock [general manager brewing] saying we had bought the Tooth brewing business that afternoon, a Thursday, and he expected me at work in Sydney on Friday morning. I can remember somebody coming from Melbourne had to go to my home, pick up a suit and meet me in Sydney with some respectable working clothes.

Pat Stone too, remembers the rush.

> It was Lou's pushing that finally got us the Tooth brewing business. We couldn't pretend to be a national brewer until we went into New South Wales. I tell you, it was chaotic. We spent two or three nights negotiating until very late. One night we were so late we couldn't even get a hamburger. We sent one of our senior legal people out and he spent two hours trying to get something to eat. We were very tired by the time we got on the plane on the 10th of August.

Bruce Siney and I went up to take over. First we went up to Dawson Waldron's offices, Tooth's solicitors, very palatial offices in the high rise central business district, and got there early at 9.30 a.m. John Spalvins arrived and after going through it for an hour or so we signed the contracts. Tim Plant [finance manager] handed over the deposit. I think he had a bank cheque for $40 million in his pocket. We had him chained to about four other people in case he caught a plane for Brazil.

The newspapers carried the news in big headlines. The *Financial Review* described it as a $160 million 'swoop' by Carlton & United. CUB actually bought all the brewing business of Tooth & Co. Ltd from the Adelaide Steamship Co. Ltd. Adelaide Steam had bought all of Tooth & Co. in June 1981 for $204 million. The present deal, however, did not include the purchase of the Tooth hotels, nor did it include the now defunct Resch's Brewery at Waverley. It did cover the Kent Brewery and the brewery at Lismore. Terry McCrann of the *Age* commented:

> For the past five years a CUB purchase of Tooth's has looked increasingly inevitable, but somewhat amusingly it appears to have taken Neville Wran's random breath testing to finally tip the balance and bring Lou Mangan and John Spalvins to the negotiating table. The legislation's impact on stagnant volume beer sales appears to have convinced Mr Spalvins there is little percentage in continuing the struggle as a poor second in NSW and an even poorer third in the national beer market.[5]

The new arrangement made CUB number one in Australian brewing, producing very nearly half of all Australian beer. At the time of the take-over newspapers were giving this breakdown of the New South Wales market: 51 per cent Castlemaine–Toohey, 35 per cent Tooth, 11 per cent CUB and 3 per cent others. Now with the Tooth capacity, and access to its brands, CUB had 46 per cent of New South Wales.[6]

Pat Stone said that after the signing of the contract they went across to the Kent Brewery. Present were Lou Mangan, Bruce Siney (group marketing manager), Alan Kemp (CUB's group industrial relations manager), and George Haines (managing director of Tooth & Co.). He was not likely to forget that day.

Bruce H. Siney, chief marketing strategist of the 1980s.

> George Haines called his management staff together in a room called the Staging Post, next to the Museum. George found a chair, stood on it and in front of about 100 people blandly told them everything had been sold to Carlton. There was nothing to worry about. They would share the facilities with us. Tooth and Carlton were as one fighting the common enemy, Toohey's. Lou Mangan then got up, said 'Hello' and how pleased he was to be there and he introduced Bruce Siney, Alan Kemp and me. Then everybody milled around wondering what the hell was going on and what was happening next.

CUB put three key people in charge of the NSW operation: Bruce Siney became general manager, Pat Stone became assistant general manager, and Ted Kunkel became brewing manager. Pat Stone recalled:

> Ted Kunkel and I stayed up there with Bruce Siney. It was a very difficult take-over. We installed a new top management and that was pretty hard for the Tooth people. We had to establish relationships with them on day one. We

had to establish relationships with the trade on day two. Then we had to start brewing properly on day three. It really was a blur. The first three or four months we worked up there we were flat out trying to fix the knots that hadn't been tied in the contract and the people problems, making sure that we treated the people who left satisfactorily. The marketing manager left, five out of seven brewers left, senior industrial relations, and production people generally left. Tooth & Co. kept their senior commercial managers so we were left with just a few commercial people. We felt we had to change things. They had been making for a long time something that was not good beer, not even at the new brewery.

Ted Kunkel and Leighton Bullock, now head brewer at Kent, also have vivid memories of those days. They were working the clock round. Ted Kunkel said:

> We had Bob Graham, general manager brewing southern region, Leighton Bullock and myself all staying down the road at Chippendale City Garden apartments. Because of schooling problems we didn't get our families to Sydney until the end of 1983. Leighton and I would take turn about. We would fly home to Melbourne every other week-end.

The night and day activity was to fix the Tooth brews like Resch's and KB and to get bulk Foster's on the market. The first pilot Foster's brew went through in an incredible four weeks. Packaged Foster's did not go through until early 1984. Kunkel and Bullock found their problem was to convince the local staff, delicately, that the CUB methods were right and what they wanted. 'We were brought up differently,' said Ted Kunkel. 'We had to make them put up with our incredible quality control.'

CUB scored a wonderful deal in buying the Kent Brewery. Its replacement cost would have been $200 million and it was only months away from completion, making it the most modern brewery in the country, everything computerised even down to the delivery of orders to the trucks at the delivery bay. The canning line operates at two thousand cans a minute, so fast the whole thing is just a blur. Bottles are filled at eight hundred a minute. Kent was also first with the latest and most efficient bulk beer methods, the 50-litre stainless steel keg, perhaps the greatest advance in bulk handling since the arrival of the steel keg some thirty years ago. The built-in spear means that a keg can be tapped almost as fast as you can raise a glass to your lips. With the old 18-gallon casks the publican or barman had to take a spear or extractor, push the valve in at the top of the keg, insert the spear, then seal it up. With the new 50-litre cask the spear is already inside; there is a cam type fitting and all one has to do is turn a handle and the barrel is tapped. Even a child can do it. The built-in spear also revolutionises the flushing and cleaning process. Those with a taste for nostalgia, however, might feel sad. Perhaps the most evocative Australian sound is the 'Wheeeeeeeeeeee' the gas makes after a keg has expired and the tap removed. The built in spear means the end of all that; it's almost like taking the pop away from the champagne bottle.

The challenge — one that continues to face all CUB off-shore operations — was to fingerprint the beer, that is to make Foster's in Sydney precisely the same as Foster's in Melbourne. Leighton Bullock said they were not satisfied with the filtration plant at Kent. The dissatisfaction cost a million dollars. They put in sand and carbon filters to make Sydney water exactly like Melbourne water. Leighton Bullock said:

Foster's Lager in production at Sydney's Kent Brewery. Two thousand cans are processed a minute.

Sydney water from a mineral point of view is good for brewing. However Sydney water has not come through good forest land and been filtered by natural vegetation as in Melbourne. It has more solids and we needed the carbon to take out the chlorine and odiferous compounds.

So Foster's in Sydney looks the same and tastes the same as in Melbourne. Cans filled in Sydney, Melbourne, or Brisbane, all have 16 Bouverie Street, Carlton on the side. You need to be a brewer and be able to read the symbols on the bottom of the can to know the brewery of origin. When asked why, Ted Kunkel said:

If you say made in Sydney or Brisbane or elsewhere, you can take it for granted some super bar expert is going to say it is not as good as the original. And everybody thinks he's an expert on beer.

Carlton continued with most of the Tooth brands. Sydney Draught which Tooth launched in late 1982 was a total disaster and gained barely more than 3 per cent of the market. Slowly it withered and died. But they continued with KB, Resch's Draught and Resch's Pilsener; they continued with the very successful Tooth LA, perhaps the best light beer on the market. This became Carlton LA. They continued with Tooth's Old, which has a dedicated following and is one of the last top-fermented beers. Pat Stone recalls that just before the take-over there were big plans to re-launch Tooth KB in a white can with the slogan GIVE AN OLD FRIEND

ANOTHER GO. The theory was that KB was always Sydney's favourite beer, and they associated it with the great times of the 1930s in the days of Kippax and McCabe, Bromwich and McGrath. David Austin said they conducted research and found that the strongest thing going for Tooth was the gold can and the slogan 'Cold Gold'. So the idea of going white was madness. Some white cans leaked on to the market, but very few. Pat Stone said all the white cans were there ready to go and they had to destroy nigh on eight million.

Kent now operates as an efficient modern brewery and Carlton products are claiming 50 per cent of the New South Wales market. There is one thing about the brewery that is unique. It is dry. That is, the employees do not have their bars where they can get a ration of four free beers during the day as at other Carlton breweries. Instead, every week, every employee gets a free case of two dozen cans. The dry brewery was one of the settlement deals after a long strike in 1980. Many of the old Tooth employees still recall remarkable days when the brewery was 'wet'. Laurie Harmey, sales manager, remembers every morning at 6 a.m. down in the racking cellars they had the 'honeypot'. It was called the honeypot because men came swarming like bees from all over the brewery. They would take a faulty keg, and if it wasn't faulty, they would find some reason for it to be faulty. 'They would drive in a stave,' said Laurie, 'and the beer would go off like a geyser, right across wall to wall. Then everyone would come running, mugs, cans, buckets, anything they could lay their hands on. The keg would be empty in no time.' The official beer ration was four 13-ounce schooners a day, morning tea, lunch time, afternoon tea, and knock off time. There would be some very happy gentlemen around the brewery. Everybody who came on to the brewery scored a beer. It was the tradition. Police and firemen, when they called, always received a beer. The record from the George Street fire station to the brewery was one and a half minutes. Nine false alarms in a day, that was another record. The alarms were a long wire with an exposed contact. If the wire was heated by fire it expanded and set off the alarm. It was known as the Grinnell system. So the thing to do when times were dull was to hit the wire, the firemen were there in a second, and everybody had a drink. Then there were the drivers. Laurie remembered if you were delivering beer by wagon it was tradition that at every pub the weary driver was to be given a free schooner of his product. Then upon arriving back at the brewery they would get another at the watchman's office. 'I often wondered how they ever got home,' said Laurie. All such amiable events disappeared when Kent became a dry brewery.

The purchase of the Tooth breweries immensely strengthened CUB, but already forces were on the move that would change the company even more dramatically. In April 1982 Robert Holmes à Court started buying shares in Carlton. He did it almost unnoticed and within a matter of days he had spent $10 million and acquired between 2 and 3 per cent of the company. Robert Gottliebsen wrote:

> Holmes à Court has quietly lit a long take-over fuse under Australia's biggest brewer. Carlton has around 191 million shares on issue and is capitalised at around $400 million. Carlton is a classic Holmes à Court target in that the real value of its assets is substantially above the market price and it has raised capital from institutions at higher prices.[7]

As soon as John Elliott read of the new move he went to the stock market and bought the Holmes à Court holding. *Business Review Weekly* commented:

> The speed with which Elliott moved was reminiscent of the days stockbroker John M. Baillieu and David Darling, both directors of Carlton & United Breweries, spearheaded the Carlton Board into backing John Elliott to take control of Elders.

This time Elliott had moved so fast he had to go back a week later to get his board's ratification. But as *Business Review Weekly* put it, he had secured for Elders a stamp of independence and helped to defend its parent. Robert Holmes à Court was happy. The move pushed up share prices and his profit was $1.2 million.[8]

John Madden Baillieu, CUB director.

CUB was not idle. It spent $160 million on purchasing the Tooth breweries and on 21 January 1983 it bought 19.67 per cent of J. Gadsden Australia Ltd for $25 million. It was a logical move as CUB was Gadsden's principal customer for three-piece steel cans. But, as Pat Stone put it, 1983 was a year when one hardly ever had a chance to sit down. At the end of November the news hit the finance pages that Ronald Brierley of Industrial Equity Ltd had been buying shares in CUB for four months. He wrote a letter to the chairman of CUB, Sir Edward Cohen, and said IEL intended to acquire fifty million CUB shares at $3.30 each for fully paid shares and $2.55 each for the contributing shares. 'We already hold 10 338 000 shares and a full acceptance of our offer will therefore increase our holding to 60.34 million shares, which represents 23.91 per cent of the issued capital,' he told Sir Edward. On 30 November 1983, CUB shares closed at $3.55, a leap of 14 per cent. The headlines read HIGH NOON RAID ON CUB . . . BOUVERIE ST UNDER SIEGE . . . BRIERLEY'S CANNY MOVE. And who was Brierley? He was another of the brilliant new breed of take-over specialists. Brierley, aged 46, was a New Zealander, and according to one businessman, worth $25 million. The *Herald* finance editor, Barrie Dunstan, described him as 'shortish and quietly spoken. If you saw him at an airport he would not be noticed among dozens of other businessmen. But over the past twenty years the appearance of IEL on share registers and the appearance of Ron Brierley outside the board room door generally had been the signal for consternation'.[9]

David Ian Darling, CUB director.

Brierley called a press conference in the Cricketer's Bar at the Windsor Hotel. While Mr Holmes à Court loved horse racing, Mr Brierley, perhaps a gambler of a different sort, was passionate about cricket. He was single, he said, but open to offers, and he also revealed with a smile that he was a failed accountancy student. He came from a 'conventional working background' in Wellington. As a schoolboy he sold his stamp collection to finance an investment newsletter which he published for six years, annual subscription, 30s in advance. At 24 he became founding chairman of R. A. Brierley Investments, which grew to become New Zealand's fourth largest company. He came to Australia and acquired IEL when it was about to go into liquidation. The $200 000 company became like a spider, eating other insects often larger than itself. Its assets grew to $250 million covering such diverse interests as insurance, oil drilling exploration, natural gas, breweries, wine, shopping centres, dairy products, fishing, canning, milling, film making and a cemetery. At the press conference a reporter

A. B. Macdougall, CUB director.

OPPOSITE PAGE:
The famous CUB logo looks down Swanston Street in Melbourne from the company's headquarters (top). The spectacular half-time entertainment (bottom) at the 1985 Foster's VFL Grand Final at the MCG.

Sir Rupert Steele, CUB director.

asked him whether he was a risk taker by nature. 'Conservative. Logical, I hope. A realist rather than a pie-in-the-sky type,' he replied.[10]

At Bouverie Street the press received just a two-sentence statement. 'There is a normal board meeting tomorrow. The board will decide if any comment is due to be made.'

The question in everybody's mind was: Is Brierley serious? The *Australian* thought it unthinkable that CUB could fall to an outsider. Here was something Melbourne felt more passionately about than anything. It was one of the two things Melbourne had that were 'best in the world' — beer and VFL football.[11] Ron Brierley was one of those who frequently won the battle, but lost the war. After all, he had seen the way John Elliott had pounced when Holmes à Court made his raid. Did he too want to make a quick profit? John Elliott, after all, was now in a check position. If Brierley gained control of CUB he would also gain 49.4 per cent of Elders IXL, control of CUB's breweries in Victoria, NSW, Queensland and the Northern Territory and potential control of J. Gadsden, SA Brewing Co. Ltd, and the Ballarat Brewing Co. Ltd.

John Elliott was in New York when Brierley made his big move. Whenever big financial crises arrived Elliott almost always seemed to be overseas. He flew home at once to do battle, and immediately announced not just a rescue bid, but a $972 million take-over for all of CUB. All the weekend there had been extraordinary comings and goings between the directors of the two companies. On the CUB board were Sir Edward Cohen, chairman, L. J. Mangan, managing director, L. F. Coulstock, J. M. Baillieu, D. I. Darling, A. B. Macdougall, Sir Rupert Steele, R. T. Morell, D. F. Smith, D. L. Hegland, C. J. Harper and H. M. McKenzie. On the quite huge Elders IXL board there was Sir Ian McLennan, chairman, J. D. Elliott, managing director, J. M. Baillieu, J. I. N. Winter, E. A. Burton, D. I. Darling, D. L. Hegland, A. B. Macdougall, H. M. McKenzie, I. M. McLachlan, L. J. Mangan, G. M. Niall, P. D. Scanlon, M. R. Nugent, A. L. McGregor and G. F. Lord. So the directors who were on both boards were J. M. Baillieu, D. I. Darling, A. B. Macdougall, D. L. Hegland, H. M. McKenzie and L. J. Mangan. The chairmen of both boards were knights, both went to Scotch College and both were outstanding scholars and won exhibitions for being the best in their state. Sir Ian McLennan rose from being a cadet to chairman of BHP, then chairman of the ANZ Bank and was famous for being a tough, aggressive operator. He was unquestionably a father figure to John Elliott. Back when Elliott was working for McKinsey's he organised the merger of the old family McLennan business of flour millers, Kimpton, Minifie & McLennan with Barrett Burston Malsters. Then Barrett Burston merged with Henry Jones. Sir Ian was there through all this gathering of power and was chairman of Henry Jones. Then Henry Jones merged with Elders IXL. Sir Ian was an original at the take-over business, he and John Elliott worked in tandem.

Terry McCrann of the *Age* called the fateful day, 4 December, 'Sunday Bloody Sunday'.

Ostensibly John Elliott is the white knight riding back from New York to save CUB from Ron Brierley's Industrial Equity. But some terse comments in a statement issued by CUB late yesterday suggest Mr Elliott may have been riding a grey charger. It is entirely possible that CUB could fight back and thereby

unleash open warfare between leading members of the Melbourne establishment.[12]

CUB had issued a statement that Sir Edward Cohen was not a party to the Elder discussions and did not agree to the bid. 'It should not be assumed from the reports that the Board of CUB had endorsed the offer by Elders.'

On 'Sunday Bloody Sunday' all sixteen members of the Elders IXL board met at the Elders Garden Street office by the old IXL Jam Factory. The meeting went for four hours, all afternoon, until 6.30 p.m. After that the CUB directors on the Elders board trooped back to Bouverie Street and had another board meeting which went to nearly midnight. John Elliott, recalling that day, said:

H. M. McKenzie, CUB director.

> We had to counter Brierley and we had to do it quickly. We had a long board meeting on the Sunday. The CUB directors wanted us to bid for 49 per cent of Carlton, so that Carlton would have owned 49 per cent of Elders and Elders would have owned 49 per cent of Carlton. Both would have remained autonomous. When you looked at all the numbers that certainly wasn't in the interest of shareholders. So the non CUB directors were unanimous that we ought to bid for the lot.
>
> By Wednesday we realised the thing would go on for a long time because we were offering paper. The bid would take months and we would have been lucky to get control. I realised we had to get a cash bid, so along with other senior guys, we worked day and night for forty-eight hours and we got $750 million. I told my chairman at the board meeting on Friday morning that we had decided we would bid for the lot. I was only changing the nature of the bid. That did stun the CUB directors. We made a cash offer, the board agreed on Friday and on Monday we had control of CUB through the market.

It was a first in Australia. Never before had so much money been raised so quickly. 'Fortunately,' Elliott continued,

> we had long connections with Citibank. The Hong Kong Bank and Chase, they came in. Luckily the chairman and chief executive of Hong Kong Bank was in Australia, just accidentally. I told him what we wanted to do. He gave me his approval next morning. Then I was able to tell the two other banks, 'You had better tell me quick smart or I will go to someone else.' Once one was in, both were in. Then we had to get it documented. We had people up all night.
>
> Worry me. No, I enjoy the cut and thrust. No, my biggest worry came on the Friday. The Reserve Bank stopped the currency for the day, stopped any foreign transactions. They partly stopped them because we had applied to bring $700 million into the country. This could have affected the state of the dollar. They had to make a decision. Luckily they opted to free the currency and we were able to bring it all in.

Colin Harper, CUB director.

Meanwhile senior staff members at CUB looked on in baffled amazement. Many could not understand if CUB had 49 per cent of Elders, why did it not go further? Tim Plant, finance manager, said:

> There was a school of thought in certain sections of management who wanted to go to 51 per cent. As I understand it, this was fundamental. However Elliott called their bluff. If you go the 51 per cent I'll pack my bags and go somewhere else.

Rodney Morell, CUB director.

Pat Stone remembers:

The senior executives couldn't understand what was happening. I don't think they will forget those days. I sat in Lou Mangan's office for twelve hours one day from 10 in the morning until 10 at night while the board sat in the board room next door. I was there with three or four other executives, plus senior financial, stockbroking and legal advisors and the board apparently had still not made a decision. It was an amazing three or four days from the executives' point of view as it was difficult to understand the board's attitude at that time. Yet time heals a lot of wounds. In retrospect, there is no doubt that the take-over was the best option for the company.

Lou Mangan said:

There was scope for a holding company, each having 50 per cent and both listed on the stock exchange. CUB's identity would have been maintained. Of course, there would have been dangers, both companies would still have been vulnerable to outsiders.

Lou Mangan felt there had been a great deal of unfair criticism, particularly in the press.

You see, it was pretty difficult. When Elders made their bid for Carlton shares within two days the institutions had sold out and given Elders control of Carlton. Within *two days*! It's all very well to talk about not giving a lead to shareholders, but what lead could you give them? Here were the professional shareholders, the professional investment people, people selling at the offer price. The deal was done before we had a chance to react. We were startled that Elliott could raise $750 million in such a short space of time. He had a big finance division with access to that sort of thing, but it was quite a feat and I give him great credit for that.

The mystery remained about why the CUB board didn't buy the few Elders shares to push their holding over 50 per cent. Sir Edward Cohen:

The media presentation of that was totally wrong. You see, we didn't own 49 per cent of Elders. My guess is that it was 47.2 per cent. As the media should have known, Elders had an employee share issue at their annual meeting just prior to the take-over. It was a simple calculation to know that our interest had been watered down. Now we could still have bought three per cent which would have taken us back over 50. But don't you see, it would have taken Elders about half an hour to issue more employees shares and bring us back under 50. Carlton decided it didn't want to make a total offer. After all, this was the advantageous thing to Carlton shareholders.

John Elliott confirmed, yes indeed he would have made a share issue, but it would not have been a staff issue. Top Elders management would not have accepted a Carlton take-over. They would have left. Elliott said: 'Carlton have competent people to run the brewery but they didn't have the breadth of experience to run a diversified company like ours. We could take over the brewery but they couldn't take over Elders.' He said that he had two days which were the biggest in the history of the stock exchange. By the night of Friday 9 December he had gone from 17 to 37 per cent of CUB. Then by lunch time on Monday 12 December he had moved to

50.1 per cent. 'We kept paying until we got to 58 then we stopped. We thought we don't need any more. We will let the offer just run on.' As it turned out he deeply regretted that he did not keep on buying and buying.

But what of Ron Brierley, the man who started it all? He sold out to Elders on Monday 5 December in a private deal with John Elliott. The price was $3.82 a share and his gross profit was between $8 million and $10 million. According to the *Sun News Pictorial* Brierley was as cool as a can of chilled Foster's. He thought CUB was a mighty fine organisation. 'Now, or some time in the future we may get a foot in the door. We'll be watching what happens. We haven't given up altogether.'[13] But in borrowing and share buying you might say there are gears within gears. Through January and early February there was a mystery buyer who was purchasing CUB shares at slightly above the $3.82 being offered by Elders IXL. On 10 February the news came out that the buyer was the giant Singapore banking and investment company Oversea Chinese Banking Corporation. It was estimated that they now held 9.3 per cent of CUB.[14] Now John Elliott was in a corner. In order to get CUB de-listed from the stock exchange to gain control of its cash flow, Elders IXL had to own more than 90 per cent of the shares. The stalemate continued for months. Elders kept extending its cash offer of $3.82. Both John Elliott and his right-hand man Peter Scanlon made a number of trips to Singapore to deal with OCBC. The expiry date for the $3.82 offer was 28 March, but still Elders had not reached the promised land. It had only 83 per cent. On 20 March Elders extended its offer for yet another month. It was not until 8 June that the Oversea Chinese Banking Corporation ended its four-month stand off. Elders gave in, raising the offer from $3.82 to $4.56 a share. Elders paid $132.3 million for 11.5 per cent of CUB bringing the total holding to 95.4, and finally putting them in a position where they could acquire the rest of the shares compulsorily. OCBC did even better than Ron Brierley; their patience meant a profit of $32.3 million.

Terry McCrann, *Age* finance writer, was critical. He said the whole affair left a bitter taste in the mouth. First Mr Elliott had said the price would not be increased. How many CUB shareholders took him at his word and having sold missed out on the extra 80 cents? 'But what of the original CUB board?' he asked. 'Almost throughout the entire affair which started at the beginning of December they have stood mute, taking no steps to force Elders to pay an adequate price for CUB and failing at every key juncture to advise their shareholders on the most appropriate course of action.'[15]

On 15 March 1984 five CUB directors resigned: Sir Rupert Steele, C. J. Harper, D. L. Hegland, A. B. Macdougall and D. Fraser Smith. Mr H. Mitchell McKenzie had already resigned on 6 March. Sir Edward Cohen remained as chairman until the following 15 November. John Madden Baillieu, the sharebroker, who was on both boards summed it up.

A lot of people said aggressively, 'Why didn't you counter bid?' It would have been a disaster for shareholders, they would have been deprived of their take home premium. We would have had to offer a big premium to Elders. That they didn't realise. We lost control of the company in 48 hours. It just went, PFUIT!, like that. It was not done with the connivance or knowledge of the CUB members on the board. I can assure you of that.

Duncan Fraser Smith, CUB director.

David L. Hegland, CUB director.

If Elliott hadn't made the move on CUB somebody else would. It was only a question of when and by whom. All we did was to defer the thing by having a short relationship with Elders. I don't see how anyone can stand alone today without interlocking shareholders. It is so easy to borrow money. But the result has been very satisfactory, both for staff and shareholders. It is my honest belief no one has been disadvantaged. If you go round CUB, the great majority are very pleased with the result. Only a few directors lost their seats. Not a very significant event.

CHAPTER SIXTEEN
Foster's Melbourne Cup

In January 1984 the *Age* newspaper, somewhat tongue in cheek, handed out its Business Honours for 1983. Those associated with brewing were high on the list.

> To Alan Bond, the Men at Work Marketing Award for venturing to America and coming back not only with its Cup but also $150 million for Swan Brewery.
>
> To Ron Brierley, whose initial bid for CUB made two corporate lovers realise marriages are truly made in heaven, the Six Million Dollar Man award for services to John Elliott.
>
> To the Board of Directors of CUB, the stunned mullet award for inertia in the face of crisis.
>
> To John Elliott, the managing director of Elders IXL who has generated so much brokerage in 1983, the OA — Order of Audacity — for services to stockbroking.[1]

John Elliott, after Bob Hawke, Paul Keating and Paul Hogan, was becoming one of Australia's best-known faces. Barely a week went by without him being the subject of an elaborate profile in the newspapers. The *National Times* described him as

> the rich man's Bob Hawke, the type of man who could enter Parliament, swiftly assume leadership and lead the Liberals back to power. He was the Treasurer for the Victorian party and any role state or federal was his for the asking.[2]

Bill Gray of the *Herald* went on about his ruggedness. He had the face of a badly mauled boxer. It had been linked, in fact, to a map of the outback, complete with Ayers Rock. The heavy jawline and pug nose reflected his tough, pugnacious approach to life. He was proud of the 247 games he put in as ruck rover and forward pocket with Old Carey Grammarians before hanging up his boots at 34.[3] Jane Sullivan of the *Age* thought he had

> an unforgettable face, every bit as strong as Hawke's, but blunt where Hawke's is sharp. The Elliott face is tough all over: fleshy nose, a sandy complexion, shrewd eyes, a wary half smile, wavy brown hair that has never seen a blow dryer. It goes with his slightly gruff voice, hunky build and big strong hands . . . not a great intellectual in the academic sense, but a quick, sharp Mr Fixit mind.

What drives him? Not any particular desire for money, according to those who knew him. An element of ego tripping perhaps, but also an altruistic desire to help his country and love for going into a situation and trying to fix it.[4]

John Elliott switched from being State Treasurer of the Liberal Party to Party Federal Treasurer. He made political statements. For example, early in 1984 he took out newspaper advertisements to promote his essay 'The Need for Deregulation in Australia'. It contained the lines: 'The Lord's Prayer has 65 words. The Gettysburg Address has 3560 words. The law relating to the distribution of cabbages in the USA has 26 793'. Australia he felt choked under such cabbage laws. Many conservatives saw him as a new Messiah, but Elliott rejected offers of safe seats, which had to be the first move if ever he was to make a run similar to Prime Minister Bob Hawke's. Yet never at any time did John Elliott say that he would like to lead the nation. He made it clear he was too busy coping with the private sector rather than the public. His ambitions were international.

With John Elliott at the wheel it was like being in an executive jet that was moving at unbelievable speed. More took place in his first three years with CUB than in the previous thirty. After the take-over there was no great letting of blood, but there were position changes on the field. Frank Harold, assistant general manager brewing, retired aged 60. Frank Harold had been one of the first of the new breed of brewers. He was not the brewer of myth and legend — rotund, ebullient, back-slapping. He was tall, elegant and an utter non-waster of words. He joined the brewery as a scientist, very cool and clinical in his approach to brewing.[5]

When he came to the brewery the shortages still hung on from the Second World War. If you wanted a dozen your publican had to love you. You had to buy two cartons of cigarettes, a bottle of Corio whisky and a bottle of port before he would look at your order. He remembered the brewery did have a science department, two university graduates and a classic old lab with two Bunsen burners. Brewing was hard labour. The men had to cart in the sacks of malt on their backs, three bushels to a bag. Sugar, too, came in by the bag, hoisted into the brewing tower by block and tackle. Then there were the coopers. Forty years before CUB had 150 coopers on the premises, who did nothing else but make beer kegs and look after wooden fermenting vats. 'You wouldn't dare let a non union man work on a barrel,' he said. 'Now we have only one cooper left and he works in the finance department.' He could remember too the old days when every barrel had to sport a fully paid excise stamp. Each stamp had to be stuck on the barrel before it went out the door. They had a deaf and dumb character on the job. He had a superbly co-ordinated two-handed action and he could slap on the stickers with the speed of light.

And the beers? In the 1950s the beers from the Victoria Brewery were quite different from the beers that came out of Abbotsford. It was all to do with plant and equipment. But when they started the packaging at Abbotsford it was necessary to get a consistency in product. 'In 1956,' he said,

R. F. G. Fogarty suggested that we should set up a research and development group. We had to fingerprint the flavour. That was a time when there was a great development in scientific analytic tools. They had the ability to trace, detect and measure the flavours of hundreds of materials. Over the years we have built up the knowledge of volatile materials, which helped us to recreate exactly beers like Foster's Lager in different places.

In 1983 the government of Hubei Province in Central China invited CUB to go there and help modernise their beer production. So Frank Harold, Lou Mangan and Fred Coulstock all went to Hubei. They found a little brewery in the city of Wuhan. It was like turning back the clock almost to the First World War; its methods dated right back to the 1920s. Beer was produced only in bottles, and Frank Harold had the terrible suspicion that the crown seals were not new but were being re-cycled. The difficulties were immense. The Chinese were looking for expansion, but they were hardly ready for the huge leap into a computerised, automatic bottling line and they were offering only a share in the profits on exported beer. It was a useful contact, however, and the first of many that CUB was to make with the Chinese Government.

In April 1984, John Elliott announced a massive re-organisation at CUB. There were to be three divisions, beer, properties and wine and spirits. Fred Coulstock, the industrial chemist, who started his career as science master at Frankston High School, would be group executive in charge of the production, distributing and marketing of beer. Lou Mangan, while remaining managing director, would be in charge of the wine and spirit division. This was no small operation. It would include Elders' wine and spirit division, CUB's Max Cohn & Co. and a new acquisition, John Cawsey & Co. which CUB bought for $13 million. CUB was not just a producer of beer. Here was one of the largest wine and spirit operations in Australia, selling a rich variety with such names as Veuve Clicquot champagne, Famous Grouse Scotch whisky, Beefeater Gin, Noilly Prat Vermouth, Jack Daniels sour mash whiskey, Bundaberg Rum, Bleasdale, Coolawin and St Hubert's wines. In the properties division, Lou Mangan would team with Nick Norgard, former chief in Queensland. Lou Mangan stayed in the job less than a year. In November he announced he would retire on 21 January, the thirty-third anniversary of his joining the company. He said he was leaving on medical advice. His doctor had told him: 'If you go now, you will have a healthier retirement'.

Many finance journalists were waiting in the wings, ready for a Mangan revelation about the take-over, but the often tough Lou Mangan was bland, happy and relaxed.

I don't think the take-over has caused any great disturbance at Carlton. We have endeavoured to ensure that everything has gone smoothly. Our people are happy with the Elders' acquisition. Yes, I suppose I wish it hadn't happened. I have a sense of personal disappointment which I have expressed to the senior people at Elders, because I felt it could have been done differently. But apart from that personal aspect I have no regrets at all. If it hadn't been Elders it could have been somebody else. That's life in the eighties.

Lou Mangan became general manager of CUB in 1972, a board member in 1976 and the company's first managing director in July 1981. He looked back at an incredible period of progress. In his last interview with the Melbourne *Herald*, he said Foster's Lager was now known all over the world, sold all over America. It had been at the Los Angeles Olympics, on tap in London and he had even bought a Foster's in China. The group now had 50 per cent of the Australian market and with beaming confidence he said it would go to 60 per cent.

The new managing director for Carlton was a surprise. He was a man totally inexperienced in brewing, Peter Bartels, 44, Elders executive director of international trading, based in Hong Kong. 'A surprising choice', said the *Business Review Weekly*. 'Head scratching,' said the *Financial Review*. Bartels did have a background in the liquor industry however. His grandfather had the Bayview Hotel in South Melbourne. His father, who originally was a moulder, had the Mountain View Hotel in Glen Waverley. Peter went to Box Hill Grammar and after school did odd jobs round the pub, like stacking bottles. He hated school. He says he was more interested in riding bicycles. He found that he could beat all the other boys riding to and from school. He was very good at it. So if Peter Bartels was not well known to some finance journalists, he was very well known indeed to sporting writers. As a 20 year old he was built like a truck with massive keg-like thigh muscles. He was never a road racer, but on the board track he was capable of extraordinary acceleration and he

Peter Bartels, managing director of CUB.

could move as fast as if he were riding a Suzuki. He won all the Victorian and Australian speed titles. In the 1962 Commonwealth Games in Perth, with considerable aplomb, he won the 1000 metres time trial gold medal. He admits that in those days he was a reluctant trainer. Not for him three or four hundred kilometres out on the road every week. He said with a knowing grin:

> In my whole cycling career I never actually wore out a pair of brake blocks. The longest training run I did was riding from the games village to the Velodrome and back daily. I preferred winning rather than training. You see, so many sportsmen prefer training. It's the same in life. It's easier to be in the middle. There are so many risks involved in winning. There's only an elite few who will take the chance of being ultra successful. In sport, it's the difference between winners and losers. The guys that win are the guys that go for it.

Like John Elliott, Peter Bartels sees many analogies between business and sport. He was 21 when he won his gold medal. He came from a cycling family: his uncle, Tassie Johnson, had been an Olympic champion and when he had seen Tassie performing at the Melbourne Olympic Games he had wanted to be a cyclist also. But Peter did not want to wait around for the next Olympic Games. 'I could see there was no future in being a cyclist star. It seemed to me that there were a hell of a lot more champions in business than in sport.' His first job was in the marketing department of the US pharmaceutical company, Abbot Laboratories. A few years later he moved to Drug Houses of Australia and his rise was remarkable. Within ten years, at the age of 31, he was a director and general manager.

When Drug Houses was in the midst of a take-over by Slater Walker, Bartels met John Elliott. It was exactly the right time. Elliott was hunting for brilliant young executives and sent Bartels to South Africa to run international food activities for Henry Jones. He was there for two years then returned to work beside John Elliott in the delicate task of performing the marriage with Elders. His next move was to Hong Kong as executive director of Elders International Trading Group. He negotiated an agreement with the Chinese to grow pineapples in Nanning, just above the old Ho Chi Minh trail. He is very proud of that. 'It was the only equity agreement between Australia and China. Actually it was the first equity agricultural joint agreement between China and the Western world.'[6]

As soon as Bartels arrived he caused a sensation in the old brewery. Much of the old R. F. G. Fogarty tradition still lingered. There was something of the atmosphere of a medieval monastery, information did not leak out easily. One had to triumph in a severe obstacle race of aides and secretaries before getting to see the top executive. The first thing Peter Bartels did was to prop open his door and leave it open. When someone went in to see him he had a habit of sitting on the edge of his desk. He still has the muscles of a cyclist, but not quite the figure. In his racing days he was 89 kilograms, at 44 he was more like 102 kilograms. Instead of racing lightweight bicycles, he was racing two thoroughbred Porsches at Calder almost every Saturday. Bartels has drive, an awesome desire to be in front. It is obvious that the race against Bond, Castlemaine, Toohey and Swan is not all that different from the Commonwealth Games or the car races at Calder. He sees Bond as a very good adversary. 'You can't be a champion unless you beat someone. The better the quality you beat,

the more delight the victory,' he said. When Bartels moved into the chair there was a series of other appointments. Walter Fisher became executive director of brewing, Pat Stone executive director southern region, John Jopling executive director Queensland and Northern Territory, Bruce Siney executive director marketing and international, Ted Kunkel executive director New South Wales, Nick Norgard executive director hotels strategy, and wines and spirits division, and Ian Fraser Smith executive director finance and administration.

Meanwhile the spread of Foster's as an international beer had continued. In July 1984 Foster's in the can, brewed by Watney's under licence, exactly the same as Foster's in Australia, went on sale in the United Kingdom through twelve thousand outlets. Foster's Draught already had captured 12 per cent of the London and south-east England draught lager market. Almost at the same time Foster's Lager draught beer, produced at the Bulimba brewery, hit the Queensland market. Foster's in cans and bottles had been launched in August 1982 and now the big hope was that the company could tackle the stolid chauvinistic Queensland taste with the bulk brew.

There was no limit to the public relations tactics used to spread the Foster's message. Foster's became the official beer for the Australian Olympic team in Los Angeles and there was an official launching on 2 July 1984 at the Melbourne Cricket Ground. CUB produced the biggest ever Foster's can, two metres tall, intending to fill it with two million messages from every pub right across Australia. There was even a message from the Santa Teresa Aboriginal community at the Boolarra Club Hotel near Alice Springs. It read: 'Run like an emu, jump like a roo, if you can't win gold, silver will do'. Foster's had quite an impact on the Los Angeles Olympics. The Mayor of Los Angeles, Tom Bradley declared a Foster's Lager Day and Paul Ormonde, Carlton public affairs manager, went to California for the big event. He said it was the first time a non American product had been so honoured. Mayor Bradley's proclamation read:

> I, Tom Bradley, Mayor of the City of Los Angeles, do hereby proclaim July 29, 1984 as Foster's Lager Day in the City of Los Angeles in recognition of the continuing contributions of Foster's Lager to the quality of life in Australia and in this city.[7]

There was yet another way of spreading the name Foster around the world. In July 1984 Sir Rupert Clarke, chairman of the Victoria Amateur Turf Club, announced the $327 000 Foster's Caulfield Cup.

In the following year CUB went further. There was a very carefully timed press conference on 1 April 1985. The information to be released was top secret, as carefully protected as a time bomb to be released in the Federal Government's annual budget. The chairman of the Victoria Racing Club, Hilton Nicholas, announced that from here on the Melbourne Cup would be worth an incredible million dollars, Australia's first million dollar event, and it would be known as the Foster's Melbourne Cup, sponsored by Carlton. This was Peter Bartel's first big decision as managing director, and was a matter entered into with great care. The Melbourne Cup is almost a religious event, sacred. All Australia stops for the Melbourne Cup. Melbourne was the first place on earth to declare a public holiday for a horse race, and it was something not to be tampered with lightly.

OPPOSITE PAGE:
Foster's being utterly British.

Hilton Nicholas, chairman of the VRC, and Carlton's managing director, Peter Bartels, with the 1985 Melbourne Cup.

Australia has never had success in finding a really true emotive national day. Australia Day has been a failure; the nation does not want to look back upon its origins. Queen's Birthday was just another excuse to have a lazy long weekend. Anzac Day went close to being a serious national day, but it eroded with time. The one day which meant something real to Australians was Melbourne Cup Day. Dare anyone tamper with it by calling it the Foster's Melbourne Cup? Bruce Siney, the marketing director at CUB thought it was possible. Foster's was a national product which related to everything Australian. You couldn't call it the Kleenex Melbourne Cup, the Aspro Melbourne Cup, the Pal Melbourne Cup, or even the Four 'n' Twenty Pie Melbourne Cup, but they would accept the Foster's Melbourne Cup. After the announcement John Elliott, Peter Bartels, and Bruce Siney waited for a cynical reaction. But the reaction was almost nil. There was only a very faint tut-tut from the *Herald* on April 3.

> The Encyclopaedia Britannica describes it as 'the greatest all-age handicap in the world'. Mark Twain was astonished when he saw it bring a nation to a standstill. It is, of course, the Melbourne Cup and it will never be quite the same again. At 2.40 p.m. yesterday the Victoria Racing Club finally cut the umbilical cord with tradition by announcing that a sponsor's name would be linked with the race that is as powerful an Australian totem as Ned Kelly or Gallipoli . . . It was inevitable; and crass though it may seem initially, it should be no real damage to the event. The old Cup is gone. Let's drink the health of the new one.

The *Financial Review* was more down to earth.

> CUB did some quick market research before taking on the Cup and the survey produced the surprising result that a large number of people believed CUB already sponsored it. No doubt the Caulfield Cup had helped that along . . . the reasoning cannot really be faulted. After all, nothing else stops Australia every year and, given what CUB expects to get out of it, a case can be mounted that the price may be on the low side.[8]

Unquestionably the *Financial Review* was correct. The 1985 Melbourne Cup celebrated Victoria's hundred and fiftieth birthday. It went by direct telecast to the east and west coasts of USA, to Hong Kong, Britain and Europe with at least sixty million viewers. The official guests were the Princess of Wales in very pure, classic, black and white, and Prince Charles in tails, a striped shirt, a spotted tie and a double-breasted waistcoat complete with watch chain. The Prince gave the best Cup speech since the days of Prime Minister R. G. Menzies. He mentioned that the chairman of the VRC, Hilton Nicholas, should have filled the gold three-handled Melbourne Cup with Foster's. Obviously there was none available; it was all being sold in England. There were at least a million Foster's pennants arranged in eight kilometres of bunting. There was a great Foster's beer can sail hanging from a cherry picker. There were Foster's blimps and Foster's on every passing helicopter. There were Foster's girls dressed as jockeys and Foster's Blue Birds, long-legged girls, handing out Foster's sun visors. The Foster's hospitality centre was composed of three huge astrodomes. As you went in you received a free racebook, Foster's pen and Foster's tie.

The battle for beer supremacy in Australia in early 1984 took a new turn, and the contest to see who could produce the tastiest, the best disguised low alcohol beer was on. In years gone by there had been many attempts to sell beer with low or no alcohol, but it had never worked. Somehow beer without alcohol did not fit the macho Australian image. CUB launched Carlton Pilsener back in August 1968, but it did not take on. In 1973 CUB tried Light Ale first in small cans and bottles then in quart cans. It had an alcohol content of 3.2 per cent. It was hardly noticed. There was a much greater effort with Carlton Light in 1979. Its alcohol content was 3.3 per cent and for the calorie conscious it contained only 122 kilojoules per 100 millilitres.

By the 1980s police everywhere were blaming the drinking driver for the high accident rate. The police in Victoria, backed by the government, were the most innovative. They were conducting random breath tests, with breathalyser units at strategic points outside hotels, race courses, football grounds, and the driver was becoming terrified. Low alcohol beer was the obvious solution. Carlton LA 2.1, inherited from Tooth, went into production in October 1984: 85 to 95 kilojoules. It was not just a Sydney beer, it had its dedicated devotees all over Melbourne. On 9 January 1985 Victoria's Health Minister, Tom Roper, launched Abbots Exxtra Light in the yellow can, alcohol content 0.9 per cent or one fifth that of regular beer with a splendid slim rating of 55 to 65 kilojoules. At the press conference CUB brewers claimed that anyone could down twenty-two 200 milligram glasses of beer in one hour and still have a blood alcohol level under 0.05 per cent. One reporter commented: 'You couldn't get drunk on this stuff because you would drown first'. Mr Roper said: 'This new low-alcohol beer gives drinkers another alternative'. He confided that he had been known to have one in his time, and on more than one occasion, but this beer had 'a good nose and a reasonable palate'. 'People will still be able to enjoy a beer or twenty-two and drive home in the knowledge that it is not an alcoholic problem they have when they are picked up,' he said.[9]

In 1985 almost everybody had a light beer. There was Swan Special Light, Birell Premium Light made by Coopers in South Australia and Abbots Exxtra Light all with an alcohol content under one per cent. There was Castlemaine Fourex Light, Carlton 2.1 and Toohey's 2.2 Lite. At first the extra light beers had a battle. Swan, for example, wanted to sell its Special Light, not as a soft drink, but as a beer, a genuine beer sold in bottle shops and bars. But this was not possible. It ran into trouble both in New South Wales and Victoria because, incredibly, it was classified as a soft drink and hotels could not sell it across the bar as beer. There had to be special legislation in state parliaments to make the sale possible. Legislation went through in Victoria in January and both Swan Special Light and Abbots Exxtra Light began selling the next day.

In February 1985 light beers had 2.5 per cent of the national market. The *Sun News Pictorial* in Melbourne ran a tasting before a panel of beer drinkers. They masked a range of bottles which included Castlemaine Fourex, Crown Lager, Abbots Lager, Carlton LA, Swan Light, Castlemaine Fourex Light, Abbots Exxtra Light, Tarax Export Light, and Birell Premium Light by Coopers of South Australia. It was an interesting experiment. The drinkers were hopeless at picking the difference between the full strength and the light 2.1 and 2.2 beers. They did not notice the change in alcohol strength. They could all pick Abbots Exxtra Light and Birell as, indeed, extra light beer. It seemed to be that if you liked light beer, it was pointless drinking anything with a higher alcohol content if you were likely to be out on the road.[10]

This was a time when capital constantly was moving round in circles. Elders was a favourite hunting paddock for Robert Holmes à Court. It was his lusty buying of Elders shares in 1981 that eventually led to the Henry Jones merger with Elders and gave Mr Holmes à Court a profit of more than $12 million. It was a Holmes à Court bid that started the ripples that caused the Elders take-over of CUB. On 26 October 1984 Mr Holmes à Court's Bell Group bought 5 per cent of Elders. He was quoted as saying that his intentions were serious and documents for a partial take-over aimed at taking the Bell stake to 20 per cent were with the printers.[11] But it wasn't to be. Three weeks later the Bell Group made a $46 million exit. There was an off-market deal when a group of Elders' corporate friends led by South Australia Brewing relieved the Bell Group of the shares. The *Financial Review* commented:

> The exercise presented Bell Group with capital profits before charges of about $5 million and about $900 000 in dividends. The takeout of Bell could be described as a variation of the practice known in the United States as 'greenmail'. Greenmail is a term coined in the United States to describe the practice of a company that repurchases its own shares at a premium from an unfriendly suitor.[12]

It was not easy to believe every strange event that took place, but it was an era of strange events. On 19 July 1985 Alan Bond's Bond Corporation launched a $500 million partial bid for 50 per cent of Castlemaine–Toohey's Ltd. Terry McCrann in the *Age* commented:

> A take-over offer by Alan Bond's Bond Corporation for giant brewing group Castlemaine Toohey's would be about as credible as Ted Turner's junkiest of junk-bond bids for the American CBS TV network or Robert Holmes à Court's first offer for BHP. It is simply not possible to attach any credibility that Bond Corp on its own could make a sensible bid for 100 per cent of Castlemaine.[13]

Terry McCrann was absolutely right. How could a company worth $200 million make a bid for a company that was worth $1.1 billion. Few people believed he could raise the money, but he had powerful backers in the Hong Kong and Shanghai Bank and the Standard Chartered and State Bank of New South Wales.

The story all began in 1983 when Alan Bond was making his big challenge for the America's Cup. Castlemaine–Toohey's managing director, Lloyd Zampatti, flew to Newport Rhode Island to discuss the purchase of Bond's Swan Brewery. The idea did not work. The Trade Practices Commission made matters spectacularly difficult by deciding that if Castlemaine–Toohey took over Swan it would have a monopoly in West Australia with 95 per cent of the market. Meanwhile many of Castlemaine–Toohey's directors became alarmed. Here was another company in a classic situation. It was doing splendidly well. It was in great financial shape, very few borrowings, an under-valued share price and rich in assets, worth around $612 million.

Had Castlemaine–Toohey been a pop record on the take-over stakes it would have been at the top of the charts. Lloyd Zampatti realised this. Back in the old days, before he went to the Swan Brewery and resigned just one week after Bond took over, Zampatti had worked for Nicholas Kiwi Ltd. Castlemaine–Toohey's directors decided they could make take-over moves more difficult if they diversified. So they launched a $307 million bid for Nicholas Kiwi at $4 a share. The bid was not big enough. The multinationals Reckitt and Colman and Consolidated Foods beat them in the scrum and won control. Castlemaine then moved into soft drinks and bought a series of Coca-Cola franchises, but it was all too late. Bond quietly entered the market in April. Through his brokers Rivkin & Co. he bought 97 000 shares at $4.80. By June rumours were buzzing and Bond was buying at $6. On 20 July Bond made his partial offer of $7.10 a share for 50 per cent of the capital, which Castlemaine–Toohey's directors rejected as 'nowhere near adequate'.

There was a hearing in front of the Trade Practices Commission, which said it would take a very serious view if one brewer gained a substantial influence upon the brewing industry as a whole. According to the *Australian*, clearly this was a message for Elders IXL.[14] Obviously the TPC was going to be amiable about the whole affair. Lloyd Zampatti must have wished it had been equally amiable when he was contemplating a take-over in the other direction back in 1983. On 26 July Bond lifted his game. He offered $7.50 for all the shares, but there was a complication. Castlemaine sold their beer in the United Kingdom through the giant English brewer Allied Lyons. Allied Lyons owned 20 per cent of Castlemaine–Toohey. Right at this time Allied Lyons bought 5 per cent of Castlemaine–Toohey in exchange for 50 per cent of their soft drink company Britvic. Would Allied Lyons be the silver knight this time and charge to the rescue?

Couriers were going in all directions, to Britain and the United States. There were rumours of a third mystery buyer, later identified as Philip Morris. Lloyd Zampatti went to London, but Peter Beckwith, Bond Corporation managing director, already was there, allegedly on holiday. Finance writer, Robert Gottliebsen, claimed that the most serious miscalculation made in the whole bid was to leave Beckwith alone with Allied. Allied was left with some unattractive alternatives. They could fight it out toe to toe with Bond, try to buy out Bond, or sell to a third party. When Lloyd Zampatti started talking about Philip Morris, they obviously took fright. If Philip Morris got control of Castlemaine–Toohey, they would have a chunk of Allied and a foothold in England.[15] Allied Lyons, impressed by Peter Beckwith, finally settled for cash at $8.25, a nice profit of around $150 million.

On 28 August Castlemaine–Toohey's directors recommended that shareholders accept the Bond bid and it was all over. 'You can now say Bond Corporation owns Castlemaine–Toohey', a jubilant Bond told reporters. Terry McCrann, who had been amazed when the offer was first made, was still amazed. He wrote it was 'without doubt the most amazing take-over in corporate history. Indeed the exercise in which — figuratively speaking — a $200 million corporate mouse was able to persuade a group of bankers to lend it a billion dollars in order to swallow a $1200 million elephant could well be the most amazing financial coup seen anywhere in the western corporate world.' McCrann went on to predict that the annual interest burden on servicing $1200 million spent to acquire Castlemaine would run to $190 million plus.[16]

Of course, all through this John Elliott was smiling. It made him realise what a bargain basement deal he had with CUB. He had bought CUB for roughly an even billion dollars and won 48 per cent of the beer market. Alan Bond paid $1200 million for 34 per cent of the market. A little quick figuring on a pocket calculator shows that Bond paid about $31.5 million for each one per cent of the market. This makes the CUB purchase worth just on 1.7 billion.

Meanwhile, all was over at Castlemaine for Lloyd Zampatti. Absolutely no one predicted that he would stay with the now hugely enlarged Bond Brewing. The interviewing team on the ABC's *Carlton Walsh Report* asked Bond whether Zampatti would remain at Castlemaine–Toohey. Bond replied: 'He will leave'. Zampatti departed from Castlemaine–Toohey Ltd less than a week after the take-over. Four other directors went at the same time, the deputy chairman Mr Lloyd Hartigan, Mr M. N. Little, Mr W. H. Perkins, and Sir John Rowell.[17] One month later Lloyd Zampatti became chief executive of Brett & Co. a Queensland timber, hardware and stevedoring business. The *Financial Review* commented: 'As a private company Brett does not publish its financial results — but it is a minnow beside the Castlemaine whale'.[18]

There were now in effect two brewery giants in Australia; back in 1890 there had been 350. Although it might be an exaggeration to say there were only two breweries left in Australia, it was no mistake to say that two huge personalities were face to face in battle for sole command, John Dorman Elliott, 44, of Elders IXL and Alan Bond, 47, of the Bond Corporation. Elders claimed 48 per cent of the market, Bond 42 per cent. According to figures published in advertising journals both were spending around $40 million a year in promotion and advertising. Big money was being laid out by both companies to make incisions in old traditional markets. Castlemaine had 73 per cent of the Queensland market, but CUB was fighting state chauvinism with Foster's in draught and bottles. It was having more success against Toohey's in Sydney with nigh on 50 per cent. But for chauvinism no one was as unshakeable as the football hardened Victorian who had been drinking his Foster's Lager and Victoria Bitter for a hundred years. CUB claimed and insisted it had 98 per cent of the Victorian market.

Even before the take-over Lloyd Zampatti had been plastering Melbourne with Fourex signs and shipping his cans across the Victorian border by semi-trailer. Prices were heavily discounted in an attempt to match Foster's can for can. Every night on television there was a commercial which depicted a semi-trailer loaded with Fourex trundling down the highway from Brisbane, lovely muted colour tones, as romantic as covered waggons discovering America. 'He makes a drop at Clarrie's', a real outback pub. The truck moves inexorably, on, on, and then passes a Sydney–Melbourne mile post. Just to make it authentic enemy territory, up pops a CUB illuminated sign. The smooth voiceover drones: 'But it doesn't come from Sydney and it isn't you know who'.

CUB counter-attacked with its line of commercials using the voice of John Meillon, a thoroughly identifiable Foster's drinker. 'You can get it riding.' Shot of a fellow pedalling hard on his bicycle. 'You can get it

OPPOSITE PAGE:
The 1985 Foster's Melbourne Cup is presented by His Royal Highness, the Prince of Wales (top). Left to right: John Elliott; Her Royal Highness, the Princess of Wales; VRC chairman, Hilton Nicholas; VRC vice chairman, Peter Armytage; His Royal Highness, Prince Charles; co-owner of What A Nuisance, Lloyd Williams: Mrs Lloyd Williams; winning jockey, Pat Hyland; and co-owner of What A Nuisance, Dennis Gowing.
What A Nuisance (bottom) wins the first Foster's Melbourne Cup in 1985.

Evonne Cawley, member of the Australian Federation Cup tennis squad sponsored by Foster's, in the early 1980s.

sliding.' Greg Chappell makes a glorious drive while Richard Hadlee slides to cut it off at the boundary. 'You can feel it coming on about four.' There's a rugged character in a steel foundry. He lifts the shield off his face, sweaty and thirsty. 'A hard-earned thirst needs a big cold beer.' Suddenly, almost by stroke of magic, out comes an arm with a bottle of Victoria Bitter. A hand whips off a top, a glass is filled. 'Ahhhh.' Another commercial featured the famous brewery Clydesdales, six of them, with a rig over 13 metres long. Noel Browne of George Patterson Advertising said getting them ready for the commercial was a task beyond belief. Their handler, Terry Goodear, started his work at 2 a.m. to get them ready. They had to be paraded back and forth through the bush. By the time the six Clydesdales had geared up for their tenth take, filming *Ben Hur* or *Cleopatra* would have seemed easier.

The going was tough for Bond Brewing; he was not doing even as well as the old-time Courage. In late 1985 CUB set up a complete marketing organisation in Western Australia with the object of making Foster's on tap available throughout the state. Soon CUB was claiming 10 per cent

OPPOSITE PAGE:
Photograph recapturing the traditions of an earlier era when beer was transported by horse and waggon.

of the market, right in the home of Alan Bond. Bond had a problem. Elliott could claim that Foster's was Australia's national beer, but if Bond was going to push for a national beer, he had to decide which one — Castlemaine, Toohey's or Swan.

In November Alan Bond invaded Melbourne. He hired a cavalcade of luxurious cars to take a battalion of interstate journalists from the airport for an official unveiling at the Melbourne Regent of Bond Brewing's 'first national beer', Swan Premium Export Lager. It was very upmarket in black cans and black stubbies, to be known as Black Swan. There was a video show with the theme 'Style is Back in Black'. There were black BMWs, languorous beauties in black gowns; black was everywhere. The *Financial Review* told of the first commercial. It depicted suave but healthy elegance, with shots of young, upwardly mobile professionals sculling on a river, night skiing at Perisher, and relaxing in a city suite with a cool glass of Swan Premium. The music theme sounded like something out of James Bond.[19]

The battle was even more widespread. The London correspondent of Melbourne's *Sunday Press* reported that England was in danger of drowning in a sea of Australian beer. There were now Fourex signs all over London and Alan Bond was using the eyebrow-raising banner: 'An Aussie wouldn't give a XXXX for any other beer'. But the correspondent added that Foster's had been available in London now for thirty years and had 5 per cent nationally of the draught lager market.[20]

Gough Whitlam, former prime minister and Australian Ambassador to UNESCO in Paris, had another angle. In a debate with Sir James Killen, he pointed out that the local Australian Trade Commission had been given the responsibility of putting before the French both Foster's Lager and Castlemaine Fourex. They had great difficulty with Fourex. Fourex was the name of a famous French condom; could the beer be publicised, particularly when it had the slogan: 'I Can Feel a Fourex Coming On'.

Alan Bond, however was determined to make an impression on Melbourne. He bought the Princes Bridge Hotel, better known as Young & Jackson's, home of the famous nude painting *Chloe*, once said to be a tourist attraction second only to the stuffed effigy of Phar Lap. Young & Jackson's was a Melbourne totem, akin almost to the Shrine. Then just before the year's end in 1985 he accepted the offer of the presidency of the Richmond Football Club. Some could have construed this as a surprising choice. After all, Alan Bond was a Western Australian entrepreneur, supposedly passionate about yachting. His interest in the future of a football team from a Melbourne industrial suburb could not have been great. Richmond's director, Andrew Fairley was frank enough.

> He wants a sporting profile in Victoria and he realises that if CUB is going to operate in the beer market in Western Australia then it is necessary for him to operate in the beer market in Victoria. It's one way he could see of taking CUB, both in the marketing context and as a high profile leader.

John Elliott was president of the Carlton Football Club, and as an old footballer himself, he could be seen watching Carlton on most Saturday afternoons. If he had a slight edge on Bond in beer sales, he also had an edge in football; Carlton was by far the better performer in 1985 and in 1986 and Richmond was languishing down in the depths of the ladder.

CHAPTER SEVENTEEN

Foster's Takes Courage

If the years 1983 to 1985 seemed an overpowering brew, the excitement really was only just starting. In early September 1986 the share prices of Allied Lyons began to leap. Allied Lyons was the second largest brewer in Britain, second only to Bass Charrington, and it had 13 per cent of the British beer market. Its interests were not only beer, however, but also catering, wine, spirits and soft drinks. The name Lyons was as well known in England as McDonalds in America. Lyons was England's oldest chain of tea houses.

Elders had been quietly picking up Allied Lyons shares since April and on 4 September the Allied Lyons chairman, Sir Derrick Holden-Brown, confirmed that Elders IXL now owned a 4.9 per cent stake.[1] The next day the *Herald* in Melbourne had a headline: ELDER'S ELLIOTT SETS A FIRE UNDER LONDON. Elders IXL with a number of unnamed partners had made the biggest take-over bid in Britain's history. The *Herald*'s London correspondent wrote, 'The first question being asked here today was where on earth is he getting the money — at least £1.75 billion of it — and who are his friends. But Mr Elliott is giving nothing away.'[2]

The reaction in London swung between shock and total disbelief. How dare these colonials move in and try to buy the ancestral home. John Elliott's remarks to the press certainly inspired feedback:

> We began looking at the UK beer market 15 months ago and we decided Allied would give us the most scope. We tend to try to find the companies we think we can manage better. Allied's beer brands are a bit tired and we think we have something to contribute.

Sir Derrick Holden-Brown said: 'For this company, which is small and heavily borrowed to think it can tilt at Allied-Lyons is impudence. We will fight it all the way.' Asked what he thought about those tired brands, he replied: 'He would say that wouldn't he? I cannot agree. There is nothing tired about our brands.'

The offer for Allied Lyons, four times the size of Elders IXL in Australian money, was worth $3.5 billion. As soon as John Eliott returned home at the beginning of October he explained his moves. It had all started six months after Elders IXL had taken over CUB. If they were going to sell

Foster's throughout Europe then they needed a brewery in England. They sent over a large team, studied the six major breweries in careful detail, and came up with Allied Lyons, the second biggest, but a poor performer. The tradition in England has been to drink ale — warm, brown and flat — but lately they have developed a taste for lager and lager had 42 per cent of the market. Of that lager market, Foster's had captured 6 per cent, varying to 12 per cent in the London area. By using Allied Lyons as a base into the Common Market Elliott could get into the great population areas of Europe. The thought of the competition of such formidable giants as Heineken and Carlsberg did not worry Mr Elliott. The British had never competed in Europe because they always made the wrong beer. CUB did not. Allied Lyons, he said, dealt in food, restaurants, wine, spirits, tea and hotels, but their actual beer operation was only the same size as CUB. CUB plus Allied Lyons would make the combine the eighth largest brewer in the world. But how did a mouse go about purchasing a lion? It was a question of knowing where to find the money.

After the Elders' take-over of CUB the company debt was $1.8 billion, but eighteen months later it was down to $600 million. John Elliott said Citibank was impressed by this, so they were prepared to back him again. He started buying shares at £1.75, but when he passed 6 per cent of Allied Lyons and made a public announcement the share price jumped to £2.75. Why did not Elders keep on buying quietly? Elliott explained:

> When you put together a consortium loan to bid $3500 million, you can't do that in forty-eight hours. We are not talking to three banks this time but seven or eight. It was an extensive exercise and it took eight weeks to put it together. And so a lot of people knew about it around the world and rumours got moving. Stock started to go up and then speculation ran riot.
>
> We had to declare our hand. The company could take defensive action which was not in the interest of shareholders. In the UK, once a company is under offer they cannot issue stock, nor can they buy another company.

That very situation did not please Sir Derrick. He commented: 'The uncertainty this creates among our employees is deplorable. We are supposed to live with that for up to six weeks while the Australian company makes up his mind.'[3] The take-over bid in England was considered 'cheeky', 'non British', even 'distasteful', but John Elliott was very determined. He was asked, 'Will you get Allied Lyons?'

'Yes.'

'How many take-overs have you made now?'

'Eleven.'

'How many have been successful?'

'Eleven.'

The bid for Allied Lyons was, of course, just part of Elliott's plan for global expansion. Where could he go in Australia? Consumption of beer was falling. The beer taxes were very nearly the highest in the world and he was running out of competitors. Any more take-overs almost certainly would receive a firm no from the Trade Practices Commission. His targets now were Europe, North America, South-East Asia and particularly China. Elliott was looking for partners in his bid for Allied Lyons. He believed his take-over would have a better chance if he could lead a powerful consortium and he made no secret that his number one interest was the

Allied Lyons brewing capacity. Allied's beer brands included Skol, Double Diamond and Ind Coope Long Life. In its spirits and wine division it had Teachers whisky, Romanof vodka and Harvey sherries, all with fairly static earnings. It was doing better with its food and beverage division, which included Tetley teas and the Baskin and Robbins ice cream chain. John Elliott said:

> Now, look at some of their brands; they are all number two in the market; none of them are the leaders. They've got the number two beer, the number two Scotch and the number two food lines. We want to be number one in everything we do and when we get the Allied brands we will be.[4]

Many names came up as possible members of the consortium, among them Suntory of Japan for the food side and Hiram Walker of Canada for the wine and spirits. All this raised fury among Allied Lyons directors, the sort of fury Robert Holmes à Court aroused in Australia when he suggested he might sell off sections of BHP.

On 21 October John Elliott, on behalf of Elders IXL, announced that he would go it alone with a bid worth $3.6 billion Australian or £1.8 billion for Allied Lyons with an offer of £2.55 a share. John Elliott said Elders would retain the brewing and wine and spirits interests, but would sell off the food, tea, ice cream, and hotel interests, plus a Mercedes Benz dealership, the largest in Britain. There was an immediate 'totally unacceptable' response from the Allied Lyons board.[5]

Some newspapers in jovial fashion described the struggle as if it were a football match with the president of Carlton competing in the beer Grand Final, but it was more serious than that. Soon the infighting in the ruck became rough indeed. The Elders ruckmen had to dodge their way through a maze of British financial watchdogs and umpires. The British Takeover Panel asked questions about the ownership of the company and the Monopolies and Mergers Commission intervened. Elders was using a British company, IXL, as a vehicle for the take-over bid. There were demands through the Takeover Panel for the names of the partners in this company. The partners were Bob Cowper and Richard Wiesener, both members of a Monaco based consultancy business. Together they held 21 per cent of IXL. Both were old friends of John Elliott. The *Financial Review* on 12 November 1986 speculated about these two. It said Richard Wiesener started business with $2000 and now he could be worth $100 million. Cowper's associates put his wealth at $50 million.

Bob Cowper was a former director of Elders, but Australians knew him better as a Test cricketer and a great one. During the 1965–66 Test series he made 307 runs for Australia against England at the Melbourne Cricket Ground. Richard Wiesener's association went back to the days when they both had their Masters of Business Administration and worked for McKinsey's. The *Business Review Weekly* even called him 'Elliott's Minder'. Wiesener told the journal that they met on Wiesener's first day at McKinsey's. 'I was ushered into his office — they had a funny system there where you had to share an office with someone — and the fellow I was asked to share a desk with was John Elliott.'[6] Together they worked out a scheme for raising $50 000 and eventually took over Henry Jones; that was how it had all started. For the next seven years Wiesener was at Elliott's side, helping engineer the growth of Henry Jones. In 1979 he resigned as executive director of Henry Jones, parted amiably, and set up a finance business with Bob Cowper in Monaco. The Monte Carlo Wiesener–Cowper team came into the Allied Lyons affair right at the start. They used a vehicle, Windermere Securities, funded by Elders, to buy the original forty million shares in Allied Lyons.

Allied Lyons scorned the Elders IXL offer. It said the price offered for their shares was absurd. John Elliott said, not so, but for his intervention they would be languishing around £2.10. Both Elders and Allied Lyons were spending heavily on big advertising campaigns, and Sir Derrick Holden-Brown, who had been almost unknown before the battle was now the subject of magazine and newspaper features. Said the *Business Review Weekly*:

> Sir Derrick, 62, is everybody's vision of the dapper gentleman businessman: short, stocky, and many believed ineffectual. But in recent weeks he has surprised both his critics and supporters with his leadership. His approach has been tough forthright and surprisingly glossy . . . he has started playing the media and he is obviously a quick learner.[7]

At press conferences he developed a display of offended indignation. The share was now £2.75, earned entirely on Allied Lyons' own value and merits, according to Sir Derrick. A former naval officer, who had his own 10-tonne sloop on the Solent, he said Allied Lyons would have reached £2.50 without Mr Elliott's help 'and he knows it'. Gearing up for another salvo, he said, 'That is why he has resorted to some quite unsavoury tactics during the build up. Most of the allegations he has made about our company are nonsense. The only reason he persists in denigrating the performance of Allied and its management is that he is trying to talk down the value of the share price.' Allied Lyons put out a formal defence document urging shareholders to reject the Elders offer. It described Elders as a 'not very successful Australian conglomerate. It is strong on one thing only — grossly extravagant ambition, which despite its bragging, is not supported by its own resources'.

Less than a week later the British Government referred the bid to the Monopolies and Mergers Commission, a move John Elliott had feared all along. He said privately that Allied Lyons was a very big company with great lobbying power. Now the whole deal would be shelved for a long time. The deliberations of the commission could take up to six months. Yet John Elliott was not giving up, Elders still wanted Allied Lyons. The *Age* commented, 'Elders' determination not to lick its wounds and pack up and go home is likely to add millions to the cost of the bid, as it will need to keep a high profile in the City if the offer is to maintain its momentum throughout the inquiry'.[8]

It was a year when nothing ever turned out as expected. Suddenly on 12 March Elders sold its shares in Allied Lyons for a handy profit of $83.5 million. The word came back from S. G. Warburg, Allied's financial advisers, and it sounded like a sigh of relief. Clearly the whole thing had been just a short-term financial speculation. 'We very much doubt that London has seen the last of John Elliott but we are confident that Allied has seen him off,' their spokesman said.[9] Nor could one be sure about that either. John Elliott sounded as determined as ever. When asked why he sold, he said, 'Well, the price has got away really. We believe Allied became overpriced and therefore we sold our shares. But I'm going to London next week and we will be pursuing the bid with the same amount of effort'.[10]

Clearly Allied Lyons was not over-confident. Several weeks later they made a bid worth £1.25 billion for the great Canadian combine, Hiram Walker. Among many other interests Hiram Walker owned Canadian Club and Ballantine's Scotch whisky. The London *Evening Standard* remarked drily that the tortoise at last had metamorphosed into a hare. There had been ten years' development in ten days and now Allied was one of the biggest drinks players in the world.[11] Hare, perhaps, was not a good term. The tortoise had turned itself into a brontosaurus or a mammoth, a creature hideously indigestible for those in the take-over stakes.

After Elders moved away from Allied Lyons it seemed like the eye of a cyclone, something else had to happen, and it did on 10 April. John Elliott created the biggest and most extraordinary day in the history of the Melbourne Stock Exchange. Elders IXL spent $1.8 billion buying 16.8 per cent of BHP. Several years earlier the brokers had been astonished by the Elders $972 million bid for CUB. This was in another league altogether, twice the size. It all came so suddenly it left the financial world baffled. What was Elliott trying to do — capture BHP, capture Bell Resources? The Melbourne *Sun* commented, 'Will John Elliott and Elders IXL truly prove to be the shining knight BHP expects? The business world was yesterday abuzz with speculation about the exact nature of the latest king size bedfellows'.[12]

At least four journals used 'Buying Spree' in their headlines. Spree according to the Oxford dictionary, was a wild piece of fun, a drunken revelry. This was rather more than that. It was a careful, brilliantly planned operation, the type of coup in which there was no room for error. The high command battle conference took place in the Elders board on Wednesday 9 April. Word already had gone round the world to arrange the finance.

Finance writer Barrie Dunstan called them the shock troops. The shock troops were the stockbrokers. There were Peter Lawrence, a close friend of John Elliott and John Gross, Elliott's second cousin from Roach Tilley Grice. There was a team from E. L. and C. Baillieu, including John Baillieu, the senior partner and Elders board member. There was John McIntosh of McIntosh Hamson Hoare Govett, a committeeman with John Elliott at the Carlton Football Club. They had to work out where they could get the shares and at what price. They agreed on $7.36, 80 cents above the closing price for the previous day. They had to work out who would talk to whom, who would persuade which BHP shareholder to sell. They had to acquire 200 million shares and it all had to work. Then they had to decide precisely at what stage they would pull out. If they went over 20 per cent even by 0.1 per cent they would be in deadly trouble. According to the rules, this would constitute a take-over bid and they would have to go all the way and make their offer to all the shareholders. The discussions went to well after 11 p.m., but for the brokers the work was only just starting. After all, they were tackling the biggest deal they had seen in their lives. They had to find the sellers, start their telephone dialling. There were 7.30 a.m. meetings to be planned before trading started on the exchange. Hardly any one at that meeting scored more than a few hours' sleep.[13]

Mr Ian Holman of McIntosh Hamson Hoare Govett was overseer of the raid. When he walked on the floor he knew that seventy million BHP shares already were there for the taking. AMP, a traditional BHP backer, was on hand to sell twenty-four million of their stake. At 10 a.m. plus ten seconds the exchange went beserk. Some thought it was like a 'volcano', some thought it was a 'madhouse'; a reporter on the *Sydney Morning Herald* had a new expression. He thought it was like a 'mugging'. First off was John 'Winnie' McDonough for McIntosh Hamson Hoare Govett. BHP, buyer $7.36, seller $7.38. Before a thoroughly startled audience he crossed four million shares at $7.36. Then came E.L. & C. Baillieu, 21 million shares. There was a wild scramble for telephones. Operators from every company were offering shares, in slabs of a million, five million or more. The *Australian* reported: 'The noise level was at such a pitch old timers were moved to recall the worst excesses of the Poseidon boom'.[14]

By 4 p.m. the brokers were beginning to relax. The total of BHP shares bought was 201 567 674. It was time to take the tops off a few bottles. The range varied, very appropriately, from Foster's Lager through to French champagne. Illustrious drinks were very appropriate, after all, the brokers had earned nigh on $14 million in commissions. But what was it all about? There was one rumour that Elliott had sold Carlton & United Breweries to BHP and he was about to become chairman. John Elliott commented: 'They're all just silly rumours. I have no particular desire to be chairman of BHP. I am chairman of Elders. We have no plans at present to sell any part of Elders.' There had been no collusion with BHP, it was just a sound 'strategic investment'. It was at 1.50 p.m. on 10 April that John Elliott gave the news of his activities to Brian Loton, managing director of BHP. Loton said it came as a complete surprise.

This serial had dramatic daily episodes. BHP decided to move very quickly indeed. Brian Loton gave the order for their contacts to start buying Elders' convertible notes in Europe. Overnight they spent $216 million. On the Friday there was a meeting at 5 p.m. at BHP. Among those present were John Elliott, John Baillieu, the chairman of BHP, Sir James Balderstone and advisers from Morgan Stanley and the Macquarie Bank. John Elliott assured the meeting that it was not his intention to take over BHP.

Robert Gottliebsen of *Business Review Weekly* reported that Elders and BHP lawyers spent the week-end toiling away at Elliott's Jam Factory headquarters in South Yarra and were in constant contact with the leading take-over lawyer David Gonski, of Freehill Hollingdale and Page. The BHP board then authorised the purchase of a billion dollars worth of redeemable preference shares, finishing with 20 per cent of Elders capital.[15] There was an onslaught of press criticism. What was in it for the share-holders? When were they consulted about buying into Elders? They were accused of hypocrisy and poor use of shareholders' money. Both Loton and Balderstone denied that there was any collusion. They had been think-ing of investing in Elders for the past nine months.

John Elliott was happy. Now he had funds plus a huge and respectable power base to pursue his interests in Europe. What's more, as the *Financial Review* put it, the back door to Elders was securely locked by the Big Australian and the company was virtually take-over proof. Furthermore as part of the new deal there was to be an exchange of directors. John

Elliott would take his seat on BHP and Brian Loton would go to Elders.[16]

The storm went further than just press comment. The chairman of the National Companies and Securities Commission ordered a public inquiry into the BHP and Elders deals and he wanted it to start immediately. The press, the public and most observers saw it all as a battle between Robert Holmes à Court and John Elliott. *Business Review Weekly* listed Holmes à Court, 49, as Australia's richest man, worth $300 million. His art collection was worth $14 million. During 1986 he bought a house in London worth $20 million, said to be the second finest after Buckingham Palace. He was suave, incredibly cool when dealing with big money, witty, and *Mode* listed him among Australia's ten best-dressed men. He owned racehorses and had substantial bloodstock interests. He was the great grandson of England's second Baron Heytesbury and a second cousin of the present Baron. He went to school with the Oppenheimer children in South Africa and his father had a farm near Bulawayo in Rhodesia.[17] When he was 19 his family moved to Perth and there he studied law, his primary training. In 1969 he initiated a $79 000 take-over of the WA Woollen Mills. It was the first of many. Most of us had never heard of him until 21 February 1984 when Bell Resources Ltd, formerly Wigmores, made a $222 million tender for sixteen million BHP shares and Robert Holmes à Court announced that he intended to take over BHP. It was a great joke at the time. Here was the flea attempting to swallow the elephant; the newspapers had great fun. They ran photographs of Bell's mundane, very ordinary offices in Perth, and compared them with the splendid black tower of BHP in Collins Street, Melbourne. But Robert Holmes à Court kept manipulating, trading, buying, selling. By 28 December 1984 BRL was the fourth largest shareholder in BHP with a 5 per cent holding of forty-eight million shares. By 5 October 1986 he had 11 per cent, then with a series of lightning raids through November he lifted the Bell ownership to 17.1 per cent. The following February he made a cash and scrip offer of $7.70 a share in a bid aimed at lifting equity to 40 per cent. However there were seven conditions and Mr Brian Loton was able to argue that the conditions made the offer unsatisfactory. On 18 February he made yet another offer, altering his bid from pro rata to proportional and seeking 50 per cent of each shareholding.

There was nobody in the country now who considered that Robert Holmes à Court was a joke. Many commentators were saying that it was as inevitable as the coming of Christmas that Robert Holmes à Court would be the next chairman of BHP. Sir James Balderstone and his directors were showing increasing signs of nerves and they gathered some remarkable allies. The steel unions demonstrated against the take-over and on 21 February Robert Holmes à Court flew to Sydney to placate them.

It was a wonderful period for the lawyers. BHP and BRL were locked in constant battles. On 27 February the Victorian Supreme Court froze the BRL bid. Then on 15 March BHP bought twenty-five million Bell shares for $150 million so that BHP could have a say at the Bell annual meeting. On 8 April BRL made an incredible formal offer of $7.70 a share with a $2 billion ceiling and so it continued. For company watchers it was fascinating to observe the two protagonists Robert Holmes à Court and John Elliott. The BHP directors would not accept Holmes à Court. They looked upon him as a company raider, a man who would use BHP for his own ends, selling off the various divisions like items in a department store. Perhaps they were wary of John Elliott, but his history was very different and he had many friends who were the core of the Melbourne establishment.

When John Elliott was a young financier, working with McKinsey's, looking for opportunities, he made his start by taking over Henry Jones IXL. The backing came from Rod Carnegie, the Myer and the Kimpton families. The CBA Bank was his biggest supporter and on the board of that bank was James Balderstone, so too was Stephen Kimpton. His association with the Kimpton and McLennan families went back a long way. After leaving university John Elliott was a BHP cadet, and of course he knew Ian McLennan, the engineer, and the architect of the huge modern expansion of BHP. Sir Ian McLennan's paternal grandfather, Donald McLennan, had started a flour mill at Mooroopna. The flour mill had blossomed into Kimpton, Minifie and McLennan, which merged with Barrett and Burston, which merged with Henry Jones. It was the young John Elliott who was called in to work the Kimpton, Minifie and McLennan merger. Elliott knew all these great wealthy families. Sir Ian McLennan was almost a father figure. He was the man who believed utterly that there was oil in Australia and pushed his company to find oil in Bass Strait. He had the thrusting, expansionist streak in his character which Elliott so much admired. Sir Ian McLennan was Elliott's chairman at Henry Jones IXL, and again at Elders IXL. It was no coincidence that he was chairman when Elders took over CUB and made its first moves towards Allied Lyons. Sir Ian retired as chairman of BHP in 1977. He was chairman of the ANZ Banking Group from 1977–1982 and he retired as chairman of Elders IXL in November 1985.

Also among John Elliott's backers were the Darling brothers, David, director of Elders and CUB, and Gordon, director of BHP. As the *Sydney Morning Herald* put it, in the black-glassed board room at 140 William Street, Melbourne, there was the OOU factor, 'one of us'. John Elliott was definitely OOU.[18]

The National Companies and Securities Commission held its hearings into the share dealings between Elders and BHP. It became a public sideshow and the stars once again were Holmes à Court and Elliott. The *National Times* described the transcripts of the inquiry as better than any movie or television series. For example there was the day Holmes à Court described conversations which took place during three meetings with John Elliott. There was 17 May, a cool day with showers, when they met on the twenty-fifth floor of Holmes à Court's penthouse apartment at 99 Spring Street; an apartment decorated with paintings by Lloyd Rees and Brett Whiteley and a glorious view across Parliament House to the Dandenongs. According to the Bell chief, the conversation went like this as each offered to buy out the other:

Elliott: 'I am in a position now to offer you $400 million profit on your holding.'

Holmes à Court: 'Well, I indicated to you earlier that $400 million was the price of a month's work. I've been on this for a lot of months. I don't think that's going to interest us at all.'

Next Holmes à Court offered to take over Elders. He said he thought Elders had debts of $1.5 billion resulting from the BHP raid. 'I said to him we would get to buy the shares and you will get to be prime minister.'

But John Elliott had his loyalties. 'I cannot sell my shares without letting people down.'

'Who specifically? Name somebody?' said Holmes à Court.

'The directors of BHP,' was the answer.[19]

The hearings under the chairman Mr Henry Bosch were always spectacular and good newspaper copy. Some sharebrokers were critical of Mr Bosch. They put forward the argument that the NCSC had no place to interfere in investment decisions made by public companies and no right to say that one investment was better than any other. Others felt shareholders needed this very protection in a climate where take-overs were as common as spring rain. There was a complete circle of legal action, a crossfire between Bell Resources and BHP. Then on 18 June Elders issued a writ in the Victorian Supreme Court, which presented eighty points — sixty-four allegations of bias, and sixteen claiming ulterior motives in the commission's actions.[20]

Ultimately, on 15 October the commission tabled a report in parliament which cleared the two companies of collusion,[21] but the cliffhanger serial continued. Would BHP take over Elders? Would Elders take over BHP? Would Bell grab first BHP then Elders or vice versa? Or would BHP confuse everything by swallowing Bell Resources? The betting always seemed to be on Holmes à Court. But then on 15 September there was the most remarkable result of all; a truce was declared. Both Robert Holmes à Court and John Elliott were accepted on the board of BHP. Under the agreement Bell and Elders could raise their shareholdings only through a cash offer for all of BHP with a 50 per cent minimum acceptance condition, through a partial bid approved by the BHP shareholders. In the meantime Elders was restricted to a 20 per cent holding in BHP and Bell to a holding of 30 per cent. The agreement stopped both companies from trading in more than 2 per cent of BHP shares. The press had great fun in describing the new scene, so full of love and friendship. The *Age* quoted all the 'Dear John', 'Dear Robert' and 'Dear Jim' letters. ' "Dear Robert," wrote Sir James Balderstone, "I am pleased to extend to you BHP's invitation to join the board of the company."

' "Dear Jim,' replied Mr Holmes à Court, "I am very pleased to accept appointment to the board of BHP".'[22]

There was joy to be had in digging up some of the old quotes. Rumour had it that the code name for Holmes à Court at BHP was 'wart hog'. Brian Loton had described him as just a share trader. Sir James Balderstone had said that the Big Australian would not be treated as a 'speculator's plaything' and in a letter to a disgruntled shareholder he said that Holmes à Court was 'not a person fit to be appointed a director of this company'. Then Mr Holmes à Court had been quoted with a lovely soft key insult for James. 'He doesn't understand this area very well . . . [He] is a leading pastoralist and knows a great deal about cattle prices.' Who was the happiest of the four heavyweights? 'I think I am,' said John Elliott, 'Carlton won on Saturday.' Some still saw it as the sort of truce reached in the Lebanon. London's *Financial Times* said:

The only clear thing to emerge from the exchange of letters is that 'Dear Robert' and 'Dear John' have now been given the chance to examine the prey at leisure from the inside and then to carve up the beast at their mutual convenience.[23]

The alliance with BHP, of course, was of immense importance to CUB. Per capita consumption of beer in Australia was now at 117 litres, way down from the optimistic 1970s when it seemed beer consumption could only continue to soar. The 1975 peak was 140 litres. Much could be made of statistics; the brewers were constantly making claims and denying each other's figures; but the domestic beer market was worth $5 billion. The two giants Bond Brewing and CUB had a fairly equal share of 45 per cent, and the others carved up the final 10 per cent.[24] CUB clearly had the advantage. It had spent millions world wide in establishing Foster's as a national brand. Foster's unquestionably was the most instantly recognised Australian brand name, so much so, that in an intensely parochial country it was not tainted by originating in Melbourne. It was being produced in Melbourne, Sydney, Brisbane, Cairns and Darwin. Bond Brewing on the other hand had a complexity of brands. There was Toohey's in Sydney, Castlemaine Fourex in Brisbane and Swan in Perth. Which was to be their national brand? Bond went for the new Black Swan with a big national campaign, but Swan was being produced only in Perth and it proved once again how desperately difficult it is to get Australians to move from their own local loves and tastes. They were as parochial as they were over their football. Only Foster's was really capable of spreading itself across State borders.

A survey by Reark Research showed that Foster's was the clear market leader with 22 per cent. Toohey's Draught, a Bond product, came second with 11 per cent. The score state by state was interesting. In Sydney it was Toohey's Draught 28 per cent (Bond), Foster's (CUB) 17 per cent, Toohey's 2.2 (Bond) 16 per cent, Resch's Pilsener (CUB) 7 per cent, Victoria Bitter (CUB) 3 per cent, Fourex (Bond) 22 per cent and Black Swan (Bond) 1 per cent. In Victoria it was practically all CUB: Foster's (CUB) 37 per cent, Carlton Draught (CUB) 16 per cent, Victoria Bitter (CUB) 15 per cent, Melbourne Bitter (CUB) 9 per cent, Fourex (Bond) 3 per cent and Black Swan (Bond) 2 per cent. In Brisbane Fourex was a phenomenon: Fourex (Bond) 64 per cent, Fourex Lite (Bond) 16 per cent, Foster's (CUB) 8 per cent, Black Swan less than half per cent. Breaking away from these percentage margins to establish any sort of dominance is difficult indeed and the two brewery combines were involved in the greatest promotion battle the nation had seen, worth more than $100 million.

Both companies had their jet aircraft. Alan Bond had an $11.8 million twin jet Falcon 200; CUB had a British Aerospace 125 series 800. CUB's jet had a Foster's beer symbol on the tailfin and it was known as 'The Flying Beer Can'. Given half an hour's notice or so, it could take Elders' chairman John Elliott or Peter Bartels to any place on earth. The aeroplane seated eight very comfortably indeed, and the seats converted into beds. A little panel on the wall reported the temperature outside and inside, the air speed and the time of arrival. Toward the rear, on the left, there was a little bar with crystal decanters. Further on there was the lavatory, decorated magnificently with a mural of the CUB team of Clydesdales. 'Our extra horsepower,' claimed the pilot, John Flynn. The top staff of CUB don't consider the jet a luxury. The southern states director, Pat Stone, says the brewery is not what it was in the old days. These times you have to make instant decisions on supplied information and events move so quickly you just can't wait for regular airline schedules.

'The flying beer can', or the Elders IXL corporate jet as it is more formally known.

There was a new verb very popular with CUB executives: 'to Fosterise'. The object was to Fosterise Australia. Peter Bartels, CUB managing director, had been known even to call Australia 'Fosterland'. Neither Bond Brewing nor CUB would reveal how much money they were spending on promotion. As with all wars, however, the cost was huge — bigger than the gross turnover of medium size companies. The 1985 expenditure on advertising was $16.6 million for Bond Brewing and $11.7 million for CUB. Between them, the companies were sponsoring almost everything that moved in the way of sport. Bruce Siney, CUB's marketing director, said it went all the way from golf and car racing to woodchopping and darts.

Bond Brewing was deeply into such things as surf lifesaving, lawn bowls, swimming, big golf and country cricket. The battle was intense on the nation's golf courses. Bond had the Golden Slipper two-year-old championship in Sydney which became a million dollar race in 1986, and the Australian Derby in Perth. CUB had the Melbourne and Caulfield Cups plus the Wellington Cup in New Zealand, another area where Foster's was flourishing. Stakes for the Melbourne Cup were more than a million and unquestionably CUB spent another million on promotion. Then there was the Adelaide Grand Prix which was on the world Formula I circuit. The deal with the South Australian Government was to sponsor the Grand Prix for three years. Again the cost was secret. But those who ought to know said that the direct sponsorship was $2 million and that the promotion costs matched that. So it was costing CUB $4 million a year. What with the Grand Prix on October 26 and the Melbourne Cup on the first Tuesday in November CUB had burned up $6 million within a week. Add to this the Grand Final of the Victorian Football League on 27 September which was sponsored by Foster's with a great half time spectacular, the cost according to CUB 'in the six figure range'.[25]

CUB had the Australian Open Golf, the Australian Olympic and Commonwealth Games, Sydney's Ironman competition, the National Triathlon titles, boxer Jeff Fenech, golfers Ian Stanley and Bob Shearer, the national basketball team the Brisbane Bullets, and the Interdominion harness racing classic. Bond Brewing had the Rugby League, Rugby Union, the Australian Cricket team, the Australian Indoor Tennis championships, the Australian National Showjumping Series, NSW country cricket, lawn bowls, and surf lifesaving.[26] Of course, the biggest promotion for Bond was the America's Cup. Who could estimate the costs? There were the yachts — *Australia I*, *Australia II*, *Australia III* and *Australia IV*. Swan Premium Lager was the official beer of the Cup and huge promotion was behind that. Swan sponsorship for the television on Channel 9 alone was $4.7 million. CUB was there too with its sponsorship of the Kookaburra Syndicate, a syndicate which laughed often at its own success.

Does all this outpouring of money really work? Bruce Siney insisted that it did. He said that CUB was looking particularly for sponsorships which would spread the international image. The Melbourne Cup was ideal because the live television went to sixty countries. It went right across the US in prime time and hit Britain for breakfast. He said it was seen by some one hundred million people. The Grand Final, televised live to fifteen countries was seen by seventy million. The Grand Prix was even better. Siney said, 'There are only two other sports in front of Grand Prix racing — Olympic Games and World Cup soccer. Even then soccer doesn't appeal to everyone. We believe 600 million watch the Grand Prix racing and usually it appeals to that element in the international market that can afford to buy an imported beer'.

The Grand Prix, at around $6 million over three years, was unquestionably CUB's best sponsorship deal. From now on the Foster's emblem would appear at every Grand Prix event throughout the world. Furthermore, Alan Jones, the 1980 Formula I World Champion, would personally spread the message. It was the enthusiasm of Peter Bartels that gained the Grand Prix sponsorship. He had to beat the Japanese industrial giant Mitsubishi who had the Adelaide sponsorship in 1985. As one newspaper put it, Bartels beat Mitsubishi to the chequered flag. Bartels was so keen because he was passionate about car racing, and had raced his Kremer Porsche at Melbourne's Calder racetrack. The Kremer brothers in Cologne specialised in re-building Porsches for car racing and their success at Le Mans had been astonishing. The Kremer Porsche would deliver around 400 horsepower, 100 hp more than normal. Bartels bought his Porsche in 1984 and never discussed the price, but a Kremer Porsche in 1987 would be worth around $200 000. Journalist Charles Wright asked Peter Bartels about his car and he spoke of love:

> When I first saw it I felt good. It's almost as much fun washing it as it is driving it. It's hard for me to explain. If you look at the corner rear of the Porsche it's more attractive than Playboy. If you're not an owner and haven't cared for one, it's hard to understand.

When asked what his chairman, John Elliott, thought about the Porsche, he replied, 'I think he'd probably prefer that I didn't do this, but he's a bit of a competitor too. He's been for a ride in it and quite enjoyed it. It's a great place to negotiate your salary package.'[27]

Adelaide on 26 October 1986 was something to see. There were five hundred great Foster's blue flags and the *News Adelaide* called it the great

Alan Jones (left), Australian Formula One driver sponsored by Foster's, with Peter Bartels and the Prime Minister, Bob Hawke, at the 1986 Foster's Australian Formula One Grand Prix.

'blue rinse'.[28] Tony Stephens of the *Sydney Morning Herald* wrote, 'If Alan Bond turned Perth into Swansville for the America's Cup, John Elliott has made a Fostersville out of Adelaide. Mr Elliott's avowed aim to Fosterise the world has begun here. It is as if the nation is chasing a beer-led recovery.'[29] There was criticism of CUB being the sponsor of a car race. The Reverend Dan Armstrong, a Uniting Church minister in Canberra, claimed that Australia needed Jesus more than a grand prix. 'I see Foster's pouring millions into this one event and then I see people with alcohol problems.' John Bannon, Premier of South Australia, responded:

> Because of the real stringency of the rules relating to alcohol and Grand Prix driving, and because the standards of safety and care are the best in the world, we can use that to promote safe driving. Criticism of the Foster's involvement is unrealistic. It is quite consistent for a brewery or a winery to be part of a major promotion.

Peter Bartels said, 'Motor sport has done more for road safety than almost any other activity. Alcohol and high speed do not go together. These are not street cars. They are specialised racing cars driven by people who are not allowed to have alcohol before an event'.[30] For clerical comment on the other side, an Adelaide Catholic priest, Father Joe Grealy, was official chaplain to the race. Father Grealy blessed the track and said he hoped he would not have to administer last rites to anybody.

The Frenchman, Alain Prost, took the honours in the Adelaide Grand Prix with a thrilling win. It was Prost's second world driver's championship in a row and the first time a driver had won consecutive world championships since Australia's Jack Brabham in 1959-60. Seconds after Prost crossed the finish line, an RAAF F-111 fighter screamed over the Grand Prix circuit with a victory roll, then lit the skies with the flames from its afterburner. There was a crowd of 120 000, twelve thousand up on the previous year. It was certainly the way to gather publicity. There was a media contingent of a thousand with four hundred overseas representatives and a dozen of the world's top sports writers.

On the same day there was the Ford TX5 Turbo Celebrity Race of five laps of the circuit. There was an all-star cast of celebrities with names like Greg Norman, Dennis Lillee, Dawn Fraser, John Blackman and Paul Cronin. They all drove Ford Turbo TX5s. Peter Bartels trained hard for this event and was determined to win. He spoke to Alan Jones, the great ex-champion, who told him what to do. He said there were five seconds between the red and green light and no matter what you did, it was vital to get a good start; count out those five seconds. 'I counted to five, but obviously I must have been counting my heart beats, and by the time you rev it up to 5000 revs and let the clutch out, there's no turning back.'[31] Notice went up almost immediately and Bartels was penalised one minute for jumping the gun. A minute is almost half a lap. From then on he had no hope, even though he finished second on the track. The winner was ironman Dwayne Thuys. Greg Norman came fourth. The Dire Straits' singer-guitarist, Mark Knopfler, spun out during the first lap, slammed into a wall and broke a collar bone. Peter Bartels defended himself later. He said a film of the start showed that when the light turned green he was actually behind the wheel of the car in front of him and he did not break the line.

The sponsorship of car racing now was a permanent thing for spreading the international name of Foster's. Local football was becoming less and less attractive, and the breweries had come into barrel to barrel conflict over the game. Castlemaine Fourex established itself as a major sponsor of Victorian Football League in Melbourne during 1986. CUB was the traditional sponsor from 1979 when it was the first firm to sponsor a VFL club, putting its weight behind Richmond. The next year, it decided to sponsor the entire sport. CUB was not happy with this dual sponsorship, it was a bit like Presbyterians trying to muscle their way into the Vatican. Bond Brewing staged its own deal with the VFL through Castlemaine by sponsoring the umpires and the goalposts. It was rare indeed to see umpires carrying advertising symbols. The clash came right at the beginning of the competition for the Foster's Cup, the television night knockout series. CUB objected to the Castlemaine goalposts, so their bottoms had to be covered with sheets to hide their message; they looked like nappies.

The way ahead was obvious both for CUB and Bond Brewing. There was no room for expansion in Australia. They were faced with some of the heaviest liquor taxes anywhere in the world. They had to go overseas.

OPPOSITE PAGE:
The roaring start to the first Foster's Australian Formula One Grand Prix, Adelaide 1986.

In January 1986 the Bond Group made a $38 million cash offer for the Pittsburgh Brewing Company in the United States. It was a small brewery, a little over half the size of the Swan Brewery in Perth. It brewed pilsener, lager, and dark and light beers under names such as Iron City, Old German and IC Golden Lager. The brewery would be a useful distribution centre and it had idle capacity for the possible production of Swan in the US.[32]

CUB was not far behind. On 20 March it announced it had moved into partnership with Carling O'Keefe Ltd of Toronto to brew Foster's under licence for the Canadian market. Carling O'Keefe, an associate of Rothmans International was one of the top three Canadian brewers.[33] By July it was ready to go. Paul Hogan, who spread the Foster's message so brilliantly in Britain, crossed the Atlantic to do the same for north America. The Canadians had to be educated to the correct vernacular. For example, they knew nothing about a 'tinnie' and when one mentioned the word 'coldie' they were inclined to think this was baby talk for an approaching session of the flu. Hogan had to make his ads in California. It would have been too depressing having to provide a fine thirsty message in the midst of the Canadian winter. The scripts came from the office of J. Walter Thompson in Toronto, but they had all the Hogan style. One showed Hoges at a really superb garden party taking place in a lovely marquee. He starts with the obligatory 'G'day', then talks a little about the similarity between Oz and Canada. He notes that they are 'roughing it under canvas' (a marquee fit for the Queen), and doing a 'bit of cookin' over an open fire' (a dazzling barbecue with all the conveniences), and tells the Canadians how lucky they are to have a drop of Foster's to make it all bearable. Now comes the sell: 'They're selling the liquid gold for the price of your regular brew'. He moves up to a gorgeous woman, who is decked out in more mink than Zsa Zsa Gabor. He runs his eye over her and says: 'Just as well, too. Looks like some of youse still has to go out and trap your own fur coats'. It all went down very well with the Canadians. Deeply indigenous terms like 'ripper' and 'it's like an angel cryin' on your tongue' moved into the language.[34]

The following month there was a launch on the west coast in Vancouver. The Vancouver *Sun* ran a big advertisement which read:

A NEW TWIST
FROM DOWN UNDER

Introducing Foster's. Australia's golden throat charmer. It's the number one beer in our country that knows a thing or two about what beer is all about. Foster's is brewed in Canada now. It tastes just like the luscious liquid back in Aus, but it only costs the same as your regular brew. And to make it that much easier to try, Foster's is available with the 'The Fast Cap'. The new easy opening top that spins off smoother than a well-bowled googly on a Sydney cricket pitch. In Australia, when you can't think of enough good things to say, they say only one thing. 'Ripper.'[35]

Carling O'Keefe gave CUB an excellent base in North America. In early 1987 CUB bought the Canadian company for nearly $400 million Australian.

In May Foster's started a multi million dollar assault on the US market using Paul Hogan commercials once again. If Foster's was the most recognisable Australian product, Paul Hogan was the most recognisable Australian, even in front of golfer Greg Norman. Americans had seen him

OPPOSITE PAGE:
Foster's supports the Australian team at the 1986 Commonwealth Games in Edinburgh (top). Photographed are three members of the Australian pursuit team — (left to right) Brett Dutton, Wayne McCarney and Glenn Clarke — on their way to gold.
Bottom: Bob Shearer, Ian Baker-Finch, Roger Davis and Ian Stanley enjoy a Foster's at the Tasmanian Open, sponsored by Foster's in 1986.

Paul Hogan on a Los Angeles billboard advertising Foster's.

in a famous series of ads for the Australian Tourist Commission and he was the star of *Crocodile Dundee*. Foster's had already done well in the US, better than all other Australian beers put together and it was in twelfth place on the list of America's favourite imports.[36] The Melbourne office of George Patterson International created and produced the commercials. The best of them showed Hoges in a cosy crowded bar with a Foster's bottle in his hand. Seated next to him is a beaut looking bird and Hoges is running on. 'Course back home our favourite sport is shark wrestling.'

A character on the other side looks boggle-eyed, 'Shark wrestling?'

Hogan fills up his pot, 'Nothing better than sitting down to a few rounds of man versus hungry white pointer . . . with a drop of the amber nectar'.

'White pointer?' says the boggled-eyed guy.

'Yeh!' continues Hoges, 'Course the hard part is getting the sharks into those tight little white shorts.'

Hoges winks, looks at his beer, 'Foster's. It's Australian for beer, mate'.

The series won a bronze medal in the alcoholic beverages section at the 1986 International Film and TV Festival in New York.

Both Bond Brewing and CUB conducted their missions to China during 1986 and there were possibilities that they would soon start producing their product there under licence, but first CUB had other dramatic ideas. There were rumours abroad in late August that CUB was tendering for the brewing assets of Courage in the United Kingdom. On 19 September it was official, Elders IXL purchased Courage Breweries for $3.3 billion. The deal included 3671 tenanted public houses, 1334 public houses under management, a wine and spirits wholesaler, Saccone and Speed, and a chain of 386 off-licences, Roberts and Cooper Ltd. It was an astonishing spread of ownership. Courage had over 5000 tied hotels, almost as many as all the hotels in Australia. The *Australian* reported that it caused a sensation in the City of London. It was the biggest ever take-over deal by an Australian company and it exceeded even BHP's purchase of Utah International. Instantly it put Carlton among the top ten brewers in the world.[37] Courage was owned by the Hanson Trust, which had taken over the Imperial Group for £2.6 billion the previous July. Hanson had made no secret that it wanted to get out of the brewing department. Courage was the sixth largest brewer in the United Kingdom with an annual output of 3.4 million barrels, rather smaller than CUB which produces 5.2 million. But the purchase meant that CUB at last had its own beachhead in England, the base from which it could make its assault on the splendid European Common Market. Now without all the hindrances of custom barriers it could move into Spain, France, Germany, Sweden, Greece . . . John Elliott and Peter Bartels had always believed that British brewers had never used proper brewing and marketing skills to do this.

Now at last after battling for almost two years without success to aquire Allied Lyons, they had what they wanted. A London press conference asked John Elliott whether he had been in touch with Allied Lyons. 'I telephoned them this morning,' he said. 'They seemed rather pleased.' That brought an uproarious laugh from the journalists.[38] John Elliott said later:

> Had we been able to buy Allied Lyons at the original share price that would have been a very good deal, but we struck the Monopolies Commission. We spent eight months making presentations to them. They produced a 125 page report that was regarded in the City as the most glowing report ever done on a company on the terms of our ability to manage. They said that we were perfectly fit people to purchase Allied. They didn't think we would take unnecessary risks, use unnecessary gearing and we would be good people to run it. That provided us with a green light to operate in the City of London. We were no longer regarded as these outlandish Australians coming in to break business up. Yes, we would have bought Allied Lyons but in the passage of time the market price had gone up so we had to make the choice of Allied or Courage. We did our numbers and Courage was the best buy. Also Courage had the advantage of being an instant purchase against an unwanted take-over.

John Elliott returned to Melbourne four days later, a very happy man. He told reporters: 'We're going to Fosterise the world'. Already CUB was the eighth biggest brewer. Market research had predicted that within five years there would be four or five 'world beers'. Today only Heineken enjoyed this status. He was sure Foster's would be up there with Heineken.[39]

There were a number of ironies. Courage distributed Alan Bond's Swan Lager in Britain; John Elliott had the feeling he might not want to continue that contract. And although it was not mentioned in any of the news stories, those with long memories had wistful thoughts. They remembered the day the ebullient Sir Maurice Nathan went to work with a bulldozer, turning the first sod of a new Courage Brewery at Broadmeadows, Melbourne, the offspring of the 'Take Courage' empire that was intended to down CUB.

As for Watney's, they still produced Foster's under licence in London, Halifax and Edinburgh, so with the new deal and control over Courage hotels they could look to: Courage + Watney's = 11 000 hotels. The Fosterisation of Britain, at least, was well under way.

CHAPTER EIGHTEEN

Fosterising the World

Few cities on earth are quite so dominated by their brewery as Melbourne is by Carlton. Perhaps Guinness in Dublin, or Carlsberg in Copenhagen; but look at Carlton, right in Swanston Street, barely the throw of a cricket ball from the Town Hall. The bluestone in Bouverie Street dates from 1864 and the date is still up there on the frieze. Back in the 1880s bluestone was the working man's stone, the stone for building warehouses, jails and factories. If you wanted something really fancy for a bank, or if your church congregation was well-heeled, then you went for the fancy sandstone from Sydney. The irony of it all was that the common Melbournian basalt bluestone was infinitely tougher than the upmarket soft sandstone. Nearly a century later churches like Scots Church in Collins Street had to spend millions to restore their glamorous sandstone, while the tougher bluestone already had passed it in trendiness. Bluestone came into its true glory when it was chosen for the Arts Centre.

In 1870 Mr Latham covered 11 000 square feet of land facing on to Victoria Street with a splendid bluestone building. It was two storeys high and had a slate roof. On the ground floor there was a large beer cellar where the Carlton brews were matured up to six weeks and on the first floor there were malt bins and a malt store. In 1882, just before Latham ceased to take an active day-to-day interest in the company, he bought land at the corner of Bouverie Street and Ballarat Street and built another bluestone warehouse with three floors and a slate roof. It had more beer cellars, an engine room and sugar storage. So the bluestone tradition was created. In 1920 CUB extended the lovely bluestone line another 23 metres, matching the three storeys and all the window details, so now the bluestone went for 49 metres without a break. In 1925 CUB demolished the old Bush Inn at the corner of Victoria and Bouverie Streets. It was one of Melbourne's oldest hotels. It began originally as a grocer's shop and Mr Timothy Sullivan took out a licence in 1867.[1] Now the Carlton Brewery extended its offices right down to the corner, and it was masterfully done. In the 1980s it is hard to tell that the whole facade was not built at the one time.

The next move came in 1954. The huge postwar expansion was under way. The company pulled down the grand old building in Victoria Street and erected a modern but perhaps less distinguished office block. Down came the warehouse building in Bouverie Street also. Everything was redesigned. The architects put in loading bays at ground level and supported the upper floors on steel and concrete pillars; the Bouverie Street bluestone facade was maintained, however. The old bluestone all came out, the blocks were carefully numbered, then put back stone by stone as if nothing had ever happened. In Edward Latham's day there were two hitching posts outside the Bouverie Street entrance. Delightful objects, they were very ornate cast iron to go with the exotic styles of 1870 Victoriana. They had brass barrels on top with his name and that of the company on either end.[2] The same posts are now over the road at the entrance to the group technical centre. Edward Latham would have to hunt to find any relics of his old brewery now. But there are a few items. On the north side of Ballarat Street just 25 metres from Bouverie Street there are the old stables, once the home for two hundred mighty Clydesdales. Back in the 1870s, even when he was rising 30 years old, the famed Coppin used to live there and after he died his tail and hooves were preserved in his memory.

One of the original hitching posts at the Carlton Brewery.

The old stables were completely gutted in 1964 to make way for the hop extract plant. The engineers, Milton Johnson and Partners, pulled out the old loft which used to house the fodder and altered the roof to provide ventilation and light, but the fabric of the building remained the same. There is still a sign on the building: 'Carlton Brewery Stables 1870'.

What's more, the old number one brew tower is still there, although that might be something of an exaggeration: the foundations and the walls are all original, and it has the same frame, stairs and fittings, all imported from England by Edward Latham.[3] Don Kelly, CUB's eloquent tour guide, always points out the 1873 foundation stone. Yet in Latham's time the tower, complete with clock, was something to see. It had a gorgeous Mansard roof like a Louis XIV French chateau. There was a look-out on top with cast-iron grill, almost like a play pen. In 1922 the brew tower was remodelled, the fancy Mansard roof came off, and plain block-like extra floors took its place. The clock was removed to a rather untidy little shed on the roof. It had two faces, one to the west for the benefit of North Melbourne and the other to the south down Swanston Street. A large bell sat on top of the shed and there was a hole in the roof so that workmen down below could pull up the weights. Later in the 1970s, when lofty fermenting vats went in next door, the face to the south was no longer visible. The weights disappeared, the clock went electric and even the old bell came down. One of the last of the ancient Latham relics now had gone.

The Carlton Brewery in 1987 was a remarkable mixture of the historic and the modern. The number one brew tower was doing the same things in principle that it did in Edward Latham's day, turning a mixture of malt, sugar, water and hops into sparkling beer. There was a brew kettle still in operation, a work of art, composed entirely of brass copper, beside the latest models in stainless steel. There was a cellar with ten fermenting tanks, each of which held 90 000 litres of wort and yeast, plus further fermenting towers which held 360 000 litres, but Carlton never again could be the great force it had been, because of the change in drinking habits.

Back before the First World War the packaging of beer was costly and even more expensive to transport. The ratio of draught to bottled was something like seventy to thirty. In the 1980s it was precisely the reverse. There were many reasons for this, the more leisurely life style, the drift away from the automatic drink at the pub on the way home, and not the least, the drink-driving legislation, with random blood alcohol tests for drivers.

CUB was involved in a huge project to streamline its Melbourne operations, and shift all brewing to Abbotsford. The Melbourne operation was in two clear divisions. Carlton looked after the bulk beer in kegs, Abbotsford produced all the packaged beer in cans and bottles. Under the new system the bulk beer was to be produced in the new 50-litre casks with the built-in spear, utterly metric. The government had decreed the end of the old measures and terms like firkins, kilderkins and hogsheads. The old coopers, who at one time were so powerful they could call a strike with the imperious style of builders' labourers, must have been weeping in their beer. That's if any still existed.

Actually, the packaging of beer at Carlton had ceased back on Friday 13 May 1949. From then on Carlton had handled all the bulk beer production. Abbotsford and Victoria looked after the packaging, all the bottling and canning.

From the brewery's point of view there was little logic in running a modern factory operation, which depended on high speed delivery of the product, in the heart of the Golden Mile. Back in 1865 when Edward Latham purchased his brewery it was wonderful. His horses had to travel only a mile or two to deliver around the city pubs and for export there was the easy trip down Elizabeth Street to Flinders Street and the wharves along the Yarra.

Not only was the Carlton Brewery on the casualty list, the grand old Victoria Brewery founded by Thomas Aitkin in 1854 went out of business. It stood there in all its glory in Victoria Parade, East Melbourne. There were great building programmes in early 1882, another in 1896 until it reached its present stage, complete with battlements like Fort Zindeneuf in *Beau Geste*. In the 1980s CUB used it only as a distribution centre and in 1985 the company sold it for future development. In the meantime it was registered by the Historic Buildings Council and in 1987 it was empty, waiting to be recycled; unlike the dead marines of old, recycling was not easy.

In 1871, when Victoria had a population of less than 800 000, there were 126 commercial breweries.[4] Now, effectively, there was one, CUB's brewery at Abbotsford. Unquestionably it was the largest brewery on earth south of the Equator, and, ironically it once housed CUB's greatest rival. It sits on 12 hectares beside the Yarra at Abbotsford, its huge white chimney stack like a finger pointing up to God. Not many people in Melbourne realise what a vast operation it is, and what a fascinating experience it is to be taken on a guided tour of Abbotsford by its head brewer, John Moffat. 'We are doing our exporting to Canada, USA, New Zealand, England. We are also going into Darwin, South Australia, Tasmania, Western Australia. We not only have our peaks of Melbourne weather, we have weather right round Australia.'

John Moffat doesn't like the suggestion that you could blindfold your beer drinker and he would have difficulty in distinguishing between any of the Carlton beers.

The brands are different. We make different varieties by using various combinations of malt and sugar. We brew a lager and a bitter. We brew lager here

and separate them as Foster's and Abbots later on. Then we brew a bitter and we separate those as Vic. and Melbourne later. Everything is bottom-fermented as opposed to the old top-fermented ales.

In old terminology what we make is lager. The brands are different because we vary the contents of malt and sugar. They are altered later too with hops. They differ in taste with hopping, tint level, colour plus the differences in malt and sugar. Difference between Foster's Lager and Melbourne Bitter? Foster's would be smoother, Melbourne Bitter slightly more bitter. Melbourne Bitter also has a darker tint. The degree of hopping causes the bitterness. Some people prefer Vic. and won't drink anything else. Others go for Draught. Carlton Draught is brewed here. The Draught is probably more different than other beer. It has quite a big difference in malt and sugar ratios and it has a fuller flavour.

We have low alcohol brands: Carlton Light, Carlton LA, Carlton Special Light. Carlton Light is 3.3, Carlton LA is 2.1 and Carlton Special Light is 0.9. To get alcohol you ferment carbohydrate. Your carbohydrate is broken down into alcohol. To get less alcohol you start off with less carbohydrate. Then we go to a stout. For this we use roasted barley and crystal malt which is normal malt dried at a higher temperature to produce a darker colour. This combination of the roasted barley and the crystal malt gives stout its characteristic flavour. Ah, yes, more calories. There is Abbots Double Extra Stout and Abbots Invalid Stout. Double Extra is taken straight through and Invalid has a small percentage of beer in it, a black and tan.

In 1987 a new keg-filling plant opened at the Abbotsford Brewery in Melbourne.

Ted Kunkel, managing director of Carling O'Keefe, Canada.

The fermenting vessels are the biggest and grandest things of their kind, like vast wheat silos with conical bottoms, except they are made entirely of quality stainless steel. One stands right on top and looks down through a glass panel. There way below is the yellowish, foaming stuff, in one vat alone enough to assuage 300 000 thirsts. Awesome indeed.

Come New Year 1987 Foster's was surging everywhere. Peter Bartels, CUB's managing director, claimed it was the best known Australian brand around the world. Its nearest rival was probably Vegemite. Although Australians might look upon Vegemite with deep mystic feelings as though it were some strange Oz initiation elixir, it was known only slightly in the US and elsewhere. Foster's however was being promoted on a scale never previously attempted for an Australian product. Peter Bartels, the man who wanted to Fosterise the world, saw no reason why Foster's should not become as well known as Marlboro. He looked upon Marlboro cigarettes as the cleverest of all promotions, the simple use of red and white. The Foster's plan also was for simplicity, the predominant blue and the uncluttered design on the can. It was no accident that Foster's executives appeared in public wearing zipper blue jackets and blue shirts.

To look back into the history of brewing: Emil Resch was the great force at Carlton before the First World War; R. F. G. Fogarty was the personality of the 1960s, the ultimate beer baron; Bartels however was the new breed, the style of the 1980s. If there was any dismay at the Elders take-over, the muscle being displayed at the brewery four years later may have been some consolation. The company had moved from being a good local brewing company with some useful international markets to being the sixth largest brewing organisation in the world behind only Anheuser-Busch, Millers, Heineken, Kirin and Stroh in total volume. A stockmarket survey in February 1987 stated: 'Under the direction of Elders the change to CUB has been dramatic'. The survey said the capital had stagnated under the previous management, but now they estimated that during the first five years under Elders there would be a 16 per cent annual compound rate of earnings.[5]

The change of staff at CUB was minimal. The big change was in approach. The brewery used to be like an old monastery housing an enclosed silent order. Not only did the executives not speak to the outside world, they did not speak to each other for fear of giving away departmental secrets. Bartels arrived with the new open-door approach. He gave information at staff conferences that they would never have told each other. Old hands could hardly believe such information was given with such freedom and such trust. Under previous regimes secrecy had been a way of life; even important staff appointments had been made without any announcements, and the shredder had been a vital instrument.

Bartels brought about a change akin to Gorbachev at the Kremlin or Pope John at the Vatican. He told a senior executive, 'You know one of the big problems here is that everyone is afraid to make a mistake. I'd rather people have a bias for action. Go and make some mistakes and learn from them. I only expect you to be right eight times out of ten.'

John Elliott became chairman of Courage and Peter Bartels the deputy chairman and managing director. They continued the Elliott policy of not indulging in too much blood-letting. Courage had a very experienced staff. Peter Bartels and Bruce Siney, his marketing chief, introduced new marketing ideas. Courage was providing everything for which they had planned and dreamed. Peter Bartels said Courage had over five thousand tied houses, almost as many hotels as in all Australia. The idea would be for Courage to brew Foster's in England as well as Watney, Mann & Truman. As Watney's also had its tied houses, putting the two together gave a tremendous result. Foster's already was one of the largest individual-selling lagers in the United Kingdom; this addition would put them way out in front.

In the old days at CUB, even as late as the 1960s, it was a serious matter if an executive ever left the country, and mostly they remained in Bouverie Street. The international telephone now made it easy to keep in touch with CUB executives. Elliott, Bartels, Bruce Siney, marketing director, and John Jopling, were for ever on the move. John Elliott was virtually half and half, half his time overseas and half in Australia. Peter Bartels became resident in London; chief executive of Elders Brewing Group worldwide. Perhaps a third of his time would be in Australia. For some it might seem a life of jet lag torture, but they insisted air travel now was easy. Ted Kunkel became managing director of Carling O'Keefe in Canada. Pat Stone, Keith Lawson and Bruce Siney became group executive directors — Pat in charge of southern states plus wines and spirits, Keith in charge of New South Wales, Queensland, New Zealand and Fiji, and Bruce in charge of national and international strategy.

In the US, thanks to the Paul Hogan advertising campaign, Foster's increased sales threefold in twelve months. The concentration first was on the east and west coasts and Chicago. There are subtle differences between the US and the Canadian markets. Peter Bartels said:

Pat Stone, group executive director, CUB.

> Americans like a genuine all-imported beer. They will go into the supermarket and buy a six-pack of Budweiser, but when they go out to a bar, that's when they want something different, like an imported beer. Market research has shown that our beer is very popular. They find the taste somewhere between Bud and Heineken.

Of course, the American market has been marvellous for Australian production. When demand starts to fall as winter approaches in Australia, beer for the US market takes up the slack.

Canadians, however, are different, according to Peter Bartels. Just as the British accept Foster's made by Watney's, Canadians are happy to take Foster's made under licence by their famous brewer Carling O'Keefe. Sales of Foster's in Toronto were exceeding all expectations and had taken 2 per cent of the market. In Vancouver it was doing even better, so now Foster's was being brewed in London, Halifax, Edinburgh, Toronto, Vancouver, Melbourne, Sydney, Brisbane, Cairns and Darwin. Samples from all breweries would constantly flow into Melbourne and be put through complex blind tastings to make sure it had the same flavour around the globe.

CUB continued to look for promotions that would get it known around the world. The Foster's Grand Prix was a superb outlet; it could not be better. The Foster's Melbourne Cup was excellent. The America's Cup was an interesting proposition, it was almost entirely in possession of Bond Brewing. Alan Bond won the Cup for Australia in 1983 and Swan Premium was the official beer of the America's Cup Defence in Perth in 1986–87.

Keith Lawson, group executive director, CUB.

Few people believed that Bond, with his two 12-metre yachts, *Australia III* and *Australia IV*, would not be there to win the Cup for us again in 1987.

There were seventeen entries for the Cup from Italy, France, Britain, Canada, New Zealand, six from the US, Sydney, Adelaide and two from Perth. In April 1986 CUB gave $250 000 to the Kookaburra Syndicate, backed by Perth millionaire Kevin Parry. The average cost — almost the membership fee for being in the America's Cup club — was over $20 million. CUB was a minor sponsor, and Kookaburra was almost unknown outside of Perth.

Kookaburra had a theme song 'Kookaburra, you're laughing, Flying over everyone'. That's what they did. Kookaburra beat the Bond boat four straight. At first there was shock, then a profound feeling of sympathy for Alan Bond. After all, it was Bond who had mounted the challenge in 1983. He had achieved the impossible by taking the Cup off the New York Yacht Club for the first time in 135 years. Had he not done this there would have been no contest in Perth in 1987.

Bond offered all assistance to Parry and the Kooka Syndicate, the use of *Australia III* and *Australia IV*, and generously he gave $100 000. Yet for a moment everything went flat. It seemed to John Elliott and Peter Bartels who had arrived in Perth that Australia was not alight with excitement, not backing the Kookaburra defence the way it should. First CUB gave a million dollars to the Kookaburra Taskforce Syndicate, and on the eve of the start of the final challenge, John Elliott gave a press conference. He made the announcement that Australia was not providing enough push. We were not getting behind the Kooka challenge. 'As any sportsman can tell you,' he said, 'it makes all the difference if the fans are fired up behind you.' So he said that in addition to the $1.25 million already given to Taskforce, CUB was now spending $100 000 to spread the Kooka message.

CUB took full page advertisements in metropolitan dailies all around Australia depicting *Kookaburra III* flying a Kookaburra spinnaker with the slogan 'Go for Australia Kooka'. There were great signs painted GO FOR KOOKA on the waterfront and come race morning CUB staff were out with supermarket trolleys distributing thousands of 'Go for Kooka' stickers and eyeshades. This was a little reminiscent of the VFL Grand Final when CUB literally swamped the Melbourne Cricket Ground with the Foster's Lager message. 'We're more subtle this time,' said John Elliott. They were indeed. There was no mention of Foster's on the stickers or the eyeshades, it was all for Kooka. A helicopter was to bring over the huge Foster's flag that was draped across the Melbourne Cricket Ground and carry it dramatically across Fremantle Harbour, but it was too heavy and no available helicopter could lift it.

As it turned out, Dennis Conner in *Stars and Stripes* was all triumphant for the San Diego Yacht Club. He won four straight. The finish was almost a riot. Fremantle Harbour could not have absorbed another spectator. There were people clinging all over the galvanised iron roofs of the restaurants. There were at least a thousand craft out on the water. *Kookaburra III* was hemmed in by every conceivable type of vessel: *Parts VI*, owned by an American spare parts millionaire, the handsome yacht of the Aga Khan, runabouts, tugs, catamarans, Bertrams, cruise ships, so many boats

OPPOSITE PAGE:
Even after her America's Cup defeat in 1987, Kookaburra III sailed home to a rousing reception, proudly flying her Foster's spinnaker.

it looked as if they were readying themselves to evactuate Western Australia.

And they were all waving to *Kookaburra III*'s skipper, Iain Murray. There were signs everywhere over the rocks: PROUD OF YOU KOOKA, DENNIS HOW ABOUT DOUBLE OR NOTHING and WELL DONE DENNIS YOU BASTARD!

Normally after races *Kookaburra III* was towed into the wharf. This time it sailed in and it must have been the finest piece of helmsmanship in Iain Murray's career. During races no advertising was allowed but now he broke out a great Foster's Lager spinnaker in dazzling royal blue. He threaded his way at speed through the spectator craft like a skier doing a slalom. The next day Kevin Parry announced a massive challenge worth $50 million for the next America's Cup in 1990. Of course, Foster's Lager would be there. It was another part of the plan to Fosterise the world.

NOTES

Chapter One

1   Sidney J. Baker, *The Australian Language*, Currawong Publishing Co., Sydney, 1966.
2   *Age*, 26 May 1855.
3   *Melbourne Morning Herald*, 28 May 1855.
4   *Argus*, 26 September 1871.
5   *Age*, 26 February 1875.
6   *Age*, 2 March 1875.
7   *Age*, 7 August 1875; *Argus*, August 1875.
8   *Australian Brewers' Journal*, 20 January 1909.
9   *Argus*, 11 March 1879.
10 *Australian Brewers' Journal*, 20 March 1889.
11 ibid., 20 December 1899.
12 Baker, op. cit.
13 H. W. H. Huntington, *Australian Cordial Maker*, 16 June 1904.
14 C. D. F., *Australian Brewers' Journal*, 21 March 1904.
15 Huntington, op. cit.
16 D. O'Hara, History of CUB, typescript, National Library, MS500.
17 ibid.
18 John Barleycorn, *A Glass of Ale*, Mitchell Library.
19 *Australian Brewers' Journal*, 20 July 1905.
20 *What's Brewing*, CUB House Journal, June 1965.
21 Barleycorn, op. cit.
22 ibid.
23 *What's Brewing*, March 1951.
24 Brian Carroll, *The Australian Stage Album*, Macmillan, Melbourne, 1976.
25 Barleycorn, op. cit.
26 *Age*, 20 January 1883.
27 ibid.
28 *Australian Brewers' Journal*, 20 May 1896.
29 George Meudell, *The Pleasant Career of a Spendthrift and his After Reflections*, Wilke & Co., Melbourne, 1924.
30 Michael Cannon, *The Land Boomers*, Melbourne University Press, Melbourne, 1966.
31 *Australian Brewers' Journal*, 20 May 1896.
32 Cannon, op. cit.

Chapter Two

1   Graeme Davison, *The Rise and Fall of Marvellous Melbourne*, Melbourne University Press, Melbourne, 1978.
2   David Dunstan, *Governing the Metropolis*, Melbourne University Press, Melbourne, 1984.
3   Geoffrey Serle, *The Rush To Be Rich*, Melbourne University Press, Melbourne, 1971.

4 *Australian Brewers' Journal*, 20 July 1888.
5 ibid., 20 December 1888.
6 ibid., 20 February 1890.
7 ibid., 20 January 1883, 29 March 1890, 20 October 1892.
8 ibid., 20 December 1900.
9 ibid., 20 December 1902.
10 ibid.
11 ibid., 20 January 1890.
12 ibid., 20 February 1885, 20 June 1890, 21 September 1908.
13 ibid., 20 October 1891, 20 June 1890.
14 ibid., 20 March 1890.
15 ibid., 20 February 1890.
16 ibid., 20 June 1885, 20 February, 20 April 1887.
17 ibid., 20 July 1885; *Argus*, 6 January 1887.
18 *Australian Brewers' Journal*, 20 October 1888.
19 *Age*, 11 July 1889, p. 5.
20 *Victorian Parliamentary Debates*, Vol. 61, pp. 1491-2.
21 *Australian Brewers' Journal*, 20 November 1889.
22 ibid., 20 February 1892.
23 ibid., 21 June, 20 July 1897.
24 ibid., 10 September 1895.
25 *Australian Brewers' Journal*, 20 February 1892.
26 *Herald*, 13 February 1891.
27 ibid., 18 February 1891.
28 Foster Brewing Co. Board Minutes.
29 *Australian Brewers' Journal*, 21 June, 20 July 1897.
30 ibid., 10 September 1895.

CHAPTER THREE

1 Keith Dunstan, *The Paddock That Grew*, Cassell, Melbourne, 1962.
2 P. G. McCarthy, 'Labour and the Living Wage', *Australian Journal of Politics and History*, Vol. B, April 1976, p. 83.
3 Cannon, op. cit.
4 Meudell, op. cit.
5 *Australian Brewers' Journal*, 20 May 1902.
6 ibid., 20 September 1902.
7 ibid., 20 February 1895.
8 Keith Dunstan, *Wowsers*, Cassell, Melbourne, 1969.
9 *Australian Brewers' Journal*, 20 January 1890.
10 Windsor Hotel, history booklet.
11 R. L. Parker, *Beer*, Mitchell Library, Sydney.
12 *Victorian Parliamentary Debates*, 24 August 1892.
13 *Australian Brewers' Journal*, 20 May 1890, 20 March 1888.
14 ibid., 20 June 1890.
15 ibid., 20 March 1889.
16 A Century of Brewing with Yeast Clones, pamphlet, United Breweries, Copenhagen.
17 *Australian Dictionary of Biography*, Melbourne University Press, Melbourne, Vol. 8, 1981; T. G. Parsons, Manufacturing in Melbourne 1870-90, Monash University thesis; Geoffrey Blainey, *The Rush That Never Ended*, Melbourne University Press, Melbourne, 1963.

CHAPTER FOUR

1 *Australian Brewers' Journal*, 20 March 1900.
2 ibid., 20 June 1900.
3 ibid., 20 April 1900.
4 ibid., 20 September 1900.
5 ibid., 20 May 1899, 21 August 1899.
6 ibid., 20 January 1900.
7 Blake & Riggall contract, Melbourne University Archives.

8   *Australian Brewers' Journal*, 21 May 1900.
9   Eric Nilan, Acorn to Oak, Unpublished manuscript, CUB Library.
10 *Australian Brewers' Journal*, 21 December 1903.
11 *Australian Dictionary of Biography*, Melbourne University Press, Melbourne, Vol. 10, 1986.
12 *Australian Brewers' Journal*, 20 March 1905, 20 October 1897.
13 Alfred Buchanan, *The Real Australia*.
14 *Lone Hand*, 1 January 1909.
15 Private papers, Sir Edward Cohen.
16 *Australian Brewers' Journal*, 20 June, 20 July 1907.
17 ibid., 20 November 1907.
18 ibid., 1903.
19 *Australian Dictionary of Biography*, Melbourne University Press, Melbourne, Vol. 8, 1981.
20 *Australian Brewers' Journal*, 20 August 1908.
21 Batman, *Bulletin*, 12 September 1974.
22 *Australian Brewers' Journal*, 20 December 1909, 20 November 1918.
23 CUB Board Minutes, 1908.

CHAPTER FIVE

1   *Australian Brewers' Journal*, 21 July 1902, 20 March 1911.
2   *Argus*, 7 November 1912.
3   ibid., 8 February 1918.
4   *Bulletin*, 12 September 1912.
5   *Australian Brewers' Journal*, 20 December 1897, 20 January 1898, 20 November 1900.
6   *What's Brewing*, March 1966.
7   *Australian Brewers' Journal*, 20 May 1903.
8   ibid., 21 November 1910.
9   CUB Board Minutes, 25 October 1907.
10 *Australian Brewers' Journal*, August 1909.
11 ibid., 20 May 1908.
12 ibid., 20 February 1908, 21 June 1909, 21 March 1910.
13 ibid., 20 November 1907.
14 ibid., 20 November 1909.
15 Nilan, op. cit.
16 *Australian Brewers' Journal*, 20 April 1909, 20 April 1916.
17 ibid., 20 November 1912; *What's Brewing*, March 1959.
18 Keith Dunstan, *Sun News Pictorial*, 28 July 1962.
19 *Australian Brewers' Journal*, 20 March 1903.
20 CUB Board Minutes, 21 July 1911.
21 *Australian Brewers' Journal*, 20 November 1911.

CHAPTER SIX

1   *Australian Brewers' Journal*, 21 September 1914, 20 November 1914, 21 December 1914.
2   ibid., 21 December 1914.
3   *Argus*, 26 March 1926.
4   CUB special report to Board, 8 February 1916.
5   Nilan, op. cit.
6   CUB Board Minutes, 22 December 1916, 1 June 1917, 10 August 1917, 30 August 1917.
7   *Australian Brewers' Journal*, 20 October 1914.
8   *Argus*, 3, 8 April 1915; *Bulletin*, 22 April 1915.
9   Dunstan, *Wowsers*, op. cit.
10 *Bulletin*, 1 June 1916.
11 *Australian Brewers' Journal*, 20 April 1922.
12 ibid., 20 December 1916.
13 Dunstan, *Wowsers*, op. cit.
14 *Australian Brewers' Journal*, 20 December 1916.

15 ibid., 20 February 1918.
16 ibid., 20 October 1915.
17 *Argus*, 9 November 1918.
18 ibid., 13 November 1918.
19 ibid., 7, 13, 20 February 1919.

CHAPTER SEVEN

1 *Australian Brewers' Journal*, 20 June 1924.
2 *Argus*, 19, 20 October 1920.
3 Dunstan, *Wowsers*, op. cit.
4 Geoffrey Blainey, *A History of Camberwell*, Jacarandah Press, 1964.
5 CUB Board Minutes, 5 January 1923.
6 Nilan, op. cit.
7 ibid.
8 *Australian Brewers' Journal*, 21 July 1924.
9 ibid., 20 February 1925.
10 Frank Cusack, *Bendigo, A History*, Heinemann, 1973.
11 *Australian Brewers' Journal*, 20 March 1925.
12 CUB Board Minutes, 8 April 1925.
13 *Dictionary of Australian Biography*, Melbourne University Press, Melbourne, Vol. 10, 1986.
14 *Australian Brewers' Journal*, 20 May 1914.
15 *Who's Who in Australia*, Herald & Weekly Times Ltd, Melbourne, 1950.
16 Nilan, op. cit.
17 *Argus*, 3 April 1925.
18 *Labor Daily*, 16 May 1928.
19 *Truth*, 28 January 1928.
20 *South Australian Parliamentary Debates*, Licensed Victuallers Bill, 14 July 1896.
21 *Australian Brewers' Journal*, 21 November 1927.
22 ibid., 20 September 1928.
23 ibid., 20 November 1928, 21 January, 20 March 1929, 20 November 1931.
24 *Argus*, 12 March 1930.
25 ibid., 20 March 1930.
26 *Australian Brewers' Journal*, 20 August 1909.
27 *What's Brewing*, June 1951, June 1952.
28 *Argus*, 31 March 1930.

CHAPTER EIGHT

1 *Australian Brewers' Journal*, 20 October 1931.
2 CUB Board Minutes, July 1931, July 1933.
3 *Australian Brewers' Journal*, 20 October 1932.
4 Nilan, op. cit.
5 ibid.
6 *Australian Brewers' Journal*, 20 December 1915.
7 Nilan, op. cit.
8 *Melbourne Punch*, 3 November 1921.
9 CUB Board Minutes, 6 July 1923.
10 *Australian Brewers' Journal*, 20 December 1932.
11 ibid., 21 June 1897.

CHAPTER NINE

1 Geoffrey Serle & James Grant, *The Melbourne Scene*, Melbourne University Press, Melbourne, 1957.
2 *Age*, 3 January 1942.
3 ibid., 25 February 1942.
4 Dunstan, *The Paddock That Grew*, op. cit.
5 Nilan, op. cit.
6 *Herald*, 27 July 1942.
7 ibid., 8 July 1943.
8 ibid., 27 June 1942.

9 Cyril Pearl, *Australia's Yesterdays*, Readers' Digest, Sydney, 1974.
10 *Herald*, 3 August 1942.
11 Interview, 'Midday with Schildberger', ABC-3LO, 23 April 1974.
12 *Argus*, 28 April 1944.
13 *Herald*, 11 November 1944.
14 *Argus*, 19 August 1943.
15 ibid., 13 December 1945.
16 *Herald*, 19 April 1944.
17 ibid.
18 ibid., 1 January 1944.
19 ibid., 23 January 1944.
20 ibid., 15 August 1945.
21 *Sun News Pictorial*, 28 December 1945.
22 Nilan, op. cit.
23 *Herald*, 27 February 1948.
24 ibid., 4 December 1947.
25 CUB Annual Report, 1947.
26 *Herald*, 1 September 1949; *Sun*, 17 December 1949.

CHAPTER TEN

1 *Argus*, 9 March 1951.
2 ibid., 14 November 1952.
3 *Herald*, 15 October 1953.
4 ibid., 31 May 1951.
5 *Sun News Pictorial*, 1 June 1951.
6 *Herald*, 10 July 1951.
7 *Argus*, 25 January 1952.
8 Nilan, op. cit.
9 *What's Brewing*, June 1956.
10 ibid., December 1956.
11 *Australian Brewers' Journal*, 20 July 1890.
12 *What's Brewing*, June 1954.
13 CUB Annual Report, 1955.
14 *Guinness Book of Records 1976*, Guinness Superlatives Ltd, London, 1976.
15 *Australian Brewing & Wine Journal*, 20 January 1936.
16 *What's Brewing*, March 1958.
17 *Sun News Pictorial*, 8 June 1958.
18 Weston Bate, *The Lucky City*, Melbourne University Press, Melbourne, 1978.
19 *What's Brewing*, September, 1960.

CHAPTER ELEVEN

1 *Sun News Pictorial, Herald*, 15 February 1961.
2 *Sydney Morning Herald*, 21 February 1961.
3 *Guinness Book of Records 1975*, Guinness Superlatives Ltd, London, 1975.
4 *Truth*, 21 April 1962.
5 ibid., 5 August 1961.
6 *Herald*, 5 January 1962.
7 *Age, Herald*, 16 January 1962.
8 *Sun News Pictorial*, 5 April 1962.
9 *Truth*, 21 April 1962.
10 *Age*, 2 February 1962.
11 *What's Brewing*, June 1966.
12 *Herald*, 21 March 1966.
13 Dunstan, *Wowsers*, op. cit.
14 *Sun News Pictorial*, 31 March 1964.
15 Liquor Royal Commission transcript, 7 April 1964, Public Archives.
16 Batman, *Bulletin*, 30 May 1964.
17 Dunstan, op. cit.
18 *Sun News Pictorial*, 28 February 1967.

CHAPTER TWELVE

1   *Herald*, 23 February 1968.
2   *Who's Who in Australia*, Herald & Weekly Times Ltd, Melbourne, 1971.
3   *Age*, 21 July 1971.
4   *Herald*, 9 September 1967.
5   *Sun*, 16 November 1967.
6   *Herald*, 4 November 1966.
7   ibid., 1 November 1966.
8   ibid., 5 November 1966.
9   *Australian*, 13 August 1969.
10 Batman, *Bulletin*, 19 October 1968.
11 *Sun*, 9 October 1968.
12 ibid., 14 October 1968.
13 ibid.
14 Batman, *Bulletin*, 19 October 1969.
15 *Australian*, 30 October 1969.
16 *Herald*, 13 March 1970.
17 *Sun*, 31 August 1968.
18 CUB Annual Report, 1969.
19 *Newsday*, 16 March 1970.
20 J. G. Beaney, Victorian Royal Commission on Employees in Shops, 1883.
21 Batman, *Bulletin*, 13 June 1970.
22 John Sorell, *Herald*, 1 August 1968.
23 *Herald*, 11 November 1972.
24 *Financial Review*, 6 December 1972.
25 *Sun*, 25 October 1972.
26 *Herald*, 15 November 1972.
27 *Herald*, 12 December 1972.

CHAPTER THIRTEEN

1   *Sun News Pictorial*, 11 November 1972.
2   Cyril Pearl, *Beer, Glorious Beer*, Thomas Nelson, Melbourne, 1969.
3   *Australian*, 20 August 1975.
4   *Sun News Pictorial*, 21 August 1975.
5   *Australian*, 25 August 1976.
6   CUB Annual Report, 1975.
7   *Financial Review*, 27 June 1975.
8   ibid., 24 December 1976.
9   *Sun News Pictorial*, 1 November 1977.
10 CUB Annual Report, 1977.
11 *Financial Review*, 27 January 1976.
12 Keith Dunstan, *Ratbags*, Golden Press, Sydney, 1979.
13 *Financial Review*, 27 January 1976.
14 John Fraser, *Herald*, 15 July 1976.
15 *National Times*, 6 June 1977; *Australian*, 30 July 1977.
16 *Sunday Press*, 13 October 1978.
17 CUB Employees Report, 1978.
18 *Age*, 17 May 1978.
19 ibid., 27 May 1978.
20 *Financial Review*, 9 March 1978.
21 *Australian*, 27 May 1978.
22 *Financial Review*, 29 May 1978.
23 *Age*, 27 May 1978.
24 *Herald*, 29 May 1978.
25 *Sun News Pictorial*, 3 November 1978.
26 *Courier Mail*, 19 September 1978.
27 ibid., 16 September 1978.
28 *Telegraph*, 28 September 1978.
29 *Australian*, 27 September 1978.
30 *Sunday Mail*, 1 October 1978.

31 *Telegraph*, 17 October 1978.
32 ibid., 20 November 1978.
33 ibid., 21 November 1978.
34 *Financial Review*, 29 November 1978.

CHAPTER FOURTEEN

1   *Age*, 16 November 1979.
2   ibid., 14 November 1979.
3   *Financial Review*, 5 February 1980.
4   ibid., 8 December 1980.
5   *Business Review Weekly*, 6-13 December 1980.
6   *Financial Review*, 24 June 1980.
7   *Age*, 7 March 1981.
8   *Australian*, 18 February 1981.
9   *Age*, 31 March 1981.
10 *Business Review Weekly*, 4 April 1981.
11 ibid., 29 August 1981.
12 *Age*, 2 April 1981.
13 *Business Review Weekly*, 24 August 1981.
14 ibid.
15 *Carlton News*, October 1982.
16 *Business Review Weekly*, 5-11 September 1981.
17 *Financial Review*, 13 January 1982.
18 *Age*, 25 September 1982.
19 *Carlton News*, June 1980.
20 *Age*, 23 December 1981.
21 ibid., 25 August 1981.
22 ibid., 13 August 1982.
23 *Herald*, 14 December 1982.
24 Dunstan, *Wowsers*, op. cit.

CHAPTER FIFTEEN

1   *Bulletin*, 12 November 1966.
2   *Age*, 6 November 1982.
3   S. Howard, A History of Brewing in New South Wales, Private work for Tooth
    & Co. Centenary, 1935.
4   *Sydney Morning Herald*, 26 November 1981.
5   *Age*, 11 August 1983.
6   *Australian*, 11 August 1983.
7   *Business Review Weekly*, 23 April 1982.
8   ibid., 7 May 1982.
9   *Herald*, 3 December 1983.
10 *Age*, 1 December 1983.
11 *Australian*, 1 December 1983.
12 *Age*, 6 December 1983.
13 *Sun News Pictorial*, 7 December 1983.
14 *Age*, 11 February 1983.
15 ibid., 9 June 1984.

CHAPTER SIXTEEN

1   *Age*, 14 January 1984.
2   *National Times*, 22-28 June 1984.
3   *Herald*, 13 September 1984.
4   *Age*, 4 May 1985.
5   *Sun News Pictorial*, 27 February 1984.
6   ibid., 6 July 1985.
7   ibid., 30 July 1984.
8   *Financial Review*, 18 April 1985.
9   *Australian*, 10 January 1985.
10 *Sun News Pictorial*, 17 January 1985.

[11] *Business Review Weekly*, 26 October 1984.
[12] *Financial Review*, 19 December 1984.
[13] *Age*, 16 July 1985.
[14] *Australian*, 31 August 1985.
[15] *Business Review Weekly*, 13 September 1985.
[16] *Age*, 28 August 1985.
[17] *Financial Review*, 3 September 1985.
[18] ibid., 2 October 1985.
[19] ibid., 7 November 1985.
[20] *Sunday Press*, 28 July 1985.

CHAPTER SEVENTEEN

[1] *Herald*, 5 September 1985.
[2] ibid., 6 September 1985.
[3] *Age*, 23 October 1985.
[4] *Australian Business*, 2 October 1985.
[5] *Financial Review*, 22 October 1985.
[6] *Business Review Weekly*, 29 November 1985.
[7] ibid., 25 October 1985.
[8] *Age*, 13 December 1985.
[9] *Financial Review*, 14 March 1986.
[10] *Sun News Pictorial*, 14 March 1986.
[11] *London Standard*, 17 April 1986.
[12] *Sun News Pictorial*, 11 April 1986.
[13] *Herald*, 11 April 1986.
[14] *Australian*, 11 April 1986.
[15] *Financial Review*, 15 April 1986.
[16] *Business Review Weekly*, 15 August 1986.
[17] *National Times*, 30 May to 5 June 1986.
[18] *Financial Review*, 19 June 1986.
[19] ibid., 17 October 1986.
[20] *Age*, 16 September 1986.
[21] *Herald*, 18 September 1986.
[22] *Financial Review*, 1 October 1986.
[23] *Age*, 18 April 1986.
[24] ibid., 8 April 1986.
[25] ibid., 18 April 1986.
[26] *Advertiser*, Adelaide, 10 May 1986.
[27] *Golden Wing*, Australian Consolidated Press, March 1987.
[28] *News Adelaide*, 17 October 1986.
[29] *Sydney Morning Herald*, 25 October 1986.
[30] *Age*, 18 March 1986.
[31] *Golden Wing*, op. cit.
[32] *Marketing*, August 1986.
[33] *Sydney Morning Herald*, 29 January 1986.
[34] *Vancouver Sun*, 14 August 1986.
[35] *Financial Review*, 25 July 1986.
[36] *Mercury*, Hobart, 19 September 1986.
[37] *Australian*, 19 September 1986.
[38] *Sydney Morning Herald*, 30 September 1986.
[39] *Age*, 23 September 1986.

CHAPTER EIGHTEEN

[1] D. Sloane & J. Sullivan, The Carlton Brewery, University of Melbourne thesis, 1966.
[2] ibid.
[3] ibid.
[4] Pearl, op. cit.
[5] *Golden Wing*, op. cit.

INDEX